Favre

His Twenty Greatest Games

By Doug Moe

TRAILS BOOKS
Madison, Wisconsin

Library of Congress Control Number: 2008934897
ISBN: 978-1-934553-03-9

Editor: Mark Knickelbine
Book Design: Rebecca Finkel
Cover Photo: Hank Koshollek

Printed in the United States of America

13 12 11 10 09 08   6 5 4 3 2 1

TRAILS BOOKS
a division of Big Earth Publishing
923 Williamson Street • Madison, WI 53703
(800) 258-5830 • www.trailsbooks.com

Contents

Introduction

Assessing the charismatic golfer Arnold Palmer, Dan Jenkins wrote: "Of all the greats who have come before him and after him, there was never one in his prime who created so much suspense and drama when he addressed a shot. One way or another, you knew something was going to happen."

So it was whenever Brett Favre stood behind center, awaiting a snap. No quarterback in the history of professional football generated a sense of anticipation like Favre. When he brought the Green Bay Packers to the line and started calling signals, something was going to happen. First down, touchdown, game-winning scramble, or costly interception, Favre's legend was anchored in his passion and unpredictability.

Passion? This was a quarterback who, after throwing his first game-winning touchdown pass for the Packers in 1992, was so overcome with excitement he grabbed his teammate Ron Hallstrom and smacked helmets. Hallstrom weighed 300 pounds. Favre gashed his forehead but didn't even notice the blood running down his face. He was too excited.

Sixteen seasons later, the exuberance was still there. Favre's beard was flecked with gray, but when he stepped on the field, he was transformed. The arm was still a rocket, the face a kid on Christmas Eve. In late 2006 *Sports Illustrated* ran a long profile of Favre titled "Huck Finn's Last Ride." It wasn't — he returned for the 2007 season, which would be his last with the Packers — but the title acknowledged the youthful spirit that, into his late 30s, Favre still brought to the game. Not to practices, perhaps, not to interviews and plane rides — not after almost two decades of pro football — but to the field and the game. The Huck Finn analogy was a good one in another way, too, for Huck has been American literature's most lovable rascal for more than 100 years. Mischief had always been part of Favre's mystique. It was as if, amid the billion-dollar corporate money machine that the National Football League has become, we needed someone to remind us that these modern-day gladiators are still playing a kids' game. It's supposed to be fun.

As with Arnold Palmer, the writers and announcers took to calling Favre a swashbuckler, a gunslinger, a riverboat gambler. Clichés become so for a reason. Favre wore those labels well, with his grizzled beard and rapid-fire right arm. Joe Montana moved his San Francisco 49ers teams down the field like a chess master. Favre might have been at the roulette table, blowing on a pair of dice. Or, better, up there next to a high-wire artist like Karl Wallenda, stepping out onto the precipice yet one more time, the crowd below holding its collective breath.

"To be on the wire is living," Wallenda said, near the end. "The rest is waiting."

One sensed much of that in Favre — the thrill he got from simply being out there competing, playing the game. The assumption was it gave him back something nothing else ever has or will. Has anyone in the NFL ever played the game with more sheer joy?

Favre's zest for life was instilled in childhood. His parents, Irvin and Bonita Favre, were colorful characters in a colorful part of the country. Brett would always maintain there was very little he missed out on growing up, a theory he traced all the way back to the womb. Bonita was seven months pregnant with Brett when 1969's Hurricane Camille struck the Gulf Coast. At birth, he weighed nine pounds. The doctor told the new mother the baby was already doing calisthenics in the nursery. Irv Favre coached football and for his first birthday, Brett got a helmet and shoulder pads. Did the parents dream that one day the little boy would be the starting quarterback of a Super Bowl champion? Most parents have dreams of one kind or another. Still, it's unlikely Irv and Bonita ever dared dream of the kind of success their son would eventually find in football. As for Brett, he's always maintained that, while as a boy he dreamed of one day playing in the Super Bowl, he never dreamed of rewriting the NFL record book.

Ever since people started playing games and keeping score, records have been kept, and many athletes over all those years have been quoted saying the records don't mean that much to them. Their sincerity in saying so is often questioned, but somehow Favre's lack of interest in the record book rings true, which is all the more unusual in that few athletes have ever put so many towering achievements on paper.

At the end of the 2006 season, Favre held several NFL records and was poised to set several more in 2007. Among those already belonging to the Packer great were the most career completions (5,021) and most consecutive starts by a quarterback (237 in the regular season, 257 including the playoffs).

When he made the decision to return for the 2007 season, Favre became a near lock to set more, including most touchdown passes (with 414, he began the year six behind Dan Marino) and most victories by a quarterback (he was one behind John Elway and tied with Marino). Also in sight was Marino's record for most career passing yards. With 57,500, Favre stood 3,861 behind the retired Dolphins star. Speaking to Favre's freewheeling style was his proximity to a more dubious record — his 273 interceptions at the end of 2006 placed him second all-time to George Blanda.

But when Favre broke Marino's career completions record in a December 2006 game against the Detroit Lions at Lambeau Field in Green Bay, he momentarily didn't understand why the veteran NFL referee Ed Hochuli was standing in front of him offering congratulations.

"I have no idea what you're congratulating me for," Favre said. "But thank you."

In an interview early in 2007, Favre tried to explain his ambivalence about records: "Individual stats are great," he said, "but when it's all said and done, those type of things are just what they are — statistics." What really mattered, Favre insisted in that interview, were his teammates — the guys he played with, who had his back as he had theirs.

In another interview several months later, he elaborated a bit more. Favre said that when a fan remarks on one of his records, he's flattered. He added: "But if the next person says, 'I love the way you play the game, win or lose,' that would mean so much more to me. I would hope 20, 30 years from now, I'm remembered for something else besides records, whether I have them or don't have them." Remember me, Brett Favre was saying, for how I played the game. (Still it should be noted that by the 14th game of the 2007 season, in mid-December, Favre had all the records, including most touchdown passes, most victories, most career passing yards, and, yes, most interceptions.)

There was also, with Favre, the sense that this was a superstar athlete who had learned, as everyone eventually must, that no list of accomplishments, not even a string of Most Valuable Player awards, riches, and worldwide fame, can shield you from life's hard knocks, some of which are delivered with much more ferocity than a safety blitz. Favre has had his share and more, and because he is famous, his grief has not been private. The deaths of loved ones and friends, serious illness, nature's wrath in the form of a devastating hurricane — all have been visited upon Brett Favre. It may have made this most human of celebrated athletes even more human in his admirers' eyes. As for the man himself, in the face of life's darker realities, a record is a record is a record — figures on paper. But between the lines on the football field, which for Favre had always been the place where he was most alive — like Wallenda's high wire, it was the place where he could most fully express himself — he might still find a sanctuary.

Speaking on a conference call with reporters in September 2007, Favre admitted as much. While playing the game, Favre said, "I am kind of able to engross myself in that and kind of get lost for those three hours."

No, it had never been about records, and it was not about records as Brett Favre's career played into twilight.

In any discussion of Favre and his legacy, what finally emerges is his deep and profound love for simply playing the game, for being on the field and living in that moment when the score is tied and the clock is running down and the Packers just got the ball back.

It was, in short, about the games. So consideration was given to a book about the games, the best games, of Brett Favre's storied career. There have been many, to be sure, so many that they can even be divided into sub-categories: the best comebacks, the best in freezing temperatures, the best when injured, the best under playoff pressure, or the best against fierce rivals.

In the end, the number settled on was 20. The 20 greatest games of one of the greatest quarterbacks to ever play the game of football.

Can you see him there, behind center, calling signals? Of course you can, and you are on the edge of your seat. It's Brett Favre, and something is going to happen.

Southern Mississippi vs. Alabama

SEPTEMBER 8, 1990
Legion Field, Birmingham, Alabama

The first thing to remember is that it was hot — really hot. Brett Favre would eventually become famous as a great cold-weather football player — winning his first 35 home starts for the Packers when the temperature at game time was 34 degrees or colder — but when Favre and his Southern Mississippi Golden Eagles took the field early in the 1990 season against the highly touted Alabama Crimson Tide, the temperature was 93, the heat index was 100, and one estimate had the temperature at field level at 115. It was stifling, and it was the last thing Brett Favre needed.

There had been considerable doubt whether Favre, who was starting his senior year at Southern Mississippi, would even play. He had sat out the Golden Eagles' first game — a 12-0 victory over Delta State — and few thought he would play in Birmingham. It was just too soon. Two months earlier, Brett Favre had almost died.

The incident — a serious car crash — almost ended Favre's senior season before it began. He had been touted as a possible All-American candidate, which meant he had come a long way since coming to Hattiesburg as a freshman — a very long way, when you consider Brett Favre was the last football recruit signed for a scholarship by Southern Miss in 1987.

"I was never recruited for college," Favre told *Sports Illustrated* in 1993. "No one really wanted me."

Few had heard of his little hometown of Kiln — pronounced Kill — Mississippi, Favre said, or the high school, Hancock North Central, that he attended.

"Coming from down here," Favre said, "nobody really knows who you are. Three days before the signing date, I was going to either Pearl River Junior College or Delta State. Southern Miss took me as a defensive back. When I went there as a freshman, I worked out both ways at first. I was the seventh quarterback on the depth chart."

He worked with the offense in the morning and the defense in the afternoon.

The coaches at Southern Miss weren't sure exactly what they had. It wouldn't be the last time that happened in Brett Favre's football life. He was in Hattiesburg at all only because a Southern Miss assistant, Mark McHale, had heard a few stories about a quarterback with a once-every-generation kind of arm who was playing for Hancock North Central High School.

As McHale later told the story, he finally decided to check it out and spoke in 1986 with the quarterback's high school coach, who also happened to be his father. Irv Favre said the kid could really throw, all right, and insisted he wasn't saying that just because Brett was his son.

McHale said, "Can we look at some tape?"

They looked at some films of Hancock North Central's games, and what McHale saw was the quarterback, Brett Favre, handing the ball off to his running backs. Hancock North Central ran an option offense that rarely called for a pass. Irv Favre would later say that it was his job as coach to win football games, and the overall talent on his squad favored the running game. He wouldn't throw the ball just because his son was the quarterback. That's not the way he coached or the way he lived his life.

Which was admirable, but it still left the Southern Miss assistant, McHale, wondering how well Brett could pass.

There are at least two stories of how McHale eventually was convinced. In his autobiography, written with Chris Havel, Favre said McHale came down at the tail end of the recruiting period, "probably as a favor to my dad more than anything."

In an interview for this book, the longtime radio voice of Southern Mississippi football, John Cox, concurred, saying, "It may have been a favor to Irvin Favre."

Because rules prohibited a formal workout, Brett "just happened" to be on the practice field the day of McHale's visit and unleashed a 65-yard bullet that McHale watched open-mouthed and wide-eyed.

"Damn," the quarterback remembered McHale, the offensive line coach at Southern Miss, saying. "We don't have anyone on our entire roster who can throw it that far."

But in 1997, when Brett Favre was famous, McHale recalled it a bit differently. The coach met the media in Hattiesburg a few days before Favre was going to play in his first Super Bowl in nearby New Orleans.

At that time, McHale recalled that he went to one of Favre's last high school games and watched from the stands. The quarterback still didn't get to pass much, but McHale saw enough.

"He ran a play action pass," McHale said. "It was the 50 yard line, right hash. He went back and threw that ball and that poor little receiver in the end zone, I mean, that ball had fire coming off it. Just drilled him. I said, 'That's it. This boy has a golden arm.'"

McHale convinced the Southern Miss head coach, Jim Carmody, to take a chance on Favre by saying the kid was athletic and could play safety if he didn't work out at quarterback. With that, Favre got the scholarship.

Favre's freshman year — which would be Carmody's only year as his coach — they were running some drills on the first day of practice when the young quarterback got his attention.

"I was standing with my back to his group," Carmody recalled. "I heard this noise, a whooshing sound. I turned around and said, 'What in the world is that?' I coached a long time and I never heard a ball sound like that."

In the second game of Favre's freshman year, Southern Miss was playing Tulane and Favre got the call to play early in the second half. Southern Miss was down 17-3 and had already gone through two quarterbacks. Favre was scared, even sick to his stomach (a bit hungover, perhaps, having played a beer-chugging game with a teammate the night before), but he threw two touchdown passes and led the Golden Eagles to a 31-24 comeback win.

"The end of this game was the start of a legend," wrote Kent Youngblood later in the *Wisconsin State Journal.*

It was a legend that grew and was built on a dazzling array of statistics amassed during college — by the time Favre was done at Southern Miss, he had school records in career touchdown passes (52), completions (613), attempts (1,169), and total offense (7,606 yards).

There was much anticipation for Favre's senior season in Hattiesburg, in part because his junior year had started with a bang — a road upset against top-rated Florida State — but then sputtered, with the Golden Eagles finishing only 5-6. Favre and his fans wanted his collegiate swan song to be better than that.

Favre had minor surgery on his throwing arm in the spring of 1990 — some bone spurs were removed — but by early summer, he recalled later, "I was throwing better than ever."

On July 14, Favre, his older brother, Scott, and a friend, Southern Miss linebacker Keith Loescher, took a day trip to Ship Island, the collective name of two barrier reefs on the Mississippi Gulf Coast. With some of the best beaches in the country (before it was decimated by Hurricane Katrina), Ship Island was an ideal place to fish, eat chicken, drink beer, and chat with girls under the hot summer sun.

They had two cars, and driving back, Brett was ahead in his Nissan Maxima, while Scott and Loescher followed a hundred yards or so behind. It was dusk.

Brett later recalled that his dad used to chastise him for speeding.

"One of the things he'd get on me for was driving too fast. I tend to have a heavy foot, unlike Dad, who drove slower than Christmas, and he worried it might catch up with me if I wasn't careful."

Favre was just a little less than a mile from his parents' house and going about 70 miles an hour, too fast for the twisting Kiln-DeLisle Road. He has over the years given more than one version of exactly what happened next. In one, he is blinded by the lights of an oncoming car. In another, his right front tire slides onto the shoulder. Perhaps both things happened.

"It was about 8:00," Favre said not long after the accident, "so it was still pretty light out, and a car came around the corner with its lights on. I caught the glare and eased to the right a little and just lost control. I ended up hitting a tree."

His visceral reaction was to straighten the car by turning the wheel sharply left, which, given his speed, resulted in the car swerving wildly across the road, where it flipped going down an embankment and struck a pine tree.

"He was just out of it, moaning, 'Scott, stay right here, don't leave me. Am I gonna be all right, Scott?"

Scott, following, had stopped his car and he and Loescher come running up to the overturned Maxima. Brett was groaning inside. At least they knew he was alive.

Scott Favre recalled the moment in a 1991 interview with the *Atlanta Constitution*: "He was just out of it, moaning, 'Scott, stay right here, don't leave me. Am I gonna be all right, Scott?' I said, 'Hell, yeah, you're gonna be all right, man.' I mean, what are you supposed to say, that he looks awful or he's bleeding or you're scared yourself? Damned right it was scary for everybody."

Brett recalled later that by the time the ambulance arrived, his mother was there too, insisting to ride with him in the ambulance to the hospital. Brett asked her, "Am I going to be able to play football again?"

Bonita Favre replied, "Honey, I don't know."

The doctor claimed to know. In his autobiography Favre recalled the moment: "When I got to the emergency room, the doctor told me I had a fractured vertebra, a lacerated liver, a severely bruised abdomen, and lots of abrasions."

The doctor said, "There is no way you're playing football this year."

Less than a year later, in May 1991, Favre recalled the days after the accident in an interview with the *Atlanta Constitution*: "I would constantly ask the doctor if I'd ever play football again. I mean, this was the big year that I'd worked so hard for. I was in the best shape of my life 'cause I'd really pushed myself the whole summer. And I lost it all in one split second. It was about the worst feeling I'd ever had. Pretty close to rock bottom."

Favre vowed to himself that he would play his senior season. He left the hospital after five days, and he began to mend. In early August, he returned to Hattiesburg, in anticipation of starting football practice.

But there was a problem: Favre was having trouble passing his food. It resulted in bad stomach aches. He'd vomit, feel OK for a time, then the ache would return.

"I was out of the hospital, and I thought I was OK," Favre recalled later. "I wasn't eating much, though, and when I did eat I was throwing up. I kept having these abdominal pains, and they started to get worse."

On Monday, August 6, Brett Favre checked himself into Forrest General Hospital in Hattiesburg.

The Memphis *Commercial Appeal* newspaper reported his hospitalization after an interview with his father.

"There seems to be an obstruction in his lower intestine," Irv Favre said. "The doctors are trying to treat it. There's a 50-50 chance it could get worse. If so, they might have to operate. If they do, he would be out for four weeks for sure. This is something new. This wasn't on the X-rays when he was released a few weeks ago."

The paper sought comment from the Southern Miss coach, Curley Hallman, who had taken over the team after Favre's freshman season. Hallman declined to speak about Favre's condition. Hallman was known for not saying two words about anything concerning his team when one would do.

Favre's dad concluded: "Brett was all keyed up because he was beginning to walk up the field, throw a little bit, get whirlpool treatments and beginning to move around more this past week while in Hattiesburg. But he is very disappointed now."

The doctors in Hattiesburg found that more than two feet of Favre's lower intestine had been crushed in the accident and had to be removed.

The surgery was August 8. Most of the early predictions had the quarterback needing at least six weeks to recover. He lost weight — at one point he was down 34 pounds from his pre-accident weight of 226 — but then slowly began to gain it back, along with his strength.

The head coach, Hallman, said Favre would not play until the coach was convinced he was ready.

"If we're on the 10 yard line," Hallman said, "and it's the last play of the ball game, against whomever he comes back against, he will not grace the field unless I think he's 100 percent."

The Southern Miss back up, a red-shirt freshman named John Whitcomb, was in the weight room at his old high school in Chipley, Florida, when a reporter tracked him down to tell him Favre had been hospitalized with complications from the accident and required surgery.

A few days later, Whitcomb was asked his feelings about taking over at quarterback, likely for the first several games.

"Everyone's been pretty positive," Whitcomb said. "I hope I can live up to their expectations."

A week prior to the season opener against Delta State, it was evident Favre could not play. But there were positive signs: early that week, he began jogging. So while Delta State was out, the far more important game, Alabama in week two, was now not an impossibility.

Whitcomb led the Golden Eagles to a 12-0 win over Delta State, hitting on 8 of 17 passes for 111 yards, but it was evident to all that the freshman was not Brett Favre. The Alabama game loomed.

Early in the week, Favre gave a TV interview that would be broadcast just prior to the start of the Southern Miss-Alabama game. Asked about his condition, Favre said:

> "It's the first time I've ever had to sit out. I know in spring I did
> [after minor arm surgery], but that's a lot different than the
> fall. To sit back and watch these other guys throw, and not be
> able to do anything, that's kind of tough. But I had to come
> back out yesterday to kind of get the feel of things. Hopefully
> in a few days I can be in full gear."

When did Favre and his teammates know he would play against Alabama? Accounts vary. In talking to reporters in the locker room immediately after the game, Favre said he knew as early as Monday of the week of the Alabama game that he would likely play. In another interview just a few days later, Favre insisted he didn't know until only hours before the kickoff in Birmingham.

In an interview for this book, I had a chance to ask the longtime radio voice of Southern Miss football, John Cox, about it, and Cox said the word around Hattiesburg was that Favre was going to play against the Crimson Tide.

"Curley Hallman always played it pretty close to the vest," Cox said. "But I don't think anyone on the inside had any doubt that Brett was going to play."

In his autobiography, Favre recalled that he and Curley Hallman cooked up a scheme that might confuse Alabama as well as fire up the Southern Miss team. What it involved, Favre wrote, was sending Whitcomb, the backup, in for Southern Mississippi's first offensive play against the Crimson Tide. Then, with some fanfare, the Golden Eagles would substitute Favre, who would come running onto the field like the cavalry coming over a hill in a Hollywood movie.

"Everything went according to plan," Favre wrote. "John took one snap, I ran onto the field, and 86,000 'Bama fans were actually clapping for me. I'd never heard of Alabama fans treating an opposing player like that. When I got into the huddle, all of the guys had tears in their eyes."

Favre liked that story so much he included it in a second autobiography, published seven years after the first one, and written this time with his mother, Bonita, and their ghostwriter, Chris Havel.

There's only one problem with the story — it didn't happen.

The newspaper accounts published the day after the game say that Favre started for the Golden Eagles. And in researching this book, I was able to watch a replay of the game — and the starting quarterback for Southern Miss was Brett Favre (though Whitcomb did sub in on a few plays in the first half).

What nobody was exaggerating was the importance of the game and the excitement in Legion Field as kickoff approached.

It was the dawn of a new era at Alabama. The Crimson Tide had struggled for years to find a head coach who could emerge from the immense shadow of legendary Alabama coach Paul "Bear" Bryant, and in Gene Stallings many thought they had found their man.

It wasn't even that Stallings' predecessor, Bill Curry, had failed. Indeed, Curry had a record of 26-10 in his three years at Alabama, including one season in which the Crimson Tide shared the Southeast Conference championship and Curry was voted the conference's coach of the year. It's just that the bar for football coaches at Alabama, thanks to Bryant's legacy, was set extremely high. Curry never beat Auburn, the Tide's most hated rival, in his three years. In early 1990, Curry was offered a contract extension that he perceived as a slap in the face — it called for no raise and actually took away some of his power to hire and fire assistants. Curry resigned and went to Kentucky.

Gene Stallings had coached in the NFL, but what made him attractive in Alabama were his close ties to Bear Bryant. Stallings had played for Bryant at Texas A&M in the 1950s — he was one of Bryant's famed "Junction Boys" — and then signed on as a Crimson Tide assistant coach when Bryant took the head coaching job at Alabama in 1958.

The excitement was running as high as the temperature on September 8, 1990, when the Stallings era began against Southern Miss. The game was at Legion Field in Birmingham, where until recently the Crimson Tide played up to three home games a year, splitting time with Bryant-Denny Stadium in Tuscaloosa, where the Alabama campus is actually located.

There were close to 76,000 fans on hand in the sweltering heat, which is what everyone was talking about as game time approached — that, and whether Brett Favre would be the Southern Miss quarterback.

They'd have to wait a few minutes to see, because Alabama — which had not lost to Southern Miss since 1982 and won the 1989 meeting 37-14 — received the kickoff.

On the first series, it looked like it might be a long afternoon for the Southern Miss defense. Alabama's quarterback, fifth-year senior Gary Hollingsworth, came out firing. On third down and eight from the Tide's 43 yard line, Hollingsworth dropped back and hit wide receiver Craig Sanderson down the right sideline to the Southern Miss 40, a gain of 17 yards.

From that point Hollingsworth was content to hand the ball off: first to fullback Kevin Turner, who took it up the middle to the 25, then to halfback Siran Stacey, who worked the right side for six more to the 19. On the next play, a sophomore running back, Derrick Lasic, scampered 19 yards through a right side hole cleared by Crimson Tide linemen Terrill Chatman and Trent Patterson. The fast touchdown and extra point put Alabama ahead, 7-0.

After the kickoff, the Golden Eagles took over at their own 25. Their senior quarterback, Brett Favre, was in the huddle. He wore number 4, just as he would later with the Green Bay Packers.

Favre had worn the number 10 in high school, and actually wanted it again when he got to Hattiesburg. An equipment manager told him that number 10 was out of the question. An earlier Southern Miss quarterback, Reggie Collier, had worn number 10 and set records while wearing it, including becoming the first Golden Eagle quarterback to pass and rush for 1,000 yards in the same season.

"We're probably going to retire his number," the equipment man said.

Next Favre suggested number 12, the number of a couple quarterbacks, Roger Staubach and Terry Bradshaw, he admired.

Those were taken.

Favre then suggested 11, the number his brother, Scott, had worn.

That was taken, too.

Finally, in exasperation Favre asked what number the Golden Eagles had left. They had one — number 4.

"Take it or leave it."

Favre took it, and he was wearing it — in the white away uniforms — when the Southern Miss offense took the field for the first time in Birmingham, down 7-0.

In his autobiography, Favre would remember the first play as a straight drop in which he got hit hard by a defensive lineman. Favre got hit, but the play was a sprint rollout to the right, in which he released the ball just before going out of bounds and hit tight end Eric Williams for five yards to the Golden Eagle 30.

Cox, calling the game in the press box, recalls "an audible gasp from the crowd" when Favre got hit after releasing the ball. "He got drilled pretty good," Cox said.

Stallings, the Alabama coach, would recall later: "The guy looked like a damned scarecrow, his uniform hanging all loose around him and stuff."

But Favre popped right up, and everyone let out a sigh of relief.

On third down and four from the 31, Favre dropped back, looked to his right, and let go a pass to the right sideline that split end Ron Baham grabbed at the 45 and took all the way to the Alabama 42, a pickup of 26 yards. The pass was not a tight spiral and it was almost picked off by Alabama defensive back George Teague, who would later be a teammate of Favre's on the Packers (and play a key role in another of Brett's greatest games, against the Lions in Detroit in January 1994).

The Favre-to-Baham first down was the only one the Golden Eagles could manage on their opening possession, and they punted into the end zone. Though Favre had started and played the first series, speculation around the stadium still centered on how long the recovering quarterback could last in the heat.

But Favre was in on Southern Miss's second series, which began after a three-and-out effort by Alabama. The Golden Eagles were set up in great field position after a dazzling punt return by running back Tony Smith, who fielded the punt at the Southern Miss 35 and took it all the way to the Alabama 32. From there, Favre and the Golden Eagles couldn't do much, and settled for a 45-yard field goal by kicker Jim Taylor, one of the last of the straight-on (as opposed to soccer-style) place kickers in big-time football. That made it 7-3, Alabama.

When the Crimson Tide got the ball back, *they* had a new quarterback — a junior named Danny Woodson, who was known for his athleticism. He took his second snap and scrambled from the Alabama 23 down the right sideline to the 46, where he was tackled, fumbled, and recovered the ball himself. A few plays later, again trying to scramble, Woodson was sacked, and the Crimson Tide had to punt.

Southern Miss got the ball back for the third series on their own 15 yard line. This time Whitcomb, the freshman, did come in, while Favre rested on the sideline.

"I really didn't feel any pain," Favre said after the game. "I was just tired, that's all. When I was in the hospital, I really wanted to come back for this game."

Whitcomb could not produce a first down, and the Golden Eagles punted from deep in their own territory. Crimson Tide running back Chris Anderson returned the punt for touchdown, but Southern Miss caught a huge break — a clipping call against Alabama. The touchdown was negated, but the Tide did get the ball first and 10 at the Golden Eagle 35.

Hollingsworth was back in to quarterback the Tide, and he picked up a first down, but then Alabama had to settle for a field goal try. Philip Doyle made it, a 35-yarder, and it was 10-3, Crimson Tide.

Favre was back in on the next series for Southern Miss. He missed a pass on third down and 14, and the Golden Eagles wound up having to punt. Favre wasn't as sharp as he might have hoped, but as his coach, Hallman, said after the game, it wasn't Farve's statistics that were important that day. It was that he had gotten out of a hospital bed to lead the team. It was a part of Brett Favre — call it guts, heart, toughness, or even recklessness, call it what you will — that the quarterback would summon again and again over the years, and it invariably inspired his teammates, maybe never more than in this early instance against the Crimson Tide.

"You could see it in practices this week," Hallman said after the game. "When he was in there, the team spirits rose.

"He has the poise and personality you need in a quarterback," Hallman continued. "You know, sometimes you see quarterbacks who have outstanding talent and they kind of nonchalant it. Brett has an energy, a chemistry, and the kids are drawn to it."

Southern Miss receiver Michael Jackson put it this way: "We were a nervous wreck and he walks in real calm-like and says, 'OK, boys, let's whip these guys, then go home to Hattiesburg and have some beers and see our girls.' The guy's got brass, that's for sure."

The game's next big play came with six minutes to go in the second quarter, with the score still 10-3. Whitcomb had run another series for Southern Miss while Favre rested, starting at the Golden Eagle 20, and it had not gone well. Whitcomb was sacked twice and Southern Miss wound up punting from its own end zone, giving Alabama a first and 10 from the Golden Eagle 36. Again the Tide was threatening to blow the game open. But on third and eight from the Southern Miss 34, Hollingsworth took the snap out of the shotgun, dropped back, and looked over the middle for Derrick Lassic. Lassic got a hand on the ball but tipped it into the arms of Golden Eagle safety Kerry Valrie at the 25. Valrie cut to the left sideline and took it all the way, 75 yards, for a Southern Miss touchdown. Game tied, 10-10.

Hollingsworth and the Tide came storming back with a razzle-dazzle flea-flicker from near midfield. Hollingsworth handed off to running back Siran Stacy, who lateraled back to Hollingsworth, who then hit wide receiver Prince Wimbley. Wimbley made a leaping catch inside the Southern Miss 10 yard line. Three plays later, Stacy carried it over for an Alabama touchdown, and that's how the first half ended, 17-10 Crimson Tide.

Still, Southern Miss, the significant underdog coming in, remained very much in the game. As the teams ran off the field, a sideline reporter grabbed their head coach, Hallman, for a comment about his quarterback.

"Are you concerned with some of the shots Favre is taking?"

"He's a tough kid," Hallman said. "He's handling it pretty good. Naturally we're concerned. But he's in pretty good shape."

Out of halftime, Southern Miss got the ball and on the second play from scrimmage Favre hit split end Ron Baham on a down-and-out route for 12 yards and a first down at the Golden Eagle 32. The drive stalled after that, however, with Favre missing a pass on third down.

But turnovers continued to haunt Alabama. The Tide's Chris Anderson fumbled the fourth-down punt, and Southern Miss recovered on the 'Bama 20. Favre audibled on first down and completed a pass that took the Eagles to the 8. On the next play, fullback Dwayne Nelson took the ball up the middle to the 5. On second down, Favre audibled again, took the snap, and pitched to Tony Smith running right, and Smith scored to make it 17-17.

Another error in judgment cost Alabama on the kickoff. Wide receiver Prince Wimbley fielded the kick eight yards deep in the end zone, but rather than down it he tried to bring it out. He was tackled on the 8 yard line. The Tide picked up a first down at the 18 on two running plays. Then Hollingsworth missed on a first-down pass, and Siran Stacy went nowhere after taking a handoff on second. On third and 10 from the 18, from the shotgun, Hollingsworth took the snap and threw over the middle, only to have Kerry Valrie, who had earlier returned a pick for a touchdown, step in front of the receiver and get his second interception of the game. Valrie took it from the 33 to the Alabama 10, where Favre and the Eagle offense took over with a first down and goal.

"We were a nervous wreck and he walks in real calm-like and says, 'OK, boys, let's whip these guys, then go home to Hattiesburg and have some beers and see our girls.'"

Southern Miss picked up five yards on two running plays, but a holding penalty took the ball back to the 17. The Eagles still needed the end zone; they could not make another first down short of it. On third and goal from the 13, Favre was forced out of the pocket, rolled right, and headed toward the right sideline, where he was forced out of bounds at the 6 by his future Packer teammate, George Teague. Favre slammed into a chain link fence, then slammed the ball to the turf, thinking the field goal team would have to come on the field. But Teague had been whistled for a late hit on the play. It was another big break for Southern Miss, the penalty yielding a first down and half the distance to the goal. On the next play Tony Smith took it in from the 3 for a touchdown, and the Golden Eagles had their first lead of the game at 24-17.

After the kickoff, Hollingsworth rallied the Tide. Had he cared to, he could have pointed out that as the third quarter neared an end, Alabama had a total of 252 yards on offense compared with only 82 for Southern Miss. Still, the Tide were behind. They needed a big play, and they got it on a third and four from their own 40, when Hollingsworth dropped back to pass and Southern Miss came with a full blitz that was picked up by the Tide line, or picked up well

enough anyway for Hollingsworth to dump an eight-yard pass over the middle
to split end Craig Sanderson, who took it the remaining 52 yards into the Golden
Eagle end zone. The score was knotted, 24-24, as the third quarter ended.

The teams traded punts as the fourth quarter wore on. With 7:22 left, and
the ball on their own 20, Brett Favre and Southern Miss stepped up.

"It was pure Brett," broadcaster John Cox told me of the drive that would
ensue. "He did it so many times that season. He just lifted the team up on his
shoulders and made something happen."

Here's what happened. There was a key play early in the drive, a third and six
from the 24. Favre hit Michael Jackson over the middle for a first down at the
31 with 5:48 left.

Then, on first down, Tony Smith lost three. That made it second and 13
from their own 28. It was then that Brett Favre delivered.

He took the snap and dropped straight back, but the rush was coming and
Favre ran up into the pocket toward the line of scrimmage. Still on the run but
short of the line, Favre spotted running back Eddie Ray Jackson and hit him
with a beautifully timed sidearm throw that Jackson carried to the Alabama 35
— a pickup of 37 yards.

It was a move — the scramble *forward* — that Brett Favre would draw on
many times in the future. It's possible no quarterback was ever better at throwing while on the run toward the line of scrimmage.

Two runs and an incomplete pass later, Jim Taylor lined up for a 52-yard
field goal from the left hash mark that Taylor drilled through the uprights.

It was the game winner. Though more than three minutes remained,
Hollingsworth would soon throw another interception — his third of the game
— and the Golden Eagles had pulled off the upset, 27-24.

In the Birmingham newspaper the next day, there was a large photograph of
Brett Favre and his coach, Curley Hallman, walking off the field arm in arm.

Yet it was the losing coach, Gene Stallings, who some days later may have best
captured what happened that afternoon at Legion Field.

"You can call it a miracle or a legend or whatever you want to," Stallings said.
"I just know that on that day, Brett Favre was larger than life."

Cincinnati Bengals vs. Green Bay Packers

SEPTEMBER 20, 1992
Lambeau Field, Green Bay, Wisconsin

Somehow, Ray Scott knew. In the days that followed, everyone else would recall it as an exciting football game, a great comeback, and a memorable victory, but that night, only Ray Scott seemed to know he had witnessed history in the making.

Why Ray Scott? Maybe it was simply that Scott, the legendary broadcaster who taught Pat Summerall the business, who always said that less is more when calling a game, had witnessed greatness from a privileged seat during the Green Bay Packers' glory years of the 1960s, and therefore felt qualified to say he had seen it again. Somehow Ray Scott knew that what happened when the Packers played the Cincinnati Bengals in the third game of the 1992 National Football League season was something very special.

At a dinner that night, the Packers' general manager, Ron Wolf, who was trying to resurrect the Packers franchise and who had gambled a number-one draft pick on an untested young quarterback from the Atlanta Falcons, heard Scott tell a story about how many people had claimed to have been present at the famous "Ice Bowl" game at Lambeau in 1967. That day, in frigid temperatures, the Packers defeated the Dallas Cowboys for the NFL championship. The game was so good and the conditions so bad that over the years more people had claimed to have been in attendance than had even watched it on television. It was a badge of honor to have been a spectator at that game and Ray Scott said that in the quarter of a century since, at least 200,000 had told him personally they were there. Scott chuckled telling the story. But then he said he felt certain that in years to come, Packers fans would be equally insistent on laying claim to having been at Lambeau on September 20, 1992. Ray Scott was sure of it. The weather wasn't terrible, a championship wasn't at stake, but Scott was sure something that would live in Packers lore had occurred at Lambeau that day.

Certainly, going into the game, there was little to recommend it as having the potential to be anything extraordinary, especially for the Packers. Green Bay was off to a 0-2 start, having dropped games to the Minnesota Vikings (23-20) and the Tampa Bay Buccaneers (31-3) in the first two weeks of the season. The loss at Tampa was particularly disheartening. A headline the next day in the Madison, Wisconsin *Capital Times* newspaper summed it up: "Inept Packers fizzle on all fronts."

The most significant thing about the Tampa Bay loss was likely the fact that the new Packers head coach, Mike Holmgren, benched his starting quarterback, Don Majkowski, after the Buccaneers took a 17-0 lead into halftime.

"Of course I'm angry," Majkowski told reporters after the game. "But it's his decision."

Speaking of Holmgren, the quarterback continued: "He told me he didn't have a quick hook. I was kind of surprised. I've been in games where we were down 28, 30 points and came back."

It may not have been that Majkowsi was so bad — and in fact, his numbers, 10-15 (though for only 75 yards), weren't terrible — but rather that Holmgren was anxious to get a look at Majkowski's backup, young Brett Favre, on whom Holmgren and his boss, Packers' general manager Ron Wolf, had gambled during the last off season.

The interest of both Wolf and Holmgren in Favre predated their arrivals in Green Bay. In hindsight, it could seem like an eerie bit of predestination. Holmgren and Wolf summoned their early excitement about Favre independently of one another. It dated back to the weeks before the 1991 NFL draft, when Wolf was a personnel specialist with the New York Jets, Holmgren a quarterbacks coach with the San Francisco 49ers, and Favre a roughhewn potential draft choice out of Southern Mississippi.

Pro teams have a chance to test the top college players prior to the draft, and there was a workout for Favre on the campus of Southern Miss. As it happened, Holmgren was there representing the 49ers, and Wolf was in attendance for the Jets.

"Ironic," Holmgren called it later.

The coach continued: "I remember going to a workout the first time I saw him. Everybody was there, and I remember leaving that day thinking this kid has tremendous strength, a powerful arm, and it was really a pleasure to talk to him. I also thought he was pretty raw. He had real high grades on our charts. He was either going to be the No. 1 or No. 2 quarterback on our list, but we weren't looking for quarterbacks."

In his book, *Green Bay Replay*, Dick Schaap reported that Holmgren's enthusiastic report on Favre included one caveat: "He throws every ball with the same velocity whether it's a five-yard pass or a forty-yard pass. He's really got to learn to discipline himself."

Holmgren said that he caught up with Favre after the workout and asked, "What are you going to do now?"

"Drink some beer and chase some women," Favre replied.

Ron Wolf was even more impressed than Holmgren with the strong-armed quarterback.

In an interview for this book, John Cox, the longtime Southern Miss football broadcaster, told me that Thamas Coleman, a Golden Eagle assistant coach who has never received a lot of credit, was responsible for putting Favre on Ron Wolf's radar screen. Coleman had insisted Wolf watch tape of Favre, not from his senior season in college — when he was coming off surgery after the car accident — but his junior year, which was more reflective of the real Favre. Did Wolf appreciate Coleman's persistence? Cox says that when the Packers went to the Super Bowl several years later, behind Favre, Wolf sent Coleman four complimentary tickets to the game.

After the pre-draft workout at Southern Miss, Wolf was sold. He said later that he'd ranked Favre as not just the best quarterback, but the best player overall in the 1991 draft. Wolf's bosses with the Jets, however, were not convinced.

So both Holmgren and Wolf liked what they saw, but neither of their teams drafted Favre, who went early, in the second round, to the Atlanta Falcons.

A year later, of course, Holmgren and Wolf were together with the Packers. They surveyed the quarterbacks available in the 1992 college draft, and came to the mutual decision that none had the potential of Favre, who'd had a disappointing, bench-riding first season in Atlanta.

Wolf and Holmgren decided to try to get Brett Favre.

Fortunately for the Packers, Favre hadn't really clicked with the Falcons' head coach, Jerry Glanville, starting with the preseason team photo shoot, which Favre missed by oversleeping.

"That will cost you $1,500," Glanville said. Favre would get $100 back some weeks later at an away game against the Los Angeles Rams, when the coach overheard Favre tell a teammate he could throw a ball into the upper deck at Anaheim Stadium. Glanville ventured that he had $100 that said Favre couldn't do it. The quarterback accepted and launched a rocket that cleared the upper deck railing. He might have smirked while pocketing the coach's money.

Favre later said he knew early they were never going to be the best of buddies.

One exchange, captured forever by NFL Films, said it all. It was a night game, and Glanville seemed to be taunting Favre, asking if the rookie quarterback thought he would get into the game.

"I will if you let me" was Favre's response.

Glanville chuckled. "I tell you what," the coach said. "We've got to have two train wrecks, four quarterbacks go down, and you're it."

Favre played in two games that counted for the Falcons, throwing five passes, with no completions.

Still, he said later, he was surprised during that first off season when the call came from Ron Wolf, telling him he was a Green Bay Packer. "I was shocked Atlanta gave up on me," Favre noted later, but pleased that Wolf believed in him enough to surrender a first-round draft choice.

In his book, *The Packer Way*, Wolf said his friendship with Ken Herock, a member of the Atlanta Falcons' personnel department, led to Wolf's realizing that Favre might be available. They talked prior to the Falcons-Packers game in 1991 and Wolf recalled that Herock told him that if he wanted to see Favre — Herock knew Wolf was high on the quarterback — he should watch him in warm-ups because Favre wouldn't play in the game. Wolf took it as a message that Favre might not last long in Atlanta and that he might be available for a trade.

Wolf's deep belief in the quarterback was further evidenced when the Packers team doctor administered a physical, which Favre flunked, due to a degenerative hip condition. "We're not failing him," Wolf said, and in Feburary 1992, Brett Favre became a Green Bay Packer.

As much as they liked Favre, the determination of Wolf and Holmgren to bring him to Green Bay also said something about their enthusiasm — or lack of it — for the current Packer starting quarterback, Don Majkowski, who had, only a few years earlier, begun carving out a legend for himself in Green Bay as the Majik Man.

There was a time when Packers fans were convinced Majkowski was the savior, the quarterback destined to lead the return to 1960s, Vince Lombardi-era glory, to again make Green Bay Titletown. And Majik — his inevitable nickname — did have one magical year with the Packers, before a contract dispute and then injuries slowed his run at history.

Born in Buffalo, Majkowski had been a three-sport star in high school in western New York State, good enough in football to earn a scholarship to the University of Virginia. He was a record-setting quarterback, despite missing some games his senior season due to injury. The injury kept Majkowski from going high in the draft — the Packers got him in round 10.

Blond, ambitious, and charismatic, Majkowski did not suffer from an inferiority complex. He felt slighted by the draft, and he was determined to prove the doubters wrong.

"I always thought I was a better quarterback than I was given credit for (in the draft)," Majkowski told Jerry Poling, in Poling's book *After They Were Packers*.

"I was a better all-around athlete than any other quarterback in the NFL, including John Elway," Majkowski said. "I had a lot of confidence in my ability. It was just a matter of time until I got an opportunity."

With the Packers, Majkowski played behind Randy Wright his first two years, showing enough flashes of brilliance that just prior to the start of the 1989 season, Lindy Infante, the Packers' second-year coach, cut Wright.

With that shot of confidence from the head coach, in 1989 the Majik Man had a year for the ages, leading the Packers to a 10-6 record, throwing for 4,318 yards and 27 touchdowns.

"That whole year was just awesome," Majkowski told the *Milwaukee Journal Sentinel* some 15 years later. "We were in the playoff hunt for the first time in years. The whole community was so charged up. It was just a great time to be a Packer."

Part of it was *how* Majkowski and the Packers won, scoring fully half of their victories with fourth-quarter comebacks. In the second game of the season, the Pack trailed New Orleans 24-7 at the half. By game's end, Green Bay was on top, 35-34, and the Majik Man was on top of the world. His stats nearly defied belief: Majkowski began the second half against the Saints by completing 18 passes in succession, winding up 25 of 32 for 354 yards.

"We were in the playoff hunt for the first time in years. The whole community was charged up. It was just a great time to be a Packer."

The game of the year, the game every Packers fan recalls from the Majkowski era, is known as the "instant replay" game, a 14-13 victory over the Chicago Bears that Mike Ditka, then the Bears coach, still can't discuss without becoming belligerent. The Majik Man had thrown a last-second, game-winning touchdown pass to Sterling Sharpe, but an official had ruled that Majkowski stepped over the line of scrimmage before throwing, negating the completion. Officials reviewed the play on the TV monitors, and the call was reversed. Ditka was furious, and the ensuing controversy made Majkowski a star. Every TV sports show featured replays of the touchdown, along with Ditka's meltdown. *Sports Illustrated* took notice with a lengthy piece headlined "The Majik Show."

Still, the Packers didn't make the playoffs. The Minnesota Vikings won the division with a season-ending victory over the Cincinnati Bengals. By the next season, 1990, the curtain began to drop on Majkowski's magic show. He was one of several Packers who held out for better contracts before the season started, precisely what a young team on the rise did not need. Majkowski eventually signed for significantly more money, but the rocky start was a foretaste of the season. The quarterback had as many bad games as good; then, in November, in a game in Phoenix, Majkowski tore the rotator cuff in the shoulder of his throwing arm. He vowed at the time to rehabilitate and come back stronger than ever, but some years later, Majkowski was able to better assess the injury's impact.

"If I had never gotten hurt in 1990," he told the *Journal Sentinel*, "maybe they would have never made the trade for Brett in the first place."

But trade they did, and by the Packers training camp in the summer of 1992, at least some in Green Bay sensed the quarterback torch might be passing from Majkowski to his younger rival.

"Majkowski did have his own mystique," said veteran Wisconsin sportswriter Rob Schultz in an interview for this book. Schultz covered that first training camp and much of Favre's career for the Madison *Capital Times*.

AP Photo/Jeff Glidden

At the start of a historic career.

"Majkowski's mystique dated to 1989 and by 1992 it had faded," Schultz continued. "With Favre in camp, there was a sense of anticipation, because they had traded a number-one pick for him."

The buzz in Green Bay about the '92 team was about more than Favre, Schultz noted. Wolf and Holmgren were new, too, and something about them also brought a sense of anticipation. Schultz felt the departed coach, Infante, had been too much a zealot for control. The team chafed under his micromanagment. The first Wolf-Holmgren camp felt more professional. Favre, Schultz said, "was Wolf's first big move."

All eyes were on the young quarterback. "There was a question of how serious Favre was because of the party reputation he brought from Atlanta," Schultz said.

But the writer noticed right away that Favre's parents were at the Packers training camp, and that the quarterback seemed truly committed. "We saw a lot of Big Irv," Schultz said.

The week before the first pre-season game of the 1992 season, Favre gave an interview to the Associated Press. Inevitably, his chances of beating out Majkowski came up.

"I'm looking to be the starting quarterback here soon if Mike Holmgren and Ron Wolf feel I'm ready to play," Favre said.

He was helped a bit by the decision of former number-two quarterback Mike Tomczak — who had started the Packers' last game of the 1991 season — to hold out for a bigger money contract. That moved Favre into the role of immediate backup to Majkowski.

Holmgren appeared to be giving mixed signals about his quarterbacks. In the Associated Press story on Favre, Holmgren said, "I think experience counts for more at quarterback than any other position," which seemed to be a nod toward Majkowski. But Holmgren added: "I'm more convinced now than when we traded for Brett that he has a bright future. He has really impressed me with his leadership."

A young Packers receiver named Kitrick Taylor, who was in his first training camp in Green Bay in 1992 (and who would figure hugely in Favre's first great NFL game), said in an interview for this book that he, like Holmgren, was impressed early with Favre as a leader.

"We were all kind of getting to know each other at that camp," Taylor said. "Mainly because of the new coach. We were getting the system down."

Of Favre, Taylor said: "I knew he threw a very hard ball. He took a lot of chances. He might throw into double coverage, but a lot of those passes got there because of the speed of his ball. I could sense that he was a leader, too, a big-time leader, and a winner."

Taylor continued: "Brett was very friendly. Just a fun guy to be around. He had a great personality and made training camp fun. But he could be serious when the time came to be serious."

Asked during camp by the Associated Press to assess his chances of earning the starting job, Favre replied, "I'd say it was close," Favre said. "Don's a really good quarterback."

Majkowski started the 1992 season opener against the Vikings, a game the Packers lost 23-20 at Lambeau. That was bad enough, but the following week, on the road at Tampa Bay, the bottom fell out. The Buccaneers blitzed the Packers, 31-3, with Holmgren having yanked his starter, Majkowski, at halftime. If Majkowski was inept in Tampa, Brett Favre, who played the second half, wasn't much better. He suffered the humiliation of having his first completed pass in the National Football League be to himself.

In his first series, Favre threw a pass that was batted right back to him. "I was thinking I'd better knock it down, but I definitely didn't want to knock it down into someone's hands," Favre said. Instead, he caught it.

In a somber locker room after the game, Holmgren, Majkowski, and Favre all commented on the game and, at least to a degree, on the state of the quarterback situation.

Holmgren: "We couldn't get anything going in the first half. That isn't always the quarterback's fault. But I thought it was a good time to put Brett into the game and see what he could do."

Favre, who threw a late interception: "I've got to learn when to hold onto the ball. Taking a sack could have meant some points at the end."

Majkowski: "Crap happens in the NFL. You've just got to take it with a grain of salt. It wasn't the first time that I've been pulled and it won't be the last. It's just part of the profession."

The Cincinnati Bengals were next for the Packers, and there might have been some controversy or even excitement about which quarterback, Favre or Majkowski, would start, but the Packers were reeling from their losses and the talk that week was more about whether the season, still young, could be salvaged. Even Wolf, the general manager, recalled years later not feeling good going into the Cincinnati game: "We'd just gotten kicked in Tampa and we thought there was never going to be a light at the end of the tunnel."

The light would appear that very weekend — though it took awhile.

As expected, Don Majkowski started for the Packers against the Bengals. Coming into Lambeau in the third week of the season, Cincinnati was off to a great start. The Bengals had begun the season on the road with an easy win, 21-3, at Seattle. The next week they returned home and nipped the Los Angeles Raiders, 24-21, in overtime. It appeared they might be a much-improved team from the one that finished last in the AFC Central in 1991.

There were 57,272 fans on hand September 20, 1992 for the Bengals game at Lambeau. It was a gorgeous autumn day, sunny and warm.

But it began to look less beautiful for Green Bay fans early in the first quarter, when on only the Packers' seventh offensive play, Bengals nose guard Tim Krumrie sacked Majkowski behind the line of scrimmage.

On third down and seven from their own 38, the Packer quarterback had dropped straight back, and Krumrie, coming from the right side, grabbed Majkowski around the left leg, falling on the quarterback's ankle as the play ended. Krumrie got up but Majkowski didn't. He had damaged some ligaments in his left ankle and was writhing in pain on the 30 yard line.

"Any time you see someone lay on the ground like that," Krumrie said later, "you know they're hurt. He was in quite a bit of pain."

There was a scuffle between a few linemen on the opposing teams, and some fans in Lambeau booed Krumrie, even though the 10-year NFL veteran had been an All-American at the University of Wisconsin-Madison and lived in Eau Claire, with his wife Cheryl, in the off season.Majkowski, in any case, was done for the afternoon. He didn't need a stretcher, but he hobbled off the field assisted by two trainers. He put no weight on his left foot. For Majkowski, 1989 must have seemed like the distant past.

Back on the field, it was fourth down for the Packers, and even as they lined up to punt, Brett Favre was on the phone to the Packer coaches in the press box.

On the Bengals' next series, Johnny Holland intercepted a Boomer Esiason pass (one of two picks on the day for Holland), and Brett Favre trotted out onto the field for the Packers. That moment would loom, in hindsight, as a seminal one in team history. So what was Favre himself thinking as he entered the game in the first quarter against Cincinnati?

"I was shaking," he said in the locker room later. "I felt like I took a laxative."

Bengals cornerback Eric Thomas would later tell the *Dayton Daily News* that most of their team didn't even recognize Majkowski's replacement.

"I played with Majokowski in the Blue-Gray Game," Thomas said. "When he went out, I'm thinking, we're going to be OK. I knew nothing about Brett Favre. I had never heard of the guy."

Favre, asked again a decade later about entering the Bengal game, recalled: "More than anything, I remember how nervous I was. It doesn't look like it, but I'd studied as much as I possibly could in preparing myself, because I'd played a little bit the week before against Tampa. So I was as ready as I was going to be."

Favre continued: "I wasn't nervous that I didn't know what to do; I was nervous because I knew that this was what I'd always wanted to do, and that this was my opportunity. I knew most of the learning was going to be on-the-job training."

Favre spoke those words in 2002 to *Wisconsin State Journal* sportswriter Jason Wilde, who in September of that year had the inspired idea to approach Favre and ask the quarterback to watch a film of the Cincinnati game from a decade earlier.

Wilde and Favre sat together in the front row of an empty auditorium inside Lambeau Field and watched the film of the game that, in Wilde's words, was "the birth of his legend...the game that started it all."

Favre told Wilde that he had watched film of the game the day after it was played, but never again.

A decade later, watching himself trot on the field for the first time against Cincinnati, Favre's initial reaction was embarrassment. "Oh, man," the quarterback said. "Look at me — shirt tail's out, dual chinstrap, holy mackerel."

If Favre was nervous and excited, so were his teammates. Edgar Bennett, a rookie running back with the Packers in 1992, expressed the mixed feelings of the team on seeing Favre come on the field in the first quarter.

"When the Majik Man went down," Bennett said, "everyone was like, 'What are we going to do now?' But as soon as Brett took the field, the confidence was there. I don't think a player in the huddle doubted him."

On his first snap after the Holland interception, Favre hit Sterling Sharpe in the right flat for a gain of seven yards. The pass gave Sharpe a reception in 58 straight games, tying a Packer record held by James Lofton.

That first pass aside, it was not going to be easy for Favre. The quarterback and his offense struggled for much of the day.

Bud Lea offered this description of Favre's start in the *Milwaukee Sentinel*: "He couldn't get the offense moving. He was rushing his passes. He was throwing into double coverage. He was fumbling the ball and taking hits.

"Four times the Packers moved inside the Bengals' 30-yard-line, and they came away with only three points....On a couple occasions Favre messed up by calling the wrong formations for plays sent in by Holmgren, forcing the coach to witness some of the strangest formations he had ever seen."

The hard numbers for the first three quarters weren't pretty: Favre hit on 13 of 28 passes for 130 yards, but he was sacked five times and had four fumbles.

On one play, Favre took the center snap, backed up, and was knocked over by his own man, fullback Buford McGee.

"That's pretty bad, getting knocked down by your own guy," Favre said, as he watched the play on film a decade later. He replayed it a second time, then a third. "See what I mean? Oh, man. Half the stuff I'm doing, you don't even see rookie quarterbacks do."

Somehow, the Packers stayed in the game, if barely, through three quarters. The Bengals weren't setting Lambeau on fire, either. The first quarter was score-less.The game's first tally came with just under 10 minutes left in the second quarter. The Bengals put together a long, 13-play drive, the highlight of which came when Esiason dropped back on third down at the Packers' 43 yard line and hit Tim McGee for 21 yards to the Packers' 22.

The drive eventually stalled and Jim Breech kicked a 20-yard field goal to put Cincinnati in front, 3-0.

The Packers couldn't move on their ensuing drive, and second-year punter Paul McJulien launched a punt that Carl Pickens, a rookie wide receiver for Cincinnati out of Tennessee, fielded at the Bengals 5 yard line and returned 95 yards for the game's first touchdown. Breech's extra point made it 10-0, Bengals.

The Packers did get on the scoreboard before halftime, but they needed a little help. After Edgar Bennett picked up two yards and a first down on fourth-and-one from the Cincinnati 41, the Packers again sputtered and were forced to punt. The Bengals' Alfred Williams roughed McJulien and the penalty gave the Packers a first down on the Cincinnati 30. Chris Jacke wound up kicking a 36-yard-field goal that sent the Packers into halftime down, 10-3.

Whatever was said in the locker room, neither team came out inspired for the third quarter, which was scoreless with less than three minutes left, when the Bengals forced a turnover. Favre, still trying to get focused, made a mistake.

On a third and six from the Packer 45, Favre dropped back to pass and was blind-sided by blitzing Bengal defensive back Darryl Williams. Favre lost the ball and a Cincinnati linebacker, Ricardo McDonald, recovered the quarterback's fumble at the Green Bay 29.

It took Cincinnati only three plays to convert. On a second and 11 from the 17, Esiason hit running back Eric Ball in the right corner of the end zone with a scoring pass that with Breech's extra point put the Bengals ahead, 17-3. That was how the third quarter ended.

The Packers needed a big play.

The first Packer hero that day was a rookie, a defensive back who Green Bay selected fifth overall in the 1991 NFL draft and who subsequently held out, demanding a big-money contract before putting on a Packers uniform and saying in numerous interviews that Green Bay should feel lucky to have him.

Terrell Buckley was like that.

The highly touted Buckley's hold out lasted into the regular season. His eventual contract was worth $7 million, huge money for the time. The Cincinnati game was Buckley's first.

Buckley missed a couple of potential interceptions in the game, but all was forgiven when he lined up to return a punt from the Bengals' Lee Johnson with just under 13 minutes left in the game.

Johnson's punt, from his own 5 yard line, was a line drive that Buckley gathered in at the Green Bay 42 yard line. He danced to his right, cut back left, then spotted a hole.

"My first concern was just catching the ball and making a first down," Buckley said after the game. "It just so happened I made a move to the right and to the left and broke it back at an angle to the right and the punter was left there."

Buckley could run 40 yards in 4.3 seconds, blazing speed which shot him through the hole and left only Johnson, the punter, to beat. It was no contest, and Buckley scored easily, but not before taunting Johnson by pointing the ball back at the trailing punter starting at about the Cincinnati 20 yard line, a hot-dog move if there ever was one.

As Buckley sat catching his breath on the Green Bay bench, Mike Holmgren walked over. The precise wording of their conversation became a matter of some dispute, though each agreed it began with the coach congratulating his talented rookie on the return.

According to Holmgren, he next said: "In the future, don't wiggle the ball around until you're in the end zone."

Buckley's recollection: "He said, 'Great job. But don't hold the ball out so far. Wait till you get to the 10 to stick it out.'"

A reporter pointed out that Holmgren's version had the coach saying wait until the end zone to celebrate.

Buckley's response: "Oh, yeah? Well, the 10's the end zone to me."

The return put the Packers back in the game. The Bengals, however, did not panic. They took the kickoff and immediately put together an 11-play drive that used up nearly five minutes on the play clock. The drive stalled just outside the

Packers' 10 yard line, and Breech kicked a 24-yard-field goal with 8:05 left to put the Bengals ahead, 20-10.

The ensuing kickoff left the Packers in poor field position, at their own 12. Rookie wide receiver Robert Brooks had actually engineered a nice return out past the 30 yard line, but an illegal block wiped out the gain.

Up to that point in the game, there had been little to suggest Favre was capable of driving his team the length of the field. But something clicked.

Holmgren, afterward, said, "Part of it was that we had a lot of inexperience on the field. Then, they settled down. We pass protected. We caught the ball. Things just started to happen."

There was also this. The Packers caught a break when the Bengals switched from the blitzing, man-to-man defense they had used so successfully for more than three quarters into a loose zone designed to prevent big play completions. Holmgren said later he recognized it immediately as a "prevent" defense that the Bengals' defensive coordinator, Ron Lynn, had used when Lynn was with the San Diego Chargers and Holmgren had been offensive coordinator for the San Francisco 49ers.

Holmgren told Favre to take what the defense gave him, and the quarterback listened, directing the Packers 88 yards in eight plays.

Favre completed five of six passes in the drive, and on another occasion scrambled for 19 yards and a first down. At one point Favre completed three straight passes: to Harry Sydney for 18 yards, Sterling Sharpe for 33, and Ed West for 10. The touchdown toss — Favre's first as an NFL quarterback — was five yards to Sharpe. Chris Jacke's extra point made it 20-17, Bengals, with just over four minutes left in the game.

On the Green Bay bench, the trainers were attending to Sharpe, who had hurt his ribs on the touchdown catch.

The Packers defense needed a stop, and they rose to the challenge. The Bengals picked up a couple of quick first downs, but then just as quickly they were forced to kick. Their fourth-down punt was caught by Buckley, who may have been thinking about another return for a touchdown. The rookie caught the ball, faked left and right, and took off up field.

"I play to win," Buckley said later. "I caught the ball and did what I normally do. I shook here, I shook there and had an opening to the left. I switched the ball from the left hand to the right hand, as you learn to do in peewee, and a guy just put his helmet right there on the ball and knocked it up in the air."

There was a collective gasp from the crowd at Lambeau, and a mad scramble for the ball, which was bouncing around on the field. Eric Ball finally fell on it for the Bengals at the Packer 35 yard line. The clock read 3:11.

The Bengals were in no hurry. They picked up one first down and ran three more plays. Then Breech came in to try a 36-yard field goal with just over one minute to play.

From the right hash mark, Breech missed wide left. The kick started straight and then hooked dramatically, missing the left upright. But there was a flag on the play. Initially, Packer fans cheered because the call was against the Bengals. But the infraction was a false start before the ball was ever snapped; there was no way for Green Bay to decline it. Cincinnati was penalized five yards and Breech got another chance, this time from 41 yards. He split the uprights and Cincinnati led, 23-17.

On the Packers' sideline, Favre and Holmgren were locked in an intense conversation.

The kickoff, and where the Packers would get the ball, was critical. They were out of time-outs. The kick sailed toward the right sideline and Brooks, the rookie, misjudged where he was on the field, catching the ball on the run at the 8 yard line, only to have his momentum carry him out of bounds. It was a huge mistake. Green Bay now had to go 92 yards. Trailing by six, a field goal was useless to them. There was 1:07 to go.

Holmgren recalled later, "I told Brett, 'Relax and throw.'"

Favre brought the Packers onto the field. On the first play, he dumped a swing pass to running back Harry Sydney, who picked up just four yards before getting out of bounds to stop the clock.

"Mike was mad about that," Favre said after the game. "He wanted me to throw the ball about 20 yards downfield and I ended up hitting it for four. But after that we pushed it down the field. I didn't want him hollering at me again."

Later, Holmgren would say that all the plays on the drive had been scripted, including that one. But in any case, the next play gave the Packers hope. Favre took a short drop, allowing the Bengal rush to circle behind him. Favre then stepped up almost to the line of scrimmage and rifled a bullet along the right sideline to his best receiver, Sterling Sharpe, who turned almost in a circle back toward Favre and caught the ball with his arms extended high over his head, falling backward with the catch and a 42-yard gain to the Bengals' 46 yard line.

The play was what the Packers call an "all go," in which they send four wide receivers sprinting down the field, generally ensuring single coverage on one or two of them. Sharpe blew by Bengals cornerback Rod Jones. "He got behind the guy and made a great catch," Favre said in the locker room afterward.

Watching film of the game a decade later, Favre said: "I'm sure before that completion, no one gave us a chance. I don't know if I even gave myself a chance."

But Sharpe had been wide open. "You'd hate to miss one like that," Favre said, "especially as excited as I was, because he was so open."

Sharpe, however, had bruised his ribs earlier in the game, and he reinjured them on that catch. Sharpe had to leave the game. On the next play Favre hit running back Vince Workman for 11 yards, to the Bengals' 35.

"That was our bread-and-butter play," Favre said afterward. "They were playing deep zone, and you hope he breaks a few tackles. It worked exactly as we had planned."

Workman, however, had not made it out of bounds and the clock was running. The Packers quickly set up at the line of scrimmage. Favre took the snap and spiked the ball, stopping the clock. There were 19 seconds left in the game.

When Favre called the next play, there was a new face in the Green Bay huddle, replacing Sharpe, injured a play earlier. The new receiver's name was Kitrick Taylor and almost no one on the Packers knew a thing about him.

Born in Los Angeles in 1964, Taylor played college ball at Washington State and knocked around with a few NFL teams — Kansas City, New England, and San Diego — before landing as a free agent with the Packers prior to the 1992 season. In Taylor's best season, 1991, he caught 24 balls for the Chargers.

He wouldn't last long in Green Bay, either; Taylor was released before the 1992 season was finished. He caught only two passes for the Packers, and the second one even he doesn't really remember. Taylor does recall his first catch in a Green Bay uniform, though. It was the one that made history.

"I was so scared I thought I was going to throw halfway up into the seats. When I threw it, I closed my eyes and I was just listening for a cheer. I didn't have to wait long."

Taylor was happy to talk about it, too, when I tracked him down in California in the late summer of 2007. He was working with at-risk youth at a center in San Bernardino, having been in and out of coaching since his last short stint as a player, a few games with Denver in 1993.

"Sterling Sharpe got hurt," Taylor said, recalling that September afternoon in 1992, "and they waved me in."

After Workman's catch and the spike of the ball to stop the clock, the Packers huddled. The ball was on the Cincinnati 35 yard line and 19 seconds showed on the clock.

Taylor said Favre looked right at him and said, "We're going to score. We're going to get it in the end zone."

Favre then called the play, again the "all go," which would send four receivers on fly patterns straight down the field. He had hit Sharpe with it just two plays earlier, but Favre had also used it earlier in the game and looked for tight end Jackie Harris streaking up the middle of the field.

Taylor recalled, "When they ran it that time, the defense keyed on Harris and the wide receiver drifted toward the sideline and was open. Brett saw it happen."

Now, with the game on the line, Favre took the snap.

Watching the film a decade later, Favre recalled the moment: "This is the first time in the game where I actually had an inkling of what was going on and what I was going to do," he said.

Favre knew the Bengals' safety, Fernandus "Snake" Vinson, was apt to key on Harris, the tight end. But since the Packers had just gone wide to Sharpe, as he dropped back Favre also pump-faked to Harris in the middle. The idea was to get rid of the safety, or just freeze him for a moment, and isolate Taylor on Rod Jones, the cornerback.

Taylor was sprinting up the right sideline.

"If you watch the replay," Taylor told me, "you can actually see their deep safety keying on Jackie Harris. It made sense. Kitrick Taylor comes in the game. Who's he? So I just turned it on and got past the cornerback."

In that moment, Favre let go of the pass.

Cincinnati coach Dave Shula saw it coming. "It was basically the same play that got them to midfield," he said later. "He looked to his left and then drilled it to his receiver who was streaking down the sideline."

Taylor broke past the defender, the ball was in the air — and then something happened that Taylor told me he had never talked about before. He looked back for the ball and couldn't see it.

"It was a weird thing," Taylor said. "I actually lost that ball in some kind of glare. Just before it got to me, I lost it. I don't know if it was the sun or the stadium lights or what it might have been, but for a moment I lost it. But it was such a perfect throw from Brett that it hit me right in stride and right in the hands and I caught it. But if you look close, it wasn't a real solid catch. It wasn't a bobble but the fact is I didn't see that ball until it was right in my hands. And then I had it and I was in the end zone and we'd won the game."

Favre, in his autobiography, says "I looked hard and pumped at one of the safeties to keep him in the middle of the field and then I threw it to Kitrick Taylor up the right sideline. I was so scared I thought I was going to throw halfway up into the seats. When I threw it, I closed my eyes and I was just listening for a cheer. I didn't have to wait long."

Lambeau went crazy, of course. The noise was deafening. Packers center James Campen, who had battled former University of Wisconsin standout Tim Krumrie all day in the trenches, stood with tears running down his cheeks. Favre was sprinting in circles, head-butting Ron Hallstrom, and then finding Taylor, who recalled the quarterback screaming at him: "Great job! You're awesome! You're awesome!"

Yet the game wasn't over. Taylor's touchdown had tied it at 23-23. Chris Jacke would need to add the extra point for the Packers to win and his regular holder, Don Majkowski, was hurt and unavailable. The backup holder? Brett Favre, who had muffed a snap the month before in an exhibition game against the New York Jets at Camp Randall Stadium in Madison, and who didn't like holding for kicks.

"That was the hardest part of the game," Favre said afterward. "I thought we were winning the ballgame after the touchdown, so I was hootin' and hollerin' and Chris Jacke says, 'Hey, we've got to kick the extra point.' Oh, my heart dropped. All I could think about was me muffing it and us missing it and going into overtime and losing."

Favre didn't muff it and Jacke didn't miss. The Packers had defeated the Bengals, 24-23.

In the locker room, head coach Mike Holmgren called the win "the happiest of my life."

Kitrick Taylor would remember it as "the most exciting moment of my career."

In 2007, Taylor told me: "It's a great thing to be associated with. It will live in history — Brett Favre's first game-winning pass. It's a great thing to be part of."

There was a poignant moment in the north end zone as the game ended. After Taylor's touchdown, a reporter saw two legendary Packers, former teammates Jerry Kramer and Fuzzy Thurston, embrace. They had been in the offensive line during the Lombardi years and were back in Green Bay for an alumni dinner that night. The comeback was enough to stir even those two aging warriors, who had seemingly seen it all.

It was at the alumni dinner that evening when Ray Scott, who had broadcast so many great Packer victories over the years, told the story about the Ice Bowl and how many people had later claimed to have been there, shivering, in the stands at Lambeau.

As the years go by, Scott said, don't be surprised if more and more people start claiming to have been in Lambeau on September 20, 1992, when Brett Favre brought the Packers back so dramatically against the Bengals.

For the ones who really were there, who were intimately involved, the drama of the day culminates in the Packer locker room afterward. In the happy bedlam, certain figures stand out. Mike Holmgren is there, of course, talking to reporters, and nearby is Brett Favre, who can't stop grinning.

The quarterback is for some reason wearing a baseball cap of the San Jose Sharks hockey team. His smile reaches his eyes and in the moment he looks like a teenager. Neither will Holmgren ever again look so young.

They are winding down, and as much as they are thinking about what just happened, they are dreaming about what might lie ahead.

"There was a buzz in that locker room," sports writer Rob Schultz would say, "like nothing I had ever felt before."

Green Bay Packers vs. Detroit Lions

JANUARY 8, 1994
Pontiac Silverdome, Pontiac, Michigan

It was the first playoff game in forever—or at least it seemed like forever to Packers fans. In the strike-shortened 1982 season more than a decade earlier, Green Bay had captured the Central Division title with a 5-3-1 record and then won their first round playoff game handily, beating the St. Louis Cardinals 41-16. The Packers were then knocked out in the next round by Dallas, 36-27.

But the strike season was an aberration, and you really had to go all the way back to 1972 to find the Packers competing in the playoffs. That year, head coach Dan Devine led Green Bay to a 10-4 record and a spot in the postseason against the Washington Redskins. The game was at Washington, and the Redskins held the great Packers' running back duo of John Brockington and MacArthur Lane to a combined 65 yards. Washington won, 16-3.

Twenty-one years later, the Packers were back in the playoffs, scheduled to play the Lions for the third time that season.

In the week prior to the game, a reporter caught up with Devine, who in 1994 was the athletic director at the University of Missouri.

Asked about the Packers and Holmgren, Devine praised the coach and then said, "They're doggone good. If I'd had Sterling Sharpe, I'd still be in Green Bay."

Sharpe was the hugely talented yet enigmatic receiver who had set a record for receptions during the season. For all his success, however, Sharpe was moody and had refused to talk to reporters all season long. Still, he was one of the big reasons the Packers were back in the playoffs after such a long absence. Another, of course, was Favre, who'd had an up-and-down sophomore year but continued to impress with his eye-popping natural talent and potential.

There was a third major star, too, on that 1993 Packer team, a player with gifts equal to Sharpe's and a likeability and charisma that rivaled Favre's. His presence on the team was as unlikely as it was valuable.

As much as anyone, Reggie White was responsible for the Packers' resurgence.

White was a phenomenon, a fearsome defensive lineman who had put up astonishing numbers during many seasons with the Philadelphia Eagles. The numbers were for sacking the quarterback — which is the glamour stat for a defensive lineman. Getting to the quarterback before he passes is the lineman's equivalent of hitting a home run. Nobody was better at it than Reggie White.

In his first year with the Eagles, 1985, White had 13 sacks in 13 games and was the conference's defensive rookie of the year. In his eight seasons in Philadelphia, White had a total of 124 quarterback sacks. His nickname, with a nod to his deep religious beliefs, was the Minister of Defense.

Reggie White became a free agent after the 1992 season and was, of course, the subject of an intense bidding-and-recruiting war among many NFL teams. White later said that one of the major factors in his decision to come to Green Bay was how impressed he was with Packer quarterback Brett Favre after a Packers-Eagles game in 1992.

"It would be fair to say that something happened in that game to change the course of my career," White wrote in his autobiography, *In the Trenches*.

It was a play early in that November 15 game at Milwaukee County Stadium, played amid a sub-freezing wind chill. There were two minutes left in the first quarter. White eluded his blocker and had a clear shot at the Packer quarterback, Favre. White put a ferocious lick on Favre that separated the quarterback's left shoulder and would have knocked just about anyone else out of the game. Favre shook it off, threw a touchdown pass to Sharpe a few plays later, and played the rest of the game at a high level despite the pain.

The Packers won the game, 27-24, and Reggie White was impressed. White would later say that when he was thinking of leaving the Eagles and considering his future, he remembered Brett Favre and how tough the quarterback had been that cold day in Milwaukee.

Which is not say the Packers were at the top of the list of teams White was interested in when he became a free agent. Green Bay wasn't, in fact, even on his original list of contenders. Small city, cold weather. Washington and Cleveland were courting him hard (the wife of Browns' owner Art Modell gave White's wife an expensive coat) and the San Francisco 49ers were in the mix as well, probably at the top of the list. In prayer, Reggie said, he heard God telling him to go to San Francisco.

It's tough to outflank God, but Holmgren and Wolf did their best. When White's scheduled visit to Green Bay was imperiled by weather that might delay commercial flights, Wolf found a private plane that delivered the star on time. Over lunch at Red Lobster (where the kitchen happily went off the menu in preparing a special catfish dish for White), Wolf said, "You're a great player. And if you play for the Green Bay Packers, you'll become a legend." There are no fans, Wolf said, like Packers fans. "They'll love you."

There were other touches. Wolf sent Reggie's wife flowers every other day. The clincher may have come when Holmgren and his defensive coach Ray Rhodes flew to White's hometown of Knoxville (born in Chattanooga, Reggie played college ball at the University of Tennessee) unannounced in late March 1993.

They accompanied White to a service club speaking engagement and joined him at home later for coffee and conversation. White mentioned how Favre had impressed him with his toughness.

The stumbling block, and it was a big one, was White's belief that God was telling him to go to San Francisco.

According to Dick Schaap in *Green Bay Replay*, when Holmgren got back to Wisconsin, he called and left a voice message on White's answering machine: "Reggie, this is God. I want you to play in Green Bay."

White laughed. And then he learned, not from God but from his agent, that the five-year, $19-million deal that he had been offered by the 49ers was actually guaranteed for only three years. White could, in theory, have been cut at that point.

It was a wake-up call for White, and it was just enough to make him dial upstairs again.

The next time Reggie prayed, he heard a voice asking him where the current brain trust, Holmgren and some of his assistants in Green Bay, had been previously. The answer was San Francisco. Reggie reasoned that Green Bay was the San Francisco of the east. And the voice said, "That's right. Reggie, I want you to go to Green Bay."

White's Packers contract called for $17 million over four years.

Sportswriters noted that signing White gave the Packers instant credibility. The magic did not, however, instantly translate to the playing field. The Packers started the 1993 season with just one win against three losses. Favre was erratic, still learning Holmgren's complex offense, complaining that the playbook was overwhelming and "a foot thick."

Meanwhile, the Packers' defense, with its new $17-million man anchoring the line, was struggling as well. After White's former team, the Eagles, came into Lambeau in game two and beat the Packers, *Philadelphia Inquirer* columnist Bill

Lyon wrote: "In the second half, Reggie White looked and played old and tired and slow…. Maybe there is truth to the whispers and speculation that the strongest, most dominant defensive player of our time has begun to lose it."

After a loss at Dallas that ran the Packer record to 1-3, Green Bay's defensive line coach, Greg Blache, went out of his way to assure White that the team was happy with his personal performance, and that the problems lay elsewhere. White, for his part, went to Holmgren and Wolf and asked for permission to address the team.

White gave an impassioned speech about the importance of hating to lose. Whether or not the speech gets credit, the Packers immediately began playing better. White sacked John Elway twice near the end of a game against Denver to preserve Green Bay's 30-27 victory.

The Packers would eventually go on a run of five wins in six games, and in late November, when *Sports Illustrated* sensed something was up and sent a writer to cover the Packers' first game of the season against the division-leading Detroit Lions, the magazine's focus was on Reggie.

"Other teams figured I was a rookie, and they let me make my own mistakes, but I didn't do that. Now they figure they'd better do something to screw me up."

"Pack on Track," the headline of the story the following week read, with this secondary headline: "Led by the bruising play of Reggie White, resurgent Green Bay battered the Detroit Lions to close in on first place in the NFC Central."

At 7-2, the Lions were the class of the NFC Central when they came into Milwaukee County Stadium that day to play the 5-4 Packers. No one knew it at the time, but it would be the first of three meetings between the two teams that season, a rarity in the National Football League.

In that first game in Milwaukee, the Packers prevailed, 26-17. The *Sports Illustrated* writer, Hank Hersch, noted that the Packer faithful were chanting "Reggie" at the end of the game, as the towering lineman jogged off the field with his helmet raised high after registering six tackles and a sack.

"Basically, Reggie stopped us at the line," Lions quarterback Rodney Peete told the magazine. "Anytime he's in the game, he's causing problems."

Mike Holmgren was quoted: "Reggie has changed everything — the way we play, the other team's offensive scheme."

Brett Favre, meanwhile, was not even mentioned until deep into the *Sports Illustrated* story, and then not altogether favorably.

"After earning a trip to the Pro Bowl last February in his first full season as a starter," the magazine noted, "the strong-armed Favre has struggled, trying to carry the load single-handedly against schemes designed to confuse him."

Favre was quoted: "Last year it was real vanilla. I'd walk up to the line, I'd look, I'd drop back, and I'd throw it. Other teams figured I was a rookie, and they let me make my own mistakes, but I didn't do that. Now they figure they'd better do something to screw me up."

In beating the Lions to cut their division lead to one game, Favre played a good game that could have been great if not for two first-half interceptions. His stats otherwise were terrific: 24 out of 33 passing for 259 yards.

When the two teams, Lions and Packers, met for the second time in the last game of the regular season, at the Silverdome outside Detroit, there was a lot on the line. The teams had identical 9-6 records, and the winner would claim the Central Division title. Most important, the victor would get home-field advantage for the following weekend, when the playoffs began. The loser would get the wild card spot and have to play on the road. For the Packers, that would mean meeting the Lions in the Silverdome twice in a week.

Sports Illustrated was there again, this time in the person of Rick Telander, a Chicago-based writer who knew football intimately, having played college ball at Northwestern. Telander was also enough of a journalist to know a story when he saw one, and he saw one in the Packers' hugely gifted but enigmatic wide receiver, Sterling Sharpe. As the last game of the regular season approached, Sharpe was poised to break the single-season NFL record for most receptions — a career-defining accomplishment. Yet Sharpe seemed to carry a chip on his shoulder, refusing to speak to even friendly reporters.

Telander noted that a few days before the second Lions game, a reporter had approached Sharpe in the Packer locker room and asked about something Sterling's brother, NFL player Shannon Sharpe, had said recently in the press about Sterling. It was Sterling, Shannon said, who talked him out of going into the military after high school and instead playing college football. Sterling was the greatest.

"He's grateful," the reporter said to Sterling. "Isn't that nice?"

"Why don't you ask him?" Sterling said.

People wondered: What is it with this guy?

There was little in Sharpe's background to indicate the source of his antagonism. Sterling and Shannon were raised by their grandparents on a farm outside Glennville, Georgia — an hour or so from Savannah — and while the boys worked hard helping out, they were loved.

In December 1993 — at the same time the Packers and Lions were battling for the Central Division title — the *Minneapolis Star Tribune* ran a lengthy piece on the Sharpe brothers and their growing up in rural Georgia.

Quoted was William Hall, head coach of the Glennville High Bulldogs, who recalled hearing about Sterling when the elder Sharpe was not yet in high school. Hall said another coach told him there was "an eighth grader at the middle school who is so fast you have to go see him."

Hall continued: "The first play I ever saw Sterling Sharpe was a kickoff, and he brought it back for a touchdown."

Sterling had a great high school career, with 2,000 yards total offense as a senior, and then set a career reception record in college at South Carolina.

He was the Packers' first-round draft choice in 1988 and began starting immediately; with his first real money, he bought his grandmother a lovely new brick home.

And yet.

In the locker room after the second Packer-Lion game, in which Sharpe set a new NFL record for receptions, a reporter said, "Sterling, could I talk to you for a moment?"

Sharpe replied, "What the _____ for?"

Asked about Sharpe's refusal to talk to reporters, his coach, Holmgren, said, "I talked to him about the positive benefits of that many, many times. I can't make him do it."

Sharpe gave one radio interview during his Green Bay career — near the end of his days as a Packer, he spoke to host Steve Rose on the Green Bay Christian station, WORQ. Rose co-hosted a program, called "Timeout," with Packer Ken Ruettgers.

In his book *Leap of Faith*, Rose said he was surprised the day Ruettgers brought Sharpe to the show. The host admitted being intimidated by the receiver, but eventually Rose asked Sharpe the million-dollar question: Why didn't he talk to the media?

"Too many times," Sharpe replied, "the media knows the slant they want to take in their stories. I feel they are looking for you to say a couple words that might support their angle and position. Then, they twist some things, and it can change the true story."

According to Rose, Sharpe said a Wisconsin paper had burned him badly early in his tenure in Green Bay, so he had simply stopped cooperating. As for autographs — another area in which Sharpe had drawn criticism for his lack of interaction with the fans — the receiver said this: "If I sign one, I have to sign a thousand, so I choose not to get involved in it."

It did not endear him to Green Bay. Even Brett Favre, who clicked so well with Sharpe on the field, had his moments with the receiver. He remembered one that came in training camp in 1994, just months after Favre and Sharpe had led the Packers in their epic 1993 battles against the Lions. Favre had signed a big new contract, and one day in practice he missed a couple of easy passes to Sharpe.

According to Favre, Sharpe came back to the huddle and said, "For $19 million, you should be able to put it right on my hands."

Favre was momentarily stunned, then furious. "Shut the —— up and catch the ball," the quarterback said. The huddle was silent.

They got past it. And somehow Sterling Sharpe got over whatever had planted that boulder-sized chip on his shoulder. After an injury caused him to retire early from football, Sharpe successfully recast his image and became, of all things, a member of the media, analyzing pro football for ESPN and the NFL Network.

Ironically, when the Packers and Lions played for the second time, in the last game of the regular 1993 season (the date of the game was actually January 2, 1994), it was Brett Favre who refused to talk to reporters after the game. (Of course, Sharpe didn't either.)

In the biggest game of his pro career up until then, Favre had a miserable day. The headline in the *Milwaukee Sentinel* the next morning read: "Favre's Mistakes Difficult to Excuse." The *Wisconsin State Journal* in Madison had a similar take: "Packers Hand Lions Central Title." It might have more accurately read "pass" the Lions the title, for Brett Favre threw a career-high four interceptions on the day, two of which Detroit converted into touchdowns. Asked about it afterward in the locker room, Favre replied, "I'm not saying anything. Why? You saw it, didn't you?"

Favre goes down. The Packers' loss on January 2 meant they'd play their first playoff game in years on enemy turf.

Rick Telander, in *Sports Illustrated*, saw it, heard it, and noted: "See how Sharpe Disease spreads?"

Those who did talk, Holmgren and quarterbacks coach Steve Mariucci, pointed to Favre's youth and relative inexperience — he was still only 24 — and his tendency to try to do too much, to force a completion when it wasn't there, to make something out of nothing.

Holmgren said: "When we have games where he doesn't attempt to do that, typically we win. But it's a thin line. I don't want to take away his aggressiveness."

In *Sports Illustrated*, Telander's assessment of the quarterback was harsh.

While conceding that Favre "can look so good at times," the writer noted the quarterback "sometimes suffers the meltdowns of a 12-year-old flag-footballer" and "looked awful" in throwing two crucial fourth quarter interceptions, the last "a dying quail late and down the middle."

Telander wondered: "Isn't that the first habit coaches break quarterbacks of in high school?"

When Holmgren described Favre's play as "careless," Telander wrote that "Holmgren would no doubt describe Rip Van Winkle as 'tired.'"

The final score was Lions 30, Packers 20, and it meant the Packers would have to return to the Silverdome the following weekend — as it turned out, the game was Saturday — and face the Lions again. It would be the first time in the long history of the rivalry that Detroit and Green Bay had met in the playoffs.

"I wanted to play at Lambeau," Packer defensive back LeRoy Butler said in the locker room. "That was my goal. I don't know what everybody else's goal was. It looked like our goal was to come back here."

The Lions had a new quarterback, Erik Kramer, for the second meeting with the Packers, and he would start again in the playoff game. Kramer had won the job from Rodney Peete in November, and the young quarterback told Telander that identifying priorities had improved his play. Kramer's infant son had recently recovered from a near fatal staph infection.

"I know what's important now," Kramer said, "and I'm more focused when it comes to the mental parts of the game."

Favre, meanwhile, ended his silence a couple of days after the game.

"They beat us, but I feel like we gave it to them," the quarterback said. "We made a lot of mistakes. We know if we can cut those out, we can beat them."

It was a familiar refrain, and as the playoff game with the Lions approached, Mike Holmgren was beating the same drum.

Of Favre, who threw his fourth interception by putting the ball up for grabs while trying to avoid a sack, the coach said, "I think he's a much-improved player. I really do. But he has got — and will — learn, however. If you throw the ball — if he was attempting to throw the ball away — then that's not how you do it. If he was trying to complete the ball to somebody, that's still not how you do it. You just take the sack."

Holmgren also said: "I want to hug him more than strangle him, but it's close."

Favre concluded: "At least we have another chance this week, and it's against Detroit again."

It was a huge game for the Packers, their first playoff game in forever. It was equally big for Favre personally. He had been stung by the criticism after the January 2 game (and would later call the week leading up to the playoff game "the toughest week I've ever had to go through"). All the hard work, the sweat and blood of the past two seasons, the run that started with the miracle win over Cincinnati in the third game of the 1992 season, would seem almost for naught if the Packers failed to beat the Lions and advance to the second round of the playoffs. A loss was worse than treading water. A win absolved everything, even interceptions. It was up to Favre.

"I haven't hid the fact that how we play is directly related to how he plays," Holmgren said during the week.

One of the key moments of Favre's second season, not revealed to fans at the time, came when the quarterback was struggling and Holmgren called him into his office for a frank discussion.

Many years afterward, Favre would tell reporter Lori Nickel of the *Milwaukee Journal Sentinel* that the coach told the quarterback that they would sink or swim together, that come what may, Brett Favre was Mike Holmgren's quarterback. In other interviews, Holmgren would recall that particular chat coming during Favre's third season, but it's likely they had more than one such talk. Favre, naturally, always appreciated the vote of confidence. Holmgren, for his part, knew how hard Favre was working in practice, knew the quarterback was trying to rein himself in. Both believed it wasn't a question of *if*, but of *when*.

Game day, Saturday, was bitter cold in Detroit — 22 below zero with the wind chill. Inside the Silverdome, however, it was a balmy 65. The Lion fans were heating up as well, sensing perhaps they had the young Packers quarterback on the ropes. In the upper deck, some Lions fans had strung a large banner with a red and white bull's-eye and this message: "Hey, Favre, I'm open."

Those fans probably knew that of all the quarterbacks in the NFC whose teams had made the playoffs, Brett Favre had the highest interception percentage — nearly five percent of all the passes Favre had thrown in the 1993 season had been intercepted. By contrast, the percentage for Dallas Cowboy quarterback Troy Aikman, who led in the category, was 1.5 percent.

As the first quarter started, however, it became evident that, for whatever reason, it was a different Brett Favre at the Packer helm, different than even just a week earlier. Maybe those four interceptions had rocked him sufficiently that he was more willing to rein himself in. Maybe all the sticky notes he wrote to remind himself not to throw into double coverage had finally sunk in. Whatever it was, in the rubber match with the Lions — the first playoff game for the Packers in a decade — Favre began the game playing well within himself, taking what the defense was giving him, including a sack when it was unavoidable, and at other times throwing the ball away for a harmless incompletion.

As the first quarter progressed, the Lions, although they didn't score, began to establish superior field position. They were helped tremendously by the return of running back Barry Sanders, back in the Lions' lineup after missing five games with a knee injury.

On the Lions' second possession of the game, with the ball on the Green Bay 47, Sanders took a handoff from Kramer and began to sweep left, then reversed his field and scampered to the right sideline, where he picked up 25 yards, and five more when LeRoy Butler was called for a facemask penalty. (On the day, Sanders would have 169 yards in 27 carries.)

The penalty put the ball on the Packer 17 yard line. On the next play it was Kramer who made a mistake. Dropping back and looking into the end zone, Kramer tried to hit wide receiver Herman Moore on a crossing route. Packer defensive back Terrell Buckley cut in front of the receiver and intercepted for Green Bay.

On the next Packer series, Favre missed on a third-and-15 pass from the Green Bay 35, but as Holmgren and countless sports writers had pointed out, the Packers could handle incomplete passes. Turnovers were another matter, and Favre was not turning the ball over. Even though the Lions dominated the first quarter, ending up with a time-of-possession advantage of 10 minutes and 12 seconds to the Packers' 4:48, the score at the end of the quarter was only 3-0 Detroit. Jason Hanson provided the three points on the last play of the first quarter with 47-yard field goal.

The Packers came back with the kind of long, sustained drive that again indicated a quarterback in control of his nerves and his game. Favre took the Packers 80 yards in 13 plays. A key play early in the drive came on third and nine at the Packer 47 when Favre hit Darrell Thompson with a swing pass that the running back took to the Lions' 41 and a first down. Two plays later, Favre hit Sterling Sharpe across the middle for 15 yards and another first. It was Sharpe's first catch of the day, but far from his last. For all his moodiness, Sharpe was a gamer, and in this game he was playing with a severely sore toe — an injury commonly referred to as "turf toe" — that might have sidelined less gritty receivers.

A few plays later, Favre hit Sharpe again, on a slant this time, and Sharpe scored, putting the Packers ahead, 7-3.

It was then time for the Lions to mount a long drive of their own. Ten plays, 94 yards, highlighted by a 44-yard run by Sanders in which he dodged an early tackle attempt by Terrell Buckley and sprinted down the right sideline to the Packer 20. The touchdown several plays later came on a Kramer pass to wide receiver Brett Perriman, who was playing his best game as a Lion, ending with 10 catches for 150 yards and the touchdown. Heading into the locker room for halftime, it was Detroit 10, Green Bay 7.

The Packers got the ball first in the third quarter, picked up a first down on a couple of Thompson runs, and then had a series that was perhaps most notable for Sharpe dropping a ball that was right in his hands along the left sideline. On third and 10, Favre tucked the ball and ran, sliding to the turf just short of a first down. The Packer punter, Bryan Wagner, then nearly shanked a punt that gave the Lions the ball on the Detroit 31. The Lions made it into Packer territory a few plays later on a 15-yard run by Barry Sanders, but their drive stalled.

The following Detroit punt, as it developed, was of great import. Jim Arnold lofted a high floater that Robert Brooks let bounce at the 2 yard line near the left sideline, anticipating a kick into the end zone. Instead, the ball careened high into the air and was downed by the Lions at the Packer 5.

It was about as bad as field position gets, and it was about to get worse. On first down Favre threw a bullet to Ed West that the tight end couldn't handle. It fell incomplete. Favre handed the ball to Edgar Bennett on second down and Bennett was stuffed for a two-yard loss. On third and 12 from there, Favre dropped back and looked right for Sharpe. The receiver had sprinted to the 15 and buttonhooked back toward Favre, who let go of the pass without spotting Lions' corner Melvin Jenkins lurking near Sharpe. Jenkins stepped in front of Sharpe, intercepted, and made it untouched to the end zone — 17-7, Lions.

The Silverdome went wild. Favre said later that as he lay on the ground in the end zone, Lion linebacker Chris Spielman taunted him, bringing up the four interceptions from the week before. Even for the Packers faithful, it was hard not to wonder if Favre's wheels were again coming off. What happened when the Packers got the ball back would say a lot about Favre, and that in turn would say much about the Packers' chances.

Even for the Packers faithful, it was hard not to wonder if Favre's wheels were again coming off.

On Green Bay's second play after the kickoff, Favre hit tight end Ed West for a pickup of 24 to the Lions' 45. A few plays later, on third and two, he found halfback Darrell Thompson for 10 yards to the Lions' 27.

On the next play, the seventh of the drive, Sharpe was the slot receiver to the left. Favre took the snap and backpedaled to the Lions' 37. He had good protection as he looked downfield. Favre stepped up to the 35 and released a beautiful tight spiral to Sharpe crossing at the goal line. The receiver caught it and the Packers were right back in the game at 17-14.

The interception for a touchdown was forgiven, if not entirely forgotten.

But Kramer, too, was on a roll. The Lions' quarterback brought his team right back down the field. He hit Perriman, who was having his monster, 10-catch game, first with a 19-yarder and then a 31-yard strike that brought the Lions to the Green Bay 13 yard line. A facemask penalty on cornerback Roland Mitchell gave Detroit a first-and-goal on the Packers' 8.

It was then, in the defensive huddle, that Reggie White, who was not having a great game (he was often double-teamed) but who had been so instrumental in the Packers making the playoffs for the first time in a decade, looked around at this teammates and said: "We need a big play. We need somebody to make a big play."

George Teague, the rookie safety and first-round draft choice out of Alabama, was listening.

On the next play, Barry Sanders ran to the left and picked up a couple of yards. Second and goal from the 5.

Kramer dropped back, looking first for wide-out Herman Moore in the right side of the Packer end zone. Moore was covered. Kramer swung his gaze back to the right middle of the field and spotted tight end Ty Hallock, who looked open about a yard into the end zone.

Kramer let loose a quick sidearm throw. Had it been to the right of Hallock (as the quarterback faced him) it likely would have been a touchdown. Instead, the ball was thrown slightly to the left of the tight end and George Teague brushed past him and intercepted. He then cut to the left sideline and, escorted by cornerback Terrell Buckley, returned the ball 101 yards for a Green Bay touchdown. It was the longest return for a touchdown in a playoff game in NFL history.

"I was just trying to get there as fast as I could," Teague said afterward. "After 30 or 40 yards, I felt like I had it. The only time I got tired was after the celebration in the end zone. People kept hitting me in the head. It felt great."

Kramer lay alone, face down on the Silverdome's artificial turf, his hands pounding the back of his helmet.

Teague made his way past his jubilant teammates to the Packer bench, where he was administered oxygen.

"Maybe the play of the game," Holmgren said later.

Chris Jacke's extra point made it 21-17, Packers. There was 1:40 left in the third quarter.

Say this for Erik Kramer: the interception didn't faze him. All the Lions did in the wake of Teague's postseason record interception return was mount a 15-play, 89-yard drive in which Kramer completed five of six passes and Barry Sanders rushed for 41 yards, including a 13-yard gain on a left sweep near the end of the drive that gave Detroit a first-and-goal at the Packer 5.

On the next play, Derrick Moore ran off right guard for a touchdown. It was 24-21, Lions, with 8:27 left in the game.

Packer cornerback Corey Harris gave Green Bay good field position when he returned the ensuing kickoff almost to midfield. The Packer offense, however, could not take advantage. On third and nine from the 50, Green Bay had a near-miss that would, later, loom large. On the play, Favre was chased out of the pocket right. As he sprinted toward the right sideline, Favre spotted receiver Mark Clayton wide open around the Detroit 10 yard line. Favre, still on the run, let loose a long pass that at first looked good but then began to drift right and out of bounds. Clayton could only watch it helplessly. Back near midfield, Favre grabbed his helmet with both hands.

Would he get another chance? For a time it looked bleak. After a Packer punt, Kramer led the Lions to a couple of first downs, including a 21-yard strike to wide receiver Willie Green that gave the Lions a first-down at their own 45.

The Packers, however, were able to hold on through the series. A couple of handoffs to Sanders didn't produce much, and then on third and 10 Kramer hit Perriman with the kind of ball the receiver had been tucking away all day. This time, near the first down yardage, he dropped it. The Lions had to punt.

Robert Brooks fielded the ball on the Packer 7 yard line, and fashioned a nifty return out to the 29.

There was 2:26 to go in the game.

Favre's first play was a screen pass to Edgar Bennett for 12 yards. Next the quarterback found tight end Ed West for nine yards to midfield. The clock showed 1:35. On second and a yard, Favre handed the ball to Bennett, who picked up a first down. Green Bay called time out with 1:25 left.

Out of the time out, Favre hit Sharpe for a six-yard gain to the Lion 40.

Now there was 1:04 to go.

Favre said later that the next play, as called, put Sterling Sharpe out wide left, but Sharpe was winded and stayed on the right side. Since the defense was overplaying the sideline routes — which the Packers wanted to stop the clock — Favre on taking the snap first looked for Sharpe to be crossing over the middle from the right. When he wasn't there, Favre next looked for Ed West, who was covered.

By this time Favre had stepped up into the pocket and the rush was beginning to close in around him. He ran left parallel to the line of scrimmage and noticed the safety, way downfield, drifting left with him.

Sharpe instead of crossing, had hugged the right sideline and was loose in the right corner of the end zone because the cornerback assigned to guard him, Kevin Scott, had also watched Favre rolling hard to the left. So Sharpe was as open as Clayton had been several minutes earlier. But this time Favre was sprinting in the other direction. The line of scrimmage was the Lion 40; Sharpe was perhaps 65 yards away.

Favre stopped, wheeled, and threw the ball as hard as he could back to the right.

"I don't want to say a hope and a prayer, but that's really what it was," Favre said afterward.

Scott, the cornerback, said, "I'm going to think about that play a lot." He knew Sharpe was in back of him, he just didn't think Favre could throw it that far across his body.

"It was just a miscalculation," Scott said.

Remember Jerry Glanville, the Falcons coach, betting a quarterback he didn't really respect $100 that he couldn't throw a ball into a stadium's upper deck?

Now in the Silverdome the ball sailed toward Sharpe in the right end zone.

"Time stopped for a minute," said Scott, the Lion corner. "I was just in awe."

Sterling Sharpe caught the pass for a touchdown.

Favre yanked off his helmet and sprinted toward the Packer sideline.

The extra point made it 28-24, Packers, and that's how it ended.

In the Packer locker room, Sterling Sharpe broke a four-year silence.

"I'm happy for my team," Sharpe said. "I think for the guys who have been through longer struggles than I have it means a lot more to them."

And the winning catch?

"They were pretty much in a zone," Sharpe said. "The safety never got over the top. The defense was just reading Brett's eyes and they just kind of drifted to their right. Brett looked over and made a great throw."

Coach Mike Holmgren, as he walked off the field, stopped to speak with a television reporter from Milwaukee.

"You're shaking," the reporter said.

"Well," Holmgren said, "I've never experienced anything quite like this before."

Someone should have told him to get used to it.

Atlanta Falcons vs. Green Bay Packers

DECEMBER 18, 1994
County Stadium, Milwaukee, Wisconsin

Whatever would have happened when Brett Favre's old team, the Atlanta Falcons, came to Wisconsin for the second-to-last regular season game of 1994, it was certain that history would be made. Not because of the inherent interest of Favre facing the team that gave up on him after one season, but because of the venue for the game. Win or lose for the Packers, it was to be their last game at County Stadium and their last game in Milwaukee, a city where the team had played at least some of its home games for more than 60 years.

In truth, the Packers coaches and players had come to dread playing the County Stadium games, but the final decision came down to what it almost always seems to come down to in modern professional sports — money.

Players and coaches and even general manager Ron Wolf disliked the Milwaukee games for a number of reasons. First was the two-hour bus ride to and from County Stadium, which made the home games in Milwaukee feel like road games. Because it wasn't built for football, the configuration of the field and stadium also presented problems. Perhaps most significantly, the north end zone nearly ran into the third base dugout. The locker rooms were insufficient for the larger rosters of NFL teams, particularly the visitors' locker room, which had only 35 lockers and eight shower heads. Finally, again due to logistics, the benches of both the Packers and their opponents were on the same side of the field. It was just — weird. Maybe it would have seemed less so if Lambeau Field in Green Bay wasn't so idyllic by comparison, but the comparison was unavoidable.

What Milwaukee had on its side was history. The Packers first played in the city on October 1, 1933, at Borchert Field. The Milwaukee dates — the Packers eventually settled on three regular season games and an exhibition game in

Milwaukee each year — were seen as a way to raise the Packers' image as a statewide team, as well as a way to increase attendance at the games in an era long before professional football had become America's Game, when football was a very tough ticket, nowhere tougher than in Green Bay.

The Packers lost that first Milwaukee game, 10-7, to the New York Giants. The following year the Milwaukee games were moved to State Fair Park, where they stayed until 1951. An NFL record was set at State Fair Park by legendary Packers wide receiver Don Hutson, who scored an incredible 29 points in *one quarter* — four touchdowns and five extra points — on October 7, 1945, as the Packers whipped the Detroit Lions, 57-21.

The Packers played one year, 1952, in Marquette Stadium before moving into County Stadium in 1953. They lost their first game there, September 27, 1953, 27-0 to the Cleveland Browns. The game drew 22,604 fans — County Stadium then held 36,000 — at a time when the Milwaukee crowds were critical to the franchise's financial survival.

The biggest game of the early County Stadium era came when Kenosha native Alan Ameche came to play in October 1955. Ameche that year was a rookie running back with the Baltimore Colts and already a Wisconsin legend. He'd attended UW-Madison and in 1954 won the Heisman Trophy, the first Badger ever to do so. More than 40,000 fans — standing room — packed County Stadium. Ameche didn't have the greatest game — 57 yards on 20 carries — but the Colts beat the Packers, 24-20.

Other on-the-field highlights at County Stadium included a December 3, 1961 game in which the Packers beat the Giants 20-17 to clinch their division title. Fullback Jim Taylor gained 186 yards in the game, a Packer record at the time. Six years later, on November 12, 1967, speedster Travis Williams returned two kickoffs for touchdowns in the first quarter against the Cleveland Browns, a game won by the Packers, 55-7. Then, in a November 18, 1984 win over the Los Angeles Rams at County Stadium, defensive back Tim Lewis made the longest interception return for a touchdown — 99 yards — in Packer history to that time.

The most significant game at County Stadium, though, was the only playoff game played there. It was December 23, 1967, and it was also legendary Packers coach Vince Lombardi's last game in Milwaukee. The Packers beat the Los Angeles Rams, 28-7 (two weeks earlier, in a regular season game in L.A., the Rams had triumphed), and Travis Williams, their kick return specialist, had a big day out of the backfield, rushing for 88 yards on 18 carries, including a 46-yard touchdown.

Less significant, but for many still memorable, was a County Stadium story out of the year of Lewis's interception return, 1984. It was a preseason game for the Midwest Shrine Association charities, an annual event in Milwaukee, and the Bears were the opponent. There was no love between the teams, never had been, and they were each led by a tough, no-nonsense former player — Mike Ditka was coaching the Bears and Forrest Gregg the Packers. As the first half wound down, the Bears had the ball and Gregg called a timeout, hoping his team might get the ball and score before the break. Ditka for some reason found himself offended by this, and began yelling at Gregg, who gave it right back. Remember: at County Stadium the benches are on the same side of the field. The argument continued when the half ended and the teams moved toward their locker rooms. Once inside, some Packer players inquired what was up between Gregg and Ditka.

Once inside, some Packer players inquired what was up between Gregg and Ditka. "You take care of the Bears," Gregg replied. "I'll take care of Ditka."

"You take care of the Bears," Gregg replied. "I'll take care of Ditka."

The man who would take the Packers out of Milwaukee, Bob Harlan, knew the history. He had been to Packer games at County Stadium when he was studying journalism at Marquette University. Years later, presiding over the move, Harlan called it the toughest decision he'd ever made in his life.

A native of Iowa, Harlan worked briefly for United Press International after graduating from Marquette, then returned to the school as sports information director. He went from there to the St. Louis Cardinals baseball team and worked in public relations for nearly four years before joining the Packers as assistant general manager in 1971. Harlan worked his way up the Packer hierarchy and in 1989 became president and CEO.

Since the mid-1980s, when Harlan's title was corporate assistant to the president of the Packers, he had been in communication with Milwaukee Brewers owner Bud Selig about getting a new stadium built in Milwaukee that would serve both the Brewers and Packers. The two were friends dating back to Harlan's time with the baseball Cardinals.

By the early 1990s, the new stadium talk in Milwaukee had stalled. The costs were staggering, in part because of the size of a stadium that would be required to cater to both football and baseball. Harlan sensed Selig wouldn't mind if the Packers decamped from Milwaukee — if anything it might make a smaller new stadium more viable. (It did — some years after the Packers moved, Miller Park was opened to great acclaim.)

"Bud said it would actually help him," Harlan told me in an interview for this book, speaking of the Packers leaving Milwaukee.

But the Milwaukee fans were another matter. Harlan and his accountants kept looking at the numbers, which, after the construction of luxury boxes and other revenue-producing measures at Lambeau Field, were by the early 1990s showing it cost the Packers nearly $2 million a year to play four games at County Stadium.

"I knew we had to get out of there," Harlan said. But would the fans understand?

In November 1993, *Sports Illustrated* took the issue national with a story that focused on Harlan's own conflicted feelings.

"Financially it makes absolutely no sense to play in Milwaukee," Harlan told the magazine. "But from a public relations standpoint, it does make sense. It would be a terrible mistake to turn our backs on Milwaukee. They've supported us over the years. In fact, I think the County Stadium crowd is louder than the Lambeau Field crowd."

Harlan said the decision was also complicated by the Brewers' ongoing and as yet unsuccessful efforts to get a new stadium. There was even talk of the baseball team leaving Milwaukee.

Harlan said: "Our preference is to stay in Milwaukee, preferably in a new stadium, but this all hinges on the Brewers. If the Brewers leave, we'll pull our entire schedule up to Green Bay."

Some 10 months after that *Sports Illustrated* story, in September 1994, the picture was clouded further when Bud Selig — not just the Brewers' owner but also acting commissioner of Major League Baseball — called off the baseball season because of an ongoing players' strike. The possibility existed that there would be no major league baseball in 1995, either, and if that happened, Bob Harlan told reporters, the Packers would also not play at County Stadium in 1995.

At the point when Selig canceled the 1994 baseball season — September 1994 — Harlan was actually two months into working on a plan that would move the Packers out of Milwaukee in 1995, no matter what happened to the Brewers. The Packers' president had made some courtesy calls — to Selig, to the NFL office, to business leaders and politicians in Milwaukee, saying a move was being discussed — but the first significant step came in October 1994, when Harlan told the Packers' Executive Committee he was thinking of pulling out of Milwaukee.

"They were more than a little startled," Harlan told me. "But they listened to my plan and they gave me their full approval."

He sold them on the idea the same way he sold the team's Milwaukee fans. Harlan had come up with a plan that was both bold and conciliatory. It called for pulling the games out of Milwaukee almost immediately — the last game at County Stadium would be in December, against the Atlanta Falcons — but the team wouldn't turn its back on the County Stadium fans. Milwaukee season ticket holders would be offered the chance to purchase "season tickets" for two regular and one pre-season game in Lambeau Field, starting the next year. While the Milwaukee fans would lose one game under the plan, Harlan felt he needed to include an olive branch for the Green Bay fans, many of whom hoped the move out of Milwaukee would mean four more games for them. The Green Bay fans got one more game.

In hindsight, Harlan's plan was brilliant, and it worked. Eventually, 96 percent of the Milwaukee fans bought the package in Green Bay. When the plan was first unveiled, however, no one was quite sure what to expect. Harlan had a press conference on October 12, and the next day's Milwaukee paper carried this headline: "The Pack Won't Be Back." A Milwaukee businessman floated the idea of bringing a professional Canadian league team to Milwaukee, but that went nowhere.

By December, happy or not, everyone seemed resigned to the fact that the Falcons game would be the Packers' finale at County Stadium. That there might be some lingering bitterness was evidenced when the Milwaukee police requested that Harlan and his wife allow officers to escort them out of County Stadium about midway through the fourth quarter. The authorities feared a disgruntled Milwaukee fan might attack Harlan physically. The Packers' president agreed, and later said that he and his wife listened to the end of the game on the radio in their car driving north on Interstate 43. As it turned out, they missed a barnburner.

By the time the Falcons got to County Stadium on December 18, it had been a strange year on the field for the Packers. Certainly it had been a year that had left Brett Favre with mixed feelings about Milwaukee and County Stadium.

The season had started with a 16-10 win over the Minnesota Vikings at Lambeau, but game two, against the Miami Dolphins at County Stadium, was a bad loss. The final was 24-14, but the game wasn't that close; the Packers scored two fourth-quarter touchdowns to make the score respectable. Favre fumbled to end a drive in the first half and was picked at the Dolphin 5 to wipe out another in the second. The quarterback was booed often by the Milwaukee fans and Holmgren told reporters afterward that he had been close to pulling Favre in favor of backup Ty Detmer.

The boos bothered Favre, who said later: "It kind of amazes me. I mean, what else do I have to do?"

He elaborated: "I just don't worry about it. A lot of it has to do with ignorance, you know? Two years I've played, two years I've been to the Pro Bowl. This team has been to the playoffs for the first time in 20 years. I mean, everything's been positive, but everyone wants to just keep looking at the negative — it's ignorance, it really is."

Holmgren was frustrated with the mistakes, the errors in judgment, the erratic play that the coach perceived as recklessness in his young quarterback. "I want him to be perfect," the coach said after the Miami loss.

Of course, he wasn't, and neither were the Packers. Things look bleakest after a 13-10 Thursday night loss at Minnesota. Favre had been injured in the first half and replaced by Mark Brunell, who had supplanted Detmer as the backup Packer quarterback. In the locker room at the half, Favre told Holmgren his bruised hip was probably good enough for him to play. "We're going with Mark," Holmgren said.

The Packers lost in overtime, their record falling to 3-4, and a day or two later the Packer coaches had a meeting in which Holmgren posed a question for the room: Favre or Brunell? The team's next game was against the archrival Chicago Bears.

"Look," Holmgren said. "We had a little chat yesterday about the quarterback position. Quite frankly, when you do some of your crazy things, you know coaches get a little nervous."

Years later, Holmgren told HBO's *Inside the NFL* that the vote by his assistants actually favored Brunell. What Holmgren did not tell HBO was why he decided not to take their advice and to stick with Favre instead. Favre said Steve Mariucci, the quarterbacks' coach with whom Favre was very close, had argued strongly against a change.

After making his decision, Holmgren told HBO, he called Favre into his office. (The quarterback once told the *Milwaukee Journal Sentinel* that his heart-to-heart with Holmgren had occurred during Favre's second season; Holmgren places it right after the Minnesota game in season three. Of course it's possible they're both right, and that there was more than one such emotional meeting on the topic of Favre's inconsistency.)

Holmgren recalled what happened when Favre sat down in the coach's office.

"Look," Holmgren said. "We had a little chat yesterday about the quarterback position. Quite frankly, when you do some of your crazy things, you know coaches get a little nervous."

The Viking game had been on a Thursday night, and Favre recalled that he used the extra couple days off to fly home to Mississippi for some soul-searching.

Apparently, he found what he was looking for; in their next game, the Packers with Favre at quarterback dismantled the Chicago Bears 33-6.

That evened Green Bay's record at 4-4, and though they split their next six games, putting their record at 7-7 as they prepared to host the Falcons in Milwaukee on December 18, 1994, Favre was on a personal roll. In the five weeks prior to the Atlanta game, he'd thrown 18 touchdown passes. If the Packers could beat Atlanta and then Tampa Bay the following week, they were almost guaranteed a playoff spot.

So along with it being an historic day — the Packers' last game in Milwaukee after 62 years — much was on the line as the Packers and Falcons took the field. By December in Wisconsin standards, it was a nice day — the temperature 33 under clear skies, although a brisk 15-to-20-mile-an-hour wind out of the northwest produced a windchill of 15.

The Falcons were 6-8 coming into the game — with somewhat less realistic playoff hopes of their own — and they had their own strong-armed quarterback as well in Jeff George, who had started the season on fire but cooled a bit lately.

George was the centerpiece of the Falcons' fast-paced, run-and-shoot attack, and Packer fans would see him right away because the Falcons received the opening kickoff.

Chris Jacke's kick was returned to the Atlanta 30, from where the Falcons went three and out, as a third-down pass from George — out of the shotgun and into the wind — was tipped by Green Bay's Sean Jones and fell incomplete.

Harold Alexander punted for Atlanta, into the wind, and caught a bad one that Robert Brooks returned to the Green Bay 47.

There were, of course, no boos when Brett Favre brought the Packer offense onto the field. He had turned his season around and the stats revealed it — a 61 percent completion rating and 28 touchdowns, third most in the NFL.

On second down in the first series, Favre dropped back, looked left, and hit Sterling Sharpe with a bullet that Sharpe gathered in at the Falcon 40, falling forward as he was tackled to the 36.

On third and 10 from the 36, Favre hit Robert Brooks over the middle for a first down on the Atlanta 22. The next play was a handoff to Edgar Bennett, who ran through a big hole off left tackle and took it near the 12, where it was second and short for the Packers. The give was again to Bennett going left, and he took it to the 8.

On first down, Favre hit Sharpe with a quick pass in the right flat. The receiver put a spin move on cornerback D. J. Johnson and ran in for the score. It had been an impressive eight-play, 53-yard drive, and the Packers led, 7-0.

Atlanta's second drive would change the entire dynamic of the game. On first down from the Falcon 37, George dropped back to pass, looking to his left, where he spotted Terance Mathis on the hash mark at the Green Bay 48. As George released the ball — which was caught by Mathis — the quarterback was blindsided by Packer linebacker Bryce Paup, who was blitzing from George's right side. There was a penalty flag on the play, but it was a defensive hold on Terrell Buckley rather than a late hit on Paup. Not that it mattered to George, who was writhing on the ground. The quarterback tried to get up, staggered, and fell again. It was hard to watch. He had fallen on his left arm and something was very wrong. Atlanta's veteran backup, Bobby Hebert, quickly began loosening up on the Falcon sideline. George was eventually taken to the Falcon locker room in a golf cart, where he would be diagnosed with a broken left finger. He was finished for the day.

Hebert, given his chance, came out firing. He missed badly on second down in the face of another Packer blitz. But on third and long Hebert found Mathis on the left side for 12 yards and a first down at the Packer 24. Next Hebert hit Bert Emanuel alone in the right flat, and the receiver took it to the Packer 8. But there the Packer defense tightened, and Atlanta had to settle for a Norm Johnson 20-yard field goal, making it 7-3, Green Bay.

On the Packers' next series, with a third and seven from their own 39, Favre dropped back and was immediately faced with the Falcons' hard-charging defensive end, Chuck Smith, who had come into the game with 11 sacks, sixth best in the NFL. Smith got a hand on Favre at the Packer 28, but the quarterback sprinted to his right and, as he neared the sideline, spotted wide receiver Anthony Morgan open over the middle. Favre threw on the run and Morgan made the catch at the Atlanta 48, taking it to the 42 for a Packer first down.

Running back Edgar Bennett, wearing three-quarter-inch spikes in his shoes — the longest allowable — carried the ball the next two plays and gave the Packers a first down at the 32.

The Atlanta game would showcase Bennett's talents as both a runner and a receiver out of the backfield. By the end he had run for 46 yards on 13 carries and also caught eight passes for 72 yards.

The receptions were a team record, and in the locker room later Mike Holmgren was full of praise: "He is a multi-purpose back for us and he fits in beautifully with what we try to do with our fullback. You're always looking for a guy who's a little bigger, or a guy who's a little quicker running the ball. But he combines a lot of the skills I think you need in what we do. He's just a good football player."

After Bennett's first down, Favre next hit Sterling Sharpe over the middle for 11 yards and another first down.

On third and 4 from the Falcon 15, after an incomplete pass and an gimmick play that had Sharpe carrying the ball on a run out of the backfield, Favre dropped back, looked right, and kept looking right as Anthony Morgan sprinted for the right end zone with a step on Falcon corner Darnell Walker. Favre's pass to Morgan was on target and as the first quarter ended, the Packers led 14-3.

On his television show a few days after the game, Holmgren called the first two drives "almost flawless." Maybe it had been too easy for the Packers. "I think we may have slacked off a little bit," Favre said later. In any case, the next eight times the Packers got the ball, not much good happened. They had four punts, two missed field goals, and an interception.

Atlanta was not a great deal better. On their first drive following Morgan's touchdown, they marched into Packer territory but linebacker George Koonce forced a fumble and Sean Jones recovered on the Green Bay 18.

After a three-and-out by the Packers, Hebert brought the Falcons back. He hit wide-out Andre Rison (who before too long would be wearing a Packer uniform) along the left sideline for a 34-yard gain to the Green Bay 23.

On third and seven, Atlanta correctly sniffed out a Packer blitz. Hebert dumped a short screen to running back Craig "Ironhead" Heyward, who carried it all the way to the Green Bay 2. On the next play, Heyward carried it across for the score.

Trailing by five, the Falcons decided to go for a two-point conversion. Hebert dropped to pass but pressure from Reggie White forced an incompletion. White's rush on the failed extra point conversion was one of the few times all day the Packer great was a factor. White would later say the Falcons were holding him on nearly every play. "These guys won't call anything," White said of the officials. "This is going to drive me out of the game early because I'm getting a little sick and tired of it."

The half ended with the Packers up 14-9. The most significant play of the second quarter had hardly been noticed, because no one at the time could have possibly recognized its significance.

On a routine Packer running play, wide receiver Sterling Sharpe had blocked Falcon safety Brad Edwards and sustained an injury to his neck. Sharpe lay momentarily motionless on the field. But he got up and at halftime gave wide receiver Anthony Morgan a thumbs-up and said, "I'm OK. I can come back and play."

He didn't, not against Atlanta. Sharpe would return the following week against Tampa Bay and put up some good numbers before again leaving the field early. Still no one knew the extent of the injury. They would find out less than six weeks later when Sharpe underwent spinal surgery. His career was over. Brett Favre would never again throw to a receiver as gifted as Sterling Sharpe. It was left to another receiver, tight end Mark Chmura, to find the silver lining in Sharpe's second-quarter departure against the Falcons in Milwaukee: Chmura years later said it proved to the offense they could win without Sharpe.

Chmura caught a ball late in the third quarter of the Atlanta game that put Favre over 10,000 yards in career passing. But neither team scored in the third quarter or for the first six minutes of the fourth.

The Falcons had a third down and 16 from their own 44, with 8:24 to go in the game, when Hebert came up with a big play. Out of the shotgun formation, Hebert took the snap on his 39 and dropped back a few more yards to the 36. From there, with good protection, Herbert hit Bert Emanuel down the right sideline to the Packer 33, a gain of 23 yards.

On second and seven from the 30, Hebert hit Andre Rison, who had beat Doug Evans, at the Packer 18. Rison spun and took it down the sideline all the way to the 5, where LeRoy Butler saved a touchdown by knocking Rison out of bounds. On the next play, Hebert again looked for Rison, in the left end zone this time, but he threw a poor pass that hit the Packers' Evans right in the hands. He dropped it. Given a second chance, Hebert hit Terance Mathis over the middle for a touchdown. Atlanta again went for two on the conversion, this time successfully on a Hebert-to-Rison pass. It was 17-14, Falcons, with 5:53 left in the game.

A message from the Packers to their fans flashed on the scoreboard at County Stadium: "The Packers extend their sincerest thanks to our Milwaukee fans for their great loyalty and support over the past 62 years. The Packers are also happy to welcome you to Lambeau Field in 1995. Merry Christmas and Happy Holidays."

The fans could not have been happy when Favre could not take advantage of a short kickoff that put the Packers in business on their own 40. Green Bay went three and out and punted it back to Atlanta.

Having left the game for security reasons and listening to it on the car radio, Packer President Bob Harlan may have begun to wonder if the team's last game in Milwaukee was going to be a loss.

Packer fans had more to worry about when Bobby Hebert, on third and seven from the Falcon 30, hit wide receiver Ricky Sanders over the middle for 10 and a first down.

There was 3:20 to go in the game.

Atlanta tried to work the clock. Two runs by Heyward gave them a third and four from their 39. The Packers used their second of three timeouts to stop the clock with 2:10 remaining. On third down, the defense came up big. Hebert missed Rison on the left sideline and the Falcons had to punt.

Harold Alexander's punt was not especially good; Robert Brooks caught it on the Packer 30 and returned it to the 33.

Favre brought the Packers onto the field with 1:58 left on the clock.

Everyone knew the first play would be a pass and it was, with Chmura somehow finding himself all alone at the Atlanta 48, where he caught a bullet from Favre and stumbled forward to the 42 for a pick up of 26.

Favre again looked for Chmura on the next play, but missed him on the right side.

Second down, with 1:33 to play.

Favre dropped to pass, couldn't find anyone downfield, and swung a safety to Brooks near the line of scrimmage on the left sideline. It gained only three and, worse, Brooks couldn't get out of bounds. The Packers came quickly to the line and on third and seven Favre fired a rocket that Brooks caught while tiptoeing down the left sideline. It was a gain of nine and a first down at the Falcon 30.

There was 1:09 to go.

Favre threw the ball away incomplete on first down, and then hit Anthony Morgan on a quick sideline route, but Morgan, too, failed to get out of bounds after a gain of just three. On another big third down with 50 seconds left, Favre found Brooks over the middle to the Falcon 18. Favre rushed down the field, tomahawking his right arm to indicate a quick snap and a spiking of the ball to stop the clock, which is what happened.

Twenty-eight seconds.

The spike had made it second down. Favre took the snap, dropped, looked left, and spotted Chmura coming across from the right. Favre threw and the tight end hung on at the Falcon 13, getting to the 9 before he was brought down. Green Bay took its last time out with 21 seconds left on the clock.

On the sideline, Favre and Holmgren were having an animated conversation. "We were going to throw it into the end zone," Holmgren said later. Any play, even a completion, would be dangerous if not in the end zone or out of bounds because the Packers had no way to stop the clock.

The ball was on the 9 at the left hash mark. Favre took the snap under center and faded straight back to pass. He was still on the left hash, at the Falcon 16, when his protection began to break down and Favre rolled to his right. When he reached the right hashmark, Favre turned upfield. Packer wide-out Terry Mickens was near the sideline inside the 10 yard line, guarded by defensive back Darnell Walker. As Favre neared the 9 and the line of scrimmage, two things were happening: Walker was deciding whether to leave Mickens, which might have opened up a pass for Favre, and Falcon defensive end Chuck Smith was closing in on Favre with an angle from the middle of the field.

In that instant, Favre did not, as might have been expected, fake a pass to Mickens. The quarterback had decided to run. Walker's moment of indecision still cost him, as Favre raced past. At the same time he eluded, at the 8 yard line, the defensive lineman Smith, who grasped desperately and got a hand on Favre before falling to the ground. At the 5, Favre launched himself toward the goal line. Simultaneously, Falcon defensive back Anthony Phillips, in the end zone, dove toward Favre and the goal line. The quarterback actually slid *under* Phillips as he crossed the goal line. The Packers had won.

In their car heading back to Green Bay, Bob Harlan and his wife yelled with joy. "We screamed like we were still at the game," Harlan told me.

When the gun sounded on the 21-17 victory, Packers head coach Mike Holmgren made an emotional circle of County Stadium. He climbed on snow drifts and waved to fans. He blew kisses and shouted "thank you."

"I had an emotional experience after the game," Holmgren said on his TV show a few days later. "I went over to the stands and just in some small way acknowledged what they've meant to us. I was quite frankly overwhelmed. It was really something special."

Holmgren always had a player as a guest on his show, and after the Atlanta game it was Brett Favre, who had once again found a way to win.

At some point late in the show, the quarterback was asked about the criticism he had received during the season's many rough spots.

"You just keep plugging along," Favre said. "You have fun. It's a tough job. I try to do my best and hope people appreciate that. I'm getting better. I also know I can play a lot better than I have."

Favre concluded: "Eventually we're going to get a Super Bowl here. Then they're all going to love me."

Chicago Bears vs. Green Bay Packers

NOVEMBER 12, 1995
Lambeau Field, Green Bay, Wisconsin

I t is the greatest rivalry in sports and anyone who tries to tell you otherwise will be proven wrong. History will overwhelm them. The Green Bay Packers and Chicago Bears have been fierce opponents dating back to 1921. Tracing the rivalry, one encounters so many true giants of the game that the merely famous are elbowed aside by the legendary.

George Halas and Curly Lambeau, pro football's founding fathers, got it started. The baton was later passed to Vince Lombardi, whose first victory as a head coach in the National Football League, September 27, 1959, was a 9-6 Packers win over the Bears on a muddy field at Green Bay's City Stadium, a field not yet renamed to honor Lambeau. The Packers carried Lombardi to the locker room on their shoulders that gray and misty day, and there the center, Jim Ringo, gave the new coach the game ball. A decade later, when the teams were celebrating the 100th game in their rivalry before a match-up at Wrigley Field in Chicago, a total of 14 Hall of Famers were present to mark the occasion, including former Packers Don Hutson and Johnny "Blood" McNally, along with Bronco Nagurski and Red Grange of the Bears. Halas himself would have been there, but he was hospitalized following hip surgery.

When the Bears invaded Lambeau in November 1995, to face a Packer team led by quarterback Brett Favre, it was another historic meeting — the 150th.

It would also prove one of the most memorable, which is saying a great deal, since it is a rivalry that has produced at least two full-length books: 1996's *Packers vs. Bears: The Story of Pro Football's Oldest Rivalry*, by Glenn Swain, and 1997's *Mudbaths & Bloodbaths: The Inside Story of the Bears-Packers Rivalry*, by Gary D'Amato and Cliff Christl.

Both note that the first-ever Packers-Bears match-up came at Cubs Park (later Wrigley Field) on November 27, 1921. One might even then have been able to predict the dawn of a rivalry for the ages. The franchises were in close physical proximity, only a couple of hundred miles apart, but for all that closeness they were also starkly different. Chicago was the big city, known to the world. Green Bay was tiny by comparison. Their football teams, as well as the fans of both, regarded one another with suspicion, and for good reason — there was controversy and bad blood right from that first game in 1921.

The game was played in front of 7,000 people at Cubs Park. A few hundred Packer fans made the trip from Green Bay on the train. The Green Bay *Press-Gazette* newspaper had been encouraging the city of Green Bay to get behind the new team. Coach Curly Lambeau had lobbied hard to get his squad into the most prestigious professional league, which in 1921 was known as American Professional Football Association. Lambeau was granted admission that August, and by November they were playing their first game against Chicago — not the Bears, in 1921, but rather the Chicago Staleys, named by coach George Halas for the businessman who first bankrolled the team. By the following year, 1922, both the team and the league would have new and enduring names — the Staleys would become the Bears and the league name would change to the National Football League.

"The greatest rivalry in football began because George Halas single-handedly engineered the revocation of the Packers' franchise for the sole purpose of stealing Heartly W. 'Hunk' Anderson away from Lambeau."

That first meeting at Cubs Park was one-sided in Chicago's favor. The final score was 20-0, but evidently that wasn't enough for Halas. Various published accounts suggest the coach was upset that Lambeau and the Packers had played, against league rules, a college player from Notre Dame who had not yet graduated. The player, "Hunk" Anderson, was a starting guard for Knute Rockne at South Bend. It was debatable whether Halas was more upset over the rules breach or the fact that Lambeau had gotten Anderson first. Many of the professional teams routinely violated the no-college-player clause.

But Halas did succeed in getting the Packers' franchise revoked, at least temporarily. Anderson subsequently graduated and signed a contract with Halas and Chicago, at which point the Green Bay franchise was reinstated.

"There you have it," wrote Glenn Swain. "The greatest rivalry in football began because George Halas single-handedly engineered the revocation of the Packers' franchise for the sole purpose of stealing Heartly W. 'Hunk' Anderson away from Lambeau."

Seventy-four years and 149 games later, as the Packers and Bears prepared to meet at Lambeau Field on Nov. 12, 1995, the rivalry had not lessened. There was still plenty of suspicion and distrust between the two teams, and in the week leading up to the game, much of it centered around Packers quarterback Brett Favre and whether he would be able to play.

The previous Sunday had not been a good one for either Favre or the Packers. Green Bay had played the Vikings in the Metrodome in Minneapolis. The Packers-Vikings rivalry might never supplant Packers-Bears, but if there was another team Green Bay and their fans hated with a relish approaching their distain of Chicago, it was the Vikings.

The week prior to the Minnesota game, Favre had thrown three interceptions in a loss to the Lions in the Silverdome. Then it was the Vikings, on the road in another dome. On the Packers' first six possessions, Favre led them to a touchdown and two field goals. On their last drive of the half, however, Favre dropped to pass and, as he stood in the pocket, the Vikings' defensive lineman Derrick Anderson overpowered Green Bay guard Aaron Taylor and forced Taylor to fall backward into Favre. The quarterback knew immediately something was wrong with his left ankle. He made it back to the Packers huddle, but once there he dropped to his knees and, eventually, went to the sideline, replaced by backup Ty Detmer.

"I felt it pop," Favre said later. "I never broke a bone, but I thought something popped, and as soon as you hear something pop, you think it's a bone."

It turned out to be a sprain and not a break, but it was an ugly sprain — shading the ankle blue by Monday, yellow by Tuesday. Water cooler chat across Wisconsin and Illinois centered on whether Favre would play. He had tried to come back on the ankle in the second half against the Vikings, but threw two interceptions, putting Detmer back in the game. The Packers eventually lost to the Vikings, 27-24, and they also lost Detmer — for the season. After throwing a pass that was eventually intercepted, Detmer was knocked to the ground and suffered torn ligaments in his right thumb.

The Green Bay third-stringer, T. J. Rubley, fumbled his first snap and was otherwise ineffectual against the Vikings.

Scrambling, the Packer general manager, Ron Wolf, signed a journeyman quarterback, Bob Gagliano, in the week leading up to the Bears game. Everyone in Packerland was hoping desperately that Favre would be all right to play. Never had so many words been spoken or written about an ankle. Favre couldn't or wouldn't say, and neither would Holmgren. The Packers' beat writers took to asking other players. Running back Dorsey Levens reported that when he asked Favre on Friday if the quarterback would be playing, Favre said he didn't know.

Center Frank Winters said Favre took some snaps at Friday's practice. The official line from the team was that both Favre and star defender Reggie White were "questionable," which is NFL-talk for 50-50.

The Bears, for their part, were dubious, and assumed both Favre and White would play.

"We're just going on the assumption they will play," Chicago coach Dave Wannestadt said. "I addressed the team about that Monday, and there hasn't been a word said about it since."

Heightening the suspense was the importance of the game from a division-lead standpoint. Though the Packers had narrowly won the teams' first 1995 meeting — a 27-24 squeaker on a Monday night in September — the Bears came into the game with a 6-3 record and a one-game lead in the NFC's Central Division over the Packers and the Tampa Bay Buccaneers, both of whom were 5-4. The Packers could scarcely afford a loss that would drop them two games behind.

The day of the game dawned cold and overcast; the lights were on at Lambeau. The air temperature was 22, the windchill was 15, and snow flurries were in the air.

How much into the game — and aware of its primary story line — the fans were was clear early when Brett Favre was introduced as the Packer starting quarterback. Favre came running out of the tunnel to a sustained roar, hands held high over his head, his right fist pumping. His teammates had formed a tunnel and the first player Favre ran past and slapped hands with was Reggie White. The fearsome defender would play but not start. Favre, who was slapping helmets and firing up his teammates on the sideline, was starting.

Packers great Jim Taylor was the game's honorary captain and would toss the coin to see who would kick off. Taylor, the punishing fullback from the Vince Lombardi era, knew full well about the high stakes of the Packers-Bears rivalry. Taylor once scored three touchdowns as the Packers buried the Bears, 49-0, for the most one-sided victory in the history of the rivalry. Then there was the year, 1962, when Taylor faced the Bears in Green Bay in late September and ran for 126 yards in 17 carries. Just five weeks later, on November 4, 1962, at Wrigley Field, Taylor rushed for 124 yards in 25 carries, including four for touchdowns. The lopsided final was Packers 38, Bears 7. Jim Taylor knew how to beat the Bears.

Chicago won his coin flip, however, and the Packers kicked off to start the game.

The Bears' quarterback, who was having a good year, was somebody well familiar to the Packers. Erik Kramer, whom they had battled when Kramer was wearing a Detroit Lions uniform in the 1993 season, had taken every snap for the Bears in 1995 — the only NFL quarterback who could say that as the 10th week kicked off. Kramer had been not just durable but effective, too — the Bear offense, statistically, was ranked second only to the Dallas Cowboys in the NFC. Going into the Packer game, Kramer had 21 touchdown throws and was completing 60 percent of his passes.

On the Bears' first series, which started from their own 26, Kramer had some success varying his snap count and drawing the Packers offside. Two penalties and a couple of Kramer-to-Nate Graham passes quickly moved Chicago into Packers territory.

On a second and three from the Green Bay 38, Kramer again looked for Graham, finding him along the right sideline for a pickup of 15 to the Packer 23, where he was tackled by Doug Evans.

On his early throws, Kramer had plenty of time to pass, and that had been a key to his season-long success — Kramer had been sacked only five times coming into the game.

On second down, after a running play gained a couple of yards, Kramer, operating out of the I formation, faked a handoff into the line and dropped straight back to pass. This time the Packers were blitzing and had some pressure on Kramer, who set up on his 28, the standard seven-yard drop. Up the field to his right, wide receiver Curtis Conway had run a straight route and then juked toward the sideline, a move that took in Packer corner Craig Newsome. Conway cut back upfield toward the end zone, and Newsome, trying to adjust, slipped to the turf. Blitzing linebacker Fred Strickland was almost to Kramer but the quarterback spotted Conway alone in the right-middle end zone and released the ball before being hit. Conway caught it, and with the extra point the Bears led, 7-0. Just over five minutes into the game, Conway's touchdown meant he had now made a scoring reception in seven straight games, which tied a Bears' team record.

Brett Favre, bringing the Packers onto the field after a short kickoff that gave them the ball at their own 41, was working on a record of his own. The Bears game was his 55th consecutive start for the Packers, an impressive statistic that was destined to grow and eventually become one of the most storied records of all time.

For now, the Packer faithful hollered their approval of their quarterback starting despite a painful ankle. The first drive, everyone sensed, would tell a lot about Favre's effectiveness. The quarterback himself wasn't truly sure what to expect. He'd been on crutches early in the week and starting on Wednesday the Packer trainers were having him alternate ice pumps and heat packs around the ankle. Favre would say later he had one therapeutic pack or another on 20 out of 24 hours a day from midweek on.

By Sunday morning, he felt he could start. When he came onto the field, the tape around Favre's ankle was thick and easily visible. He later compared it to a cast. It would allow him to play but seriously compromise his mobility. Favre would be, on this day, a pocket passer.

On the Packers' first play from scrimmage, Favre handed off to Edgar Bennett, who lost a yard. The next play was a reverse to wide receiver Robert Brooks, who was instantly in trouble and might have lost as much as 15 yards had he not cut and slithered his way back and forth across the field, covering substantial real estate for what in the end was no gain.

On third and 11 from the 39, Favre dropped straight back with good protection and hit receiver Mark Ingram on the left side at the Bear 37. Ingram ran it to the 32 before being shoved out of bounds; it was a gain of 28 yards, and Favre did not appear to be having a problem with his left ankle.

"It was probably hard to tell," the quarterback said later. "But I was favoring it a little bit and didn't scramble on some plays that I probably could have. We cut the game plan down."

He was also helped by a Bear defense that inexplicably rarely blitzed.

The Packers fully expected an array of blitzes, since Favre could do little should his protection break down. To counter, they would call a number of screen passes, as they did on first down from the Bear 32 after Ingram's catch. Dorsey Levens caught the screen but was stopped for no gain. Second down was a nine-yard completion to tight end Mark Chmura, and on third and one, Favre hit the team's second tight end, Keith Jackson, for a first down at the 17. Jackson had refused to report for the first six weeks of the season after being traded from Miami in the off-season, citing his intense dislike of cold weather. Now he was beginning to contribute. "It was big," Jackson said later, "because they came to me a few times on third down, which means they're getting more comfortable with what I can do."

On first down from the Bear 17, Favre dropped, let the rush come, and then dumped a screen over the middle to Bennett, who caught it at the 20 and then sprinted upfield and toward the left sideline. Bennett launched himself toward the end zone from the 3-yard line and his left foot actually pulled loose the pylon marking the goal line. It was a touchdown, and with Chris Jacke's extra point, the game was tied, 7-7.

It was going to be a day for the offenses.

Chicago's, however, sputtered on their second possession. A holding penalty on the kickoff started them deep in their own territory and they wound up three and out — with the punt taken for the Packers by Antonio Freeman at the Green Bay 45 and no Bear within 10 yards of him. Todd Sauerbrun had gotten off a line drive and Freeman took advantage, cutting to the left and taking it all the way to the Bear 29 before being tackled near the sideline.

On first down, with four wide receivers, Favre took a short drop, faked a handoff to Bennett, and fired in the direction of wide receiver Robert Brooks, who was open on the left hash mark at the Chicago 12. Brooks caught it and high-stepped into the end zone untouched.

It was a great start for the Packers' offense. The pass was Favre's 89th touchdown throw as a Packer, tying him for third all-time with Tobin Rote, behind Lynn Dickey (who had 133) and Bart Starr (155). It was huge, too, for Brooks, who was putting up receiving numbers that were making Packer fans forget about Sterling Sharpe.

"He's a heckuva football player," Favre said later. "I don't know how long it's going to take to convince everyone in this league that he's a go-to guy. I'll just keep throwing to him and believing in him until someone stands up and says, 'Hey, you're right.'"

It was 14-7 Packers, but not for long. After the Packer kickoff, the Bears drove 79 yards in seven plays, the big one coming on the first play of the drive, when Kramer hit Conway for a 38-yard reception to the Packer 35. The Bears eventually scored four seconds into the second quarter on a two-yard run by Rashaan Salaam, who vaulted over the middle of the line for the score.

"He has been good before. But I thought he was really something today. He was in a zone."

Next, with the game tied, the teams traded punts, after which the Packers started in good field position at their own 42. On second down Favre hit Ingram with a beautifully timed pass on an out pattern to the sideline, Ingram going up on tiptoe to catch it and stay in bounds for a gain of 14.

A short time later, on third and six from the Bear 40, Favre hit Keith Jackson over the middle for 12 and first down at the 28.

Favre, who connected on his first eight passes of the game, was fashioning something special this day, despite his gimpy ankle.

"He has been good before," quarterbacks coach Steve Mariucci would say afterward. "But I thought he was really something today. He was in a zone. It was like when Michael Jordan was hitting all those threes and couldn't believe they were going in."

As good as Favre's numbers were, they might have been better. On first and 10 from the 28 after Jackson's reception, Favre dropped back and from the 34 threw to the left side where Brooks was sprinting up field and angling slightly to the sideline on a "go" route. Brooks had his arms outstretched and the ball arrived directly over his helmet — an admittedly tough catch that, though the ball hit him in the hands, Brooks did not make.

On third down, after another incompletion, Favre found a diving Anthony Morgan at the Bear 7. It was otherwise notable in that it was the first time that day that Favre had been forced out of the pocket, having rolled to his right. It must be said his ankle simply did not appear to be bothering him. Holmgren would feel compelled to insist later that the Packers had not been, in his words, "sandbagging" — Favre really was hobbled and had been questionable right up until game time. "It was an ugly thing," Holmgren said of the ankle. "A running back probably wouldn't have been able to play."

The Packers, with a first down inside the Chicago 10, nearly failed to take advantage. On third and goal from the 3, out of an I formation, Favre rolled left and flipped an inelegant "shovel" pass toward Dorsey Levens at the goal line. It appeared at first to have been intercepted by Chicago safety Anthony Marshall, though whether Marshall made the pick or not quickly became moot because the Bears were called for defensive holding on Packer receiver Mark Ingram in the end zone. That made it first and goal from the 1. Favre took the snap, rolled a bit right, and threw to Levens in the right corner of the end zone. Packers 21, Bears 14.

In the Lambeau stands, fans unveiled a banner that linked two of Wisconsin's great passions:

"WELCOME HUNTERS! BEAR SEASON HAS OFFICIALLY
OPENED IN GREEN BAY."

Favre would finish the first half with 16 completions in 21 attempts, for 191 yards and three touchdowns.

Say this for the Bears, however; they did not quit, nor even limp to halftime to regroup. As the first half wound down, the Bears found themselves with a first down on their own 14 yard line with just a minute remaining in the second quarter.

Not for nothing were the Bears ranked second offensively behind the Cowboys. On first down, Kramer hit his tight end Ryan Wetnight for 13 yards and a first down to the 27. The Bears had only one time out left and went without a huddle. Kramer handed off to Robert Green, who gained 12 to the Chicago 39. Only 30 seconds remained in the half. Kramer hit wide receiver Jeff Graham, who managed to get out of bounds, stopping the clock, at the Packer 46. Next was a quick screen, intended for Green, that fell incomplete.

In the final 13 seconds, Kramer took the snap, dropped straight back, and had time. He lofted a long floater down the right side, where Curtis Conway had single coverage from cornerback Craig Newsome. Newsome had slipped slightly and that was all Conway needed. He took Kramer's pass right in stride at the Packer 7 and ran easily into the end zone. Just like that, the teams went into halftime tied, 21-21.

"Inexcusable," Holmgren said later of the last-second score.

The Bears were to prove in the third quarter that they could travel by land as well as air. On a drive that started from their own 32 with a little more than nine minutes left in the quarter, the Bears opened up with seven straight runs, gaining a total of 39 yards to the Packer 28. On second and 10 from there, Kramer hit Conway on a short pass for five yards to the 23. On third and five, Kramer faked a handoff into the line, then handed off to wide receiver Michael Timpson, who swept wide on an end-around and picked up 16 to the Green Bay 7. A Packers off-side call brought it inside the 4, where on first down Rashaan Salaam took it to the one. On the next snap Salaam leaped over the middle of the line for a touchdown.

It was 28-21, Bears, with 2:47 left in the quarter.

But the Packers came storming back. Antonio Freeman caught the Bear kick-off at the 11 and took it up the right sideline all the way to the Chicago 44. After the tackle, Freeman jumped to his feet and began waving his arms to incite the crowd, and maybe his teammates, too.

It worked. On first down, the Bears blitzed two linebackers as Favre backpedaled looking to pass. He was falling backward on his own 49 when he lofted a pass to Robert Brooks, who was running a streak route down the right side. That Favre got the pass off at all was due to a great block by Dorsey Levens, who nailed linebacker Vincent Smith as he drew a bead on Favre from the quarterback's right side.

Probably due to the pressure on Favre, the ball was underthrown slightly, but Brooks was open enough that he could wait a second or two on the Bears 16 to gather it in. A diving Bears defender, James Burton, got a piece of Brooks' jersey, but the receiver eluded him and took it for the score. On a one-play drive, the Packers had tied it at 28.

It was Favre's fourth touchdown pass of the day, and, as mentioned, the quarterback was quick later to praise his receiver.

Brooks was elated himself afterward, and a bit modesty-impaired when some-one brought up the departed Sterling Sharpe.

"Like I said when the season first started, Sterling had big numbers, but where are the Super Bowls?"

Of course, Brooks hadn't taken the Packers to that particular promised land yet either, though after the game Holmgren joined Favre in praising the receiver: "He's having a great year. I really believed in Robert Brooks. I knew he was a great football player. You can't have a guy with a better work ethic. My question was his durability."

On this day, Brooks was durable. He would catch two key passes on the Pack-ers' next sustained drive, early in the fourth quarter. The first was a third-and-eight play from the Packer 33, in which Favre found Brooks along the right side-line for a first down at the Packer 48.

The next came just two plays later, on the left side this time, when Favre, with good protection that picked up a Bears blitz, hit Brooks at the Bear 22 and the receiver carried it to the 16.

On first down from there, Favre handed to Bennett, who was stopped at the line of scrimmage. There was now less than 10 minutes to play in the game. On second down from the left hash mark, Favre looked for Brooks over the middle at the goal line, but the pass sailed high.

On third and 10, Favre took the snap and rolled right, a bit of misdirection that worked when he looked back left where Bennett and several blockers were waiting for a screen pass. Bennett caught it at the 19 and, on a play remarkably similar to his earlier touchdown, the running back dashed toward the left corner of the goal line, finally launching himself from the 3 yard line, with the ball extended in front of him, and scored.

The extra point made it 35-28 with 9:10 to go, and Favre's five touchdown passes had tied a Packers' record.

It had not been a great day for the Packers' defense, and the Bears weren't done. A drive that began at their own 20 brought the Bears to the Packers 30 with a first down and 3:20 on the clock. The Bears had run 11 plays in the drive to that point. On third and five from the Packers' 25, Kramer handed to Robert Green, who gained three yards but not a first down. On fourth and two, after the two-minute warning time-out, the Bears decided against a field goal. They also decided against merely trying to pick up a first down. Instead, Kramer threw to the end zone, looking for Wetright, his tight end, but LeRoy Butler intercepted — the first turnover of the game.

It had been an up-and-down year for Butler, but he came up big in the first half against the Bears as well, with a quarterback sack that ended a drive. Defensive leader Reggie White said of Butler later: "I think it was just a thing where he came out and showed up for us today. He played an aggressive game."

Yet the Bears still weren't finished. After the touchback the Packers tried to work the clock and succeeded in draining the Bears of their time-outs, but there was still 1:22 left when Green Bay punted from its 28.

Kramer brought the Bears onto the field, starting from their 36 with 1:13 left. Kramer hit two passes, to Conway and Wetright, taking Chicago to the Packers' 47 with 32 seconds left. On second and six from there, Kramer hit a diving Jeff Graham over the middle at the Green Bay 22. Time was now critical and the clock was running. The Bears rushed up to the new spot of the ball and quickly snapped it, though many Packers had just made it to their side of the line and defensive end Sean Jones had not. Consequently, when the ball was snapped, several yellow flags flew into the air. Jones was clearly offside, but had he, as the rules require, been given a reasonable chance to get back to his side of the ball? That was questionable, but the penalty stood, and it also stopped the clock with 17 seconds remaining. The Bears, with a first and five from the Packer 19, needed the end zone to tie the game.

On first down, Kramer threw incomplete for Conway in the end zone, but there was another Packer penalty — defensive holding against corner Doug Evans.

First and 10, now from the 14. Eleven seconds to go.

On the next play Kramer threw incomplete for Graham in the end zone. Six seconds left.

On second down, Kramer threw to the back left corner of the end zone for Michael Timpson, but the ball sailed high.

Two seconds.

On what would be the game's last play, Kramer threw into traffic around the goal line in the middle of the field, but the pass again sailed high, toward the end zone seats. It was over. In his joy, LeRoy Butler followed the ball out of the end zone and into the stands, making his second "Lambeau Leap" of the game's last two minutes.

Later, musing over Brett Favre's five touchdown passes on a badly sprained ankle, Bears defensive back Jeremy Lincoln said: "Today was the same old Favre."

Intended or not, it was quite a compliment.

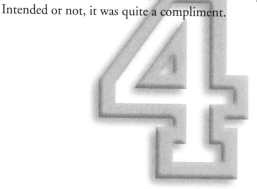

Green Bay Packers vs. San Francisco 49ers

JANUARY 7, 1996
3Com Park, San Francisco, California

It was just a few minutes before kickoff in a game that would send the winner to the National Football Conference championship game. Down on the field, a television reporter grabbed the visiting head coach, Mike Holmgren, and asked for a word.

"This has been a very emotional week for me," Holmgren said.

It could not have been otherwise. Holmgren, in his fourth season as the Packers head coach, retained so many ties to San Francisco and the Bay Area that four years or even four times four years couldn't unravel them.

It was more than the fact that Holmgren had come to the Packers from the 49ers, where he had served as an assistant coach, first under Bill Walsh and then George Seifert.

Mike Holmgren was a San Francisco native, born June 15, 1948, the year the great San Francisco columnist Herb Caen published his ode to the city in a book titled *Baghdad by the Bay*.

Holmgren grew up there, acting in school plays before he even hit high school. (Holmgren once told a magazine writer, tongue perhaps only partly in cheek, that he might have been the next John Wayne had he stayed in acting.) By high school he was, in any case, a local star — at San Francisco's Lincoln High Holmgren was both class president and all-city quarterback. The real world and its hard knocks intruded only after he went south to play college ball for the University of Southern California, where he rode the bench for three years and felt the Trojans coach, the flamboyant John McKay, had misled him. A shoulder injury took the luster off his senior season, though Holmgren played enough to be a late-round draft choice with the St. Louis Cardinals, who cut him during training camp.

Holmgren retreated to San Francisco, where he took a job teaching history at his alma mater, Lincoln High. This was 1971, the same year he married Kathy Bowman, whom Holmgren had first met at a religious retreat when they were in junior high school. They stayed in touch and married after Kathy returned from a year as a church missionary in the Congo.

In San Francisco, she worked as a nurse while her husband, who had moved on to teach at Sacred Heart High School, added the offensive coordinator for the football team job to his duties. The team was a perennial doormat in a tough parochial league; during Holmgren's time there, they suffered through a 22-game losing streak. Holmgren later told *Sports Illustrated* that at one point he quit; his players talked him into staying. "I owe them a debt of gratitude to this day," said Holmgren, by then coach of the reigning Super Bowl champions.

After three years at Sacred Heart, Holmgren moved to a school in San Jose that was a high school football power; then it was back to San Francisco where, in 1981, he became offensive coordinator and quarterbacks coach for San Francisco State University.

He was learning on the job, but Holmgren has said that his eyes really got opened the next year, when he began a four-year run as quarterbacks coach for Brigham Young University. BYU had a reputation as the best passing team in college football, and their quarterback during Holmgren's time in Salt Lake was none other than Steve Young, with whom he would re-team later in San Francisco. Later still — on January 7, 1996, at 3Com Park — they would find themselves on opposite sidelines.

Of his years at Brigham Young, Holmgren said, "The time at BYU really expanded my mind as to what was possible in this game."

Bill Walsh, who plucked Holmgren from the college ranks and made him the 49ers' quarterbacks coach, expanded it more.

Once, when asked what he had gleaned from Walsh, Holmgren responded, "Anything he gave me. He went out on a limb to hire me and I was like a sponge. I bothered him because I was in his office all the time, asking questions."

When Walsh retired, Holmgren became the 49ers' offensive coordinator under new head coach George Seifert. Holmgren was still learning, but he was also nearing the peak of his powers. In Super Bowl XXIV in 1990, his 49ers offense gave one of the most dominant post-season performances ever against the Denver Broncos, emerging with a 55-10 victory that kept Holmgren busy with reporters so long after the final whistle that he missed the team bus back to the hotel. He liked telling the story on himself about how the only official vehicle around the Superdome to give him a lift back was a stretch limo, so Holmgren climbed in, feeling pretty high and mighty. When the limo dropped him at the Hilton, a crowd of starry-eyed onlookers rushed up to see which celebrity was unloading. When Holmgren stepped out, no one had a clue who he was. Being offensive coordinator is a good way to stay anonymous.

Of course, Holmgren wouldn't stay that way long. His star was in ascendance. Following that stirring Super Bowl, both the Phoenix Cardinals and the New York Jets put out serious feelers toward Holmgren about a head coaching position. Since he and Kathy had twin daughters who wanted to finish high school in California, the offers weren't all that hard to decline. His time would come. Still, Holmgren was able to parlay all the outside interest into a landmark deal for an assistant coach at the time — a three-year contract for $900,000. One aspect of the deal that would become relevant later was that it required Holmgren to remain in San Francisco for all three years, unless his head coach, Seifert, left first and Holmgren didn't get the head job. That requirement wasn't insurmountable, but it would make the Packers' courtship of Holmgren more interesting when the time came.

Wolf watched practice, didn't say much, then went up to Harlan's office, where he said plenty. "They're walking around like they're 10-3," Wolf said. "It's a country club atmosphere."

Which it did, quickly enough. Toward the end of the 1991 season, after team president Bob Harlan had hired Ron Wolf as general manager, Wolf was on the field for a team practice. The Packers' record at the time was 3-10. Wolf watched practice, didn't say much, and then went up to Harlan's office, where he said plenty. "They're walking around like they're 10-3," Wolf said. "It's a country club atmosphere." On December 22, 1991, Wolf fired head coach Lindy Infante.

Mike Holmgren was still the 49ers offensive coordinator, though even more teams were interested in him now than in 1990, Green Bay included. But there was, in late 1991, another 800-pound gorilla in the room named Bill Parcells. Parcells had won two Super Bowls as head coach of the New York Giants, then retired early when the stress of coaching took a toll on his health. Parcells went from the sideline into a television studio as an NFL analyst, but few in the business doubted that he would one day coach again. Wolf knew and admired Parcells, and wondered, after Infante's dismissal, if the time might be right for the coach to get back to the sidelines. Parcells was choice 1, but Mike Holmgren was choice 1A, and Wolf had to find out if Parcells was legitimately thinking about returning, while at the same time courting Holmgren. Wolf would later say he figured out pretty quickly that Parcells wasn't ready. The coach was only a year removed from angioplasty surgery, a procedure Wolf himself had undergone.

Still, the recruitment war became a bit of a circus after another team, the Tampa Bay Buccaneers, became involved. Holmgren had flown to Green Bay for an interview with Wolf on December 29. The general manager told Holmgren that he'd talked informally with Parcells — that was hardly a secret — but the day before, December 28, Parcells had tentatively agreed to a five-year, $6.5-million deal to coach Tampa Bay. Incredibly, during the first meeting between Holmgren and Wolf, word arrived that Parcells had backed out of the Tampa deal, at one point mentioning his possible interest in the Packers.

Wolf later said the horse had left the barn by that time, that he assured Holmgren his talks with Parcells had never even reached the negotiation stage, and that Holmgren was the Packers' number-one choice. Holmgren, for his part, said he took Wolf at his word. But, as the saying goes, you trust your mother, but you cut the cards. Holmgren left Green Bay full of good vibes from Wolf and the organization, but before the week was out he was in talks with the Colts. Wolf checked in regularly, not wanting to suffocate Holmgren, but to let him know of Green Bay's sincere interest. For Holmgren, his interviews with other teams didn't do anything but convince him Green Bay was the right place at the right time.

Once they were talking particulars, getting a deal done took a little longer than anticipated. There was the three-year contract Holmgren had signed with the 49ers in 1990, calling for the coach to stay in San Francisco for the contract's duration. Should he leave early, Holmgren's new team would be required to compensate the 49ers with either players or draft choices.

In his autobiography, Wolf recalled angrily that both he and Packer president Bob Harlan got calls from the NFL office informing them of that clause in Holmgren's contract. Later, Wolf said — after the Packers had agreed to give the 49ers a second-round draft choice for allowing Holmgren to leave early — Holmgren's agent insisted that Holmgren had never signed the contract with the compensation clause. Wolf felt the league was trying to help the 49ers, then one of the NFL's glamour franchises, at the expense of the Packers. Maybe that's how it worked, but in retrospect it seems odd that Holmgren and his agent wouldn't have been in the loop and mentioned the signature issue during the draft-choice negotiations.

There was, in any case, already some bad blood in the relationship between the two teams, something Wolf chose not to mention in his own assessment of the situation. That may have been because it was the 49ers who were upset. The dispute predated Wolf's arrival as the Green Bay general manager, and it concerned a trade the Packers had made early in the 1991 season, when they dispatched linebacker Tim Harris to the 49ers for two second-round draft picks. After the trade was made, a Packers executive made a comment at a booster luncheon about Harris having off-the-field issues that made Green Bay happy to be rid of him; when that comment made it into the media, the 49ers cried foul.

The net result, after the dust all settled in January 1992, was that the Packers gave back one of the second-round draft choices they had received for Harris and Mike Holmgren was free to join Green Bay.

Holmgren and his agent, Bob LaMonte, met in Chicago on Friday, January 10, and the Packers faxed out a copy of the proposed contract, to which both sides had tentatively agreed. That night the coach and agent came up to Green Bay and checked into a hotel under different names to keep it quiet. Saturday morning, in the Packer offices, Holmgren signed the contract, which called for $2.5 million over five years.

That afternoon, they met the media, Wolf and Holmgren seated next to one another in front of a gaggle of microphones. Holmgren was wearing a blue suit coat and purple tie.

"I got the job I wanted," Holmgren told the reporters.

It turned into a great, if at times unlikely, fit. One would be hard pressed to find two cities less alike than Green Bay and San Francisco. Madison television producer John Roach, who shot a dozen or more commercials with Holmgren during the coach's time in Wisconsin, said in an interview for this book that Holmgren was conscious of the enormous role the Packers play in the daily life in Green Bay, no matter the season. "He was aware of being under the microscope," Roach said, but Holmgren was helped in that he was also the

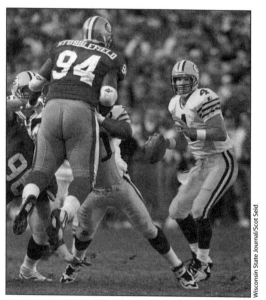

A victory over the 49ers would take the Pack to the NFC Championship game.

rare football coach who could immerse himself in something other than the game. Holmgren was a student of history, a voracious reader (Roach said they shared a passion for the mystery novels of John Sandford and Dennis Lehane), and a family man devoted to his wife, daughters, and mother, whom he relocated to a nursing home in Green Bay and with whom he lunched every Tuesday.

Holmgren was, of course, also a teacher, of football and life beyond football, and this too was a part of his relationship with his prized pupil. Brett Favre, while making tremendous strides on the field, would, by the off-season following 1995, also come to grips with an addiction to painkillers, and gain control of his life off the field. Mike Holmgren would visit Favre twice during his weeks in a rehabilitation center.

That was still some months away when the Packers traveled to San Francisco for an NFC semi-final playoff game in January 1996. Favre and the Packers were flying high — the quarterback had been named the NFL's most valuable player, and the Packers had followed up an 11-5 regular season with a trouncing of the Atlanta Falcons, 37-20, in the playoffs' first round.

"If they were watching us today," Favre said after the Falcons game, speaking of the 49ers, "they know not to take us lightly."

Inevitably, the big story of the week was Holmgren's return. In the days before the game, the 49ers players were were gracious about their former coach. "He played a huge part in my development," San Francisco quarterback Steve Young said of Holmgren.

Of all the attention focused on the coach, Packers tight end Keith Jackson said later: "You could see it getting to him. He was a little quieter this week than usual. He was intense this week."

The stakes could not have been higher: The winner would play the following week for the NFC championship and a berth in the Super Bowl, where the 49ers were defending champions.

Somehow, the Packers managed to stay loose. A reporter from Wisconsin spotted receiver Mark Ingram checking out of the team's hotel just hours before the game. Everything's cool, Ingram said. It's going to be a good day.

The biggest question mark for the Packers was probably rookie offensive guard Adam Timmerman, who would start in place of the injured Aaron Taylor and have to face San Francisco all-pro Dana Stubblefield. The 49ers defense overall was ranked number one in the league, with six players headed for the Pro Bowl. Their defensive coordinator was Pete Carroll, who would go on to lead USC to a national college championship a decade later. Carroll, for his part, was worried about containing Brett Favre: "He can make plays even when we do things well."

It was a bright, sunny day with a temperature of 59 degrees at kickoff time. The Packers won the coin toss and after the kick started first and 10 from their own 26.

Favre hit Dorsey Levens on a swing pass for seven yards on first down. On second and three, Favre handed off to Edgar Bennett running right, and Bennett in turn handed the ball to Robert Brooks, who was sweeping back left on a reverse. Reverses tend to work on good defenses that pursue well, and this one worked. Brooks gained 15 to the Packers 48.

The Packers rarely utilized the reverse, but Holmgren felt a few gambles might throw his former team off balance. "He told us going into the week that he was going to let it all hang out, and he did," Packers' tight end Mark Chmura said later. "He didn't hold back at all."

Off the first down, Bennett ran twice for a net loss of a yard, and Favre faced third and 11. He dropped to pass and was quickly pressured by 49ers' defensive end Ricky Jackson, who snagged Favre's right arm as he threw. The pass wobbled a bit but Antonio Freeman made a good grab for the first down at the San Francisco 42.

Favre quickly faced third down again after two plays had picked up only four yards. So far that season, the Packers were converting a league-leading 49 percent of their third down chances, and now Favre took a quick drop and again found Freeman over the middle, this time for eight yards and another first at the 49ers 30. Bennett gained four yards in two rushes as the Packers tried to establish a ground game. Then on third and six from the 26 Favre's pass was batted down by Dana Stubblefield.

On fourth, the Packers lined up for a Chris Jacke field goal. Jacke was 17 out of 23 on the year, but had missed three of his last eight. After the snap, the 49ers' safety Tim McDonald found a hole in the interior of the Packer line and darted through, catching Jacke's kick on the helmet and bouncing it sideways.

San Francisco had first down on its own 34, and one of the biggest plays of the game was about to unfold.

Later, the 49ers' offensive tackle Steve Wallace said the ensuing play took much of the fire out of the 49ers.

"We had all the emotion behind us," Wallace said. "We were ready to play. The very next play, boom, it just turned that quick."

On that first-down play, Young dropped back, looked to his right, and threw a swing pass out to fullback Adam Walker, who caught it behind the line at the 29, crossed the 30 and was hit by Packers linebacker Wayne Simmons. Simmons jarred Walker hard enough that the ball popped loose. Packers defensive back Craig Newsome bent to retrieve the ball, but caught it with his toe, finally picking it up at the 31 and sprinting untouched along the left sideline all the way to the end zone. It was a tremendous start for the Packers, giving them a 7-0 lead with 7:40 to go in the first quarter.

"You don't try to make a big play," Simmons said later. "You go out there and see somebody running the ball or catching the ball and you try to hit the hell out of them, and that's what I did."

The 49er coach, Seifert, said this: "That was a big play for them because it gave them such an emotional lift."

It also appeared to have a big effect on the emotions of the 49ers, who went three and out after receiving the kickoff. Antonio Freeman took the punt on the Green Bay 37, and Favre wasted no time capitalizing on the Packers' momentum.

On first down, Favre took a straight drop and found tight end Keith Jackson open over the middle for 35 yards to the San Francisco 27. It would be a huge day for the Packers tight ends, who caught 10 balls between them. The 49ers were so concerned with getting beat deep that the tight ends, running shorter routes, were open time and again over the middle. Jackson alone went over 100 yards in receiving.

The wide-outs didn't do badly, either. On first down from the 27, Favre found Robert Brooks in a single coverage down the right sideline and put the pass on the money to the 49ers' 7. On the next play he looked for Brooks in the right end zone and wound up with a defensive holding call on cornerback Marquez Pope, making it first and goal again from just outside the 3. Favre took the next snap and threw quickly while backpedaling to Jackson over the middle in the end zone for the score.

"The guy didn't throw one bad pass the whole game. It's amazing what a good team can do behind a hot quarterback."

In stunning fashion, the Packers led 14-0, with 4:13 to go in the first quarter. It was the first time the defending champions had trailed by two touchdowns in a game all year. Favre at that point was seven for eight passing, for 87 yards and a touchdown.

"The guy didn't throw one bad pass the whole game," San Francisco linebacker Gary Plummer said later of Favre. "It's amazing what a good team can do behind a hot quarterback."

Holmgren would concur. "Brett executed very well," the coach said afterward. "It starts with him. When he makes the plays like he did, normally we do OK. He has worked very hard to become a great player, and he really is."

The 49ers finally got a first down on their next possession, when Young hit the great receiver Jerry Rice for a first down at midfield. But the Packers defense seemed to be feeding off the offense's success. LeRoy Butler blitzed from his safety spot on first down, forcing an incompletion, and then on third and long Young scrambled out of the pocket and was tackled back at his own 40, bringing up a fourth down and 20.

The Packers' hole card on defense may have been defensive coordinator Fritz Shurmer, who while with the Los Angeles Rams in 1990 had utilized a "nickel" defense — five defensive backs —to help upset the 49ers, 28-17.

The same strategy helped the Packers. "We tried various combinations and had some good success mixing up our looks," Shurmer said later. "But yeah, we were pretty much nickel the whole way."

Holmgren was asked afterward when he had seen his defense play better. "I can't remember a time," the coach said.

He might have said the same of the offense.

After the 49ers punted, Robert Brooks returned it to the Packer 28, and Favre went back to work. On third and nine, under pressure from onrushing defensive end Alfred Williams, Favre found Anthony Morgan along the right sideline for a gain of 20.

Then, on second and eight from the San Francisco 49, Favre dropped, found himself pressured, and rather than roll out of the pocket, ran forward toward the line of scrimmage. It's a move that many quarterbacks use to make some rushing yards off an abandoned pass play — sometimes it's even a called "quarterback draw" — but few if any have used it as effectively as Favre in keeping a pass play alive. Favre's instinct was to keep looking downfield even as he approached the line of scrimmage and the point of no return. On this play he spotted tight end Keith Jackson, again in the middle of the field, and drilled it to him at the 49ers' 25. Jackson then carried it to the 14 for another Green Bay first down.

Edgar Bennett got a yard on first down, and then on second and nine from the 13, Favre dropped to pass. The play was a down-and-out route to the end zone and tight end Mark Chmura, but the key to the play was a move by Packer wide-out Robert Brooks. Chmura's route took him seven yards straight up the field toward safety Tim McDonald. There, at the 6 yard line, Chmura cut it to the outside. But the play was made by Brooks. Just as Chmura cut right, Brooks, coming across from his far right split end position, managed to bump McDonald, the defender, which gave Chmura a two-step edge as he ran toward the right corner of the end zone. The move is similar to a "pick" in basketball and in this case it worked to perfection, as Favre found Chmura in the end zone for six points.

The visiting Packers now led, 21-0. There was still 11:21 to go in the first half.

A bit later in the second quarter, the 49ers would finally mount a drive. On a third and 10 from their own 20, still down by three touchdowns, Young stayed cool under pressure and found Brent Jones down the middle for a gain of 29 to near midfield. Packer corner Doug Evans had good coverage on the tight end, but never looked back for the ball; the first time Evans saw it was when Jones caught it.

The 49ers were now passing on nearly every down. On first from their own 49, Young dropped back, slipped, regained his feet, and fired for Jerry Rice coming over the middle from the left side. Rice had just two catches for 16 yards before this play, and the sure Hall of Famer thought this was his third, but the officials weren't so sure. They huddled and ruled it incomplete, much to Rice's dismay.

Young found Rice on second down just short of the first-down yardage, but on third and one running back Derek Loville lost two yards after running into a fired-up Sean Jones.

The 49ers now faced a critical fourth-and-three from the Packers' 44. Out of field goal range, they elected to go. Young took the snap and the Packers blitzed. Loville, in the backfield, let a Packer defender slip past him, then Loville slipped out over the middle, where Young found him for eight yards and the crucial first.

Young was not about to stop firing. On first down he hit Jerry Rice inside the left sideline and Rice took it all the way to the Green Bay 4, where Evans finally brought him down. It would prove to be Rice's longest catch of the day.

There was a just under three minutes to play in the half and the 49ers sorely needed a touchdown. On first and second downs, however, Young threw incomplete into the end zone. On third and goal from the 4, Young faked a handoff right to Loville and then turned back to his left, with the intent of either passing or running a bootleg. Almost immediately, though, Young was hounded by Sean Jones and Fred Strickland, who got a piece of Young's jersey and nearly dropped him for a loss. The quarterback managed to make it back to the line of scrimmage, but that was it. The 49ers ended their 12-play drive by settling for a Jeff Wilkins 21-yard field goal, making it 21-3 Packers.

The 49ers would have one more shot before halftime. After getting the ball back deep in their own territory, Young scrambled for 41 yards — the longest run by a 49er all season — which brought it to the Green Bay 49. From there Young could only manage a short swing pass to Loville before time expired in the half, with the Packers up 21-3.

It was only the second time all season the 49ers had failed to score a touchdown in the first half. The Packers had sacked Young only once, but they had hurried the quarterback 11 times. Favre, meanwhile, had been masterful, hitting 15 of 17 passes for 222 yards and two touchdowns in the first half.

The 49ers would say later there was a lot of emotion in their locker room at halftime, players reminding one another that they were the Super Bowl champions.

What they probably needed out of halftime was a quick score; they didn't get it, but they got the next best thing, a sustained drive.

Starting from their own 20 after the second-half kickoff, Young engineered an impressive 14-play drive that included yet another pass out of the backfield to Loville on second and 23, one that gained 24 yards to the Packer 35. Again Young seemed determined to pass on every down; he would end the game with a team record 65 pass attempts. Young missed on first down from the Packer 35, but then hit Rice on a slant for a first down at the 25. Next he found Jones, the tight end, over the middle for another first at the Packer 9. Strickland had blitzed on the play and nearly got to Young, who was shaken up but stayed in the game.

On first and goal, Young hit Jones short in the right flat, where LeRoy Butler stuffed the tight end after a gain of three. Then Young hit UCLA rookie J.J. Stokes over the middle inside the one. But on third and less than a yard, Loville got nothing off the right side; Strickland was again there first for the Packers. Fourth and goal, and the 49ers took a time out. Young returned from a sideline conference with Seifert and called his own number, scoring on a quarterback sneak that made the score 21-10, Packers.

The teams exchanged punts in the next two series, and the exchange left the Packers with good field position at their own 42.

The first-down play was quintessential Favre. He took the snap, spun right, and faked a handoff to Bennett, the lone running back. Favre then continued to spin, a move that would have taken him back to the left, but as he planted his right foot Favre slipped and fell down at the Green Bay 35. In college, the play would have been whistled dead. Instead, Favre popped back up, looked downfield, and winged it to Keith Jackson alone over the middle for a gain of 28 to the San Francisco 30.

On second down from the 26, Favre was forced from the pocket and picked up eight yards before stepping out of bounds at the 18. The Packer drive stalled there and a Jacke field goal put them up 24-10 as the third quarter ended. When Favre had missed Ingram in the left end zone on second down, it was only his fourth incomplete pass of the day. His stats at the end of the quarter: 21-25, 296 yards, two touchdowns. His protection had been, for the most part, excellent, and Favre would later give high marks to Adam Timmerman, the rookie, who handled Dana Stubblefield well most of the day. "Adam played great," the quarterback said.

The 49ers were still in it — down two touchdowns with a quarter to go — but the Packer defense forced a three-and-out after the kickoff. The Packers had to punt on their next possession as well, but after two Young-to-Rice passes brought the 49ers to their own 40 with a first down, Packer tackle John Jurkovic hit a scrambling Young, whose subsequent fumble was recovered by Green Bay's Darius Holland.

It was a huge turnover, with a little over 11 minutes to go in the game. Turnovers are critical in any NFL game, and their importance only magnifies in the playoffs. In the 32 playoff games preceding this Packers-49ers match-up, a time span covering three seasons, the team with the fewer turnovers had won 30 of the 32 games. Holmgren had said as much in a sideline interview just before game time. After talking about how emotional he was coming back to San Francisco, he said his team had to avoid turning the ball over. They did.

Now, as the Packers offense came back on the field, some fans began to leave 3Com Park. That seemed premature, with 11 minutes to go, but Favre and the Packers managed to eat up another four and a half minutes with a drive that culminated in a Chris Jacke field goal that put the Packers ahead 27-10 with seven minutes left.

Favre's statistics continued to amaze. At this point in the playoffs, counting the Atlanta game and three and a half quarters against the 49ers, Favre was 45 of 63 passing for 498 yards, five touchdowns, and no interceptions. He was continuing his MVP year into the postseason.

The game was essentially over. San Francisco would score a consolation touchdown with just 50 seconds left, but the drive had taken 11 plays. The final score was 27-17.

The seconds ticked down. On the Packers sideline, Mike Holmgren and Reggie White embraced.

Then, with 18 seconds left, Holmgren found himself face to face on the sideline with Brett Favre. Coach and quarterback smiled and shook hands. No doubt there would be more celebrating later, but for the moment what that handshake seemed to signify was that as good a win as this was, there was more work yet to do. It would, as things turned out, take one more year. But Mike Holmgren, Brett Favre, and the Green Bay Packers were setting their sights on the highest mountain of them all.

Green Bay Packers vs. Tampa Bay Buccaneers

SEPTEMBER 1, 1996
Houlihan Stadium, Tampa, Florida

In December 1995, the magazine *Texas Monthly* published a harrowing story about a former star NFL football player who was hooked on painkillers. The author of the piece was in the player's home when the player, who had swallowed many pills, slumped unconscious to the floor. The writer called an emergency hotline. A few minutes later the paramedics arrived. The player was still on the floor, conscious, though barely. His eyes kept rolling back into his head.

A paramedic asked if he knew what day it was. The player said Tuesday. It was Saturday.

They took him away on a stretcher. As they left, one of the paramedics looked at a framed photograph on the wall that showed the wide receiver Golden Richards catching a touchdown pass for the Dallas Cowboys.

One paramedic said to the other, "This is Golden Richards?"

"Yeah," the other said.

"This is sad. This is really sad."

Richards would recover, though the doctors would later say he may have had a grand mal seizure.

The *Texas Monthly* article, written by Joel Reese, who had grown up idolizing Richards, said that by 1995 Richards had been addicted to painkillers, off and on, for two decades. The article vividly, and terribly, illustrated the pills' grip and potential for serious harm. What few knew reading the story about a former Cowboy by then 15 years out of the NFL was that within weeks a prominent current player — the Most Valuable Player in the NFL for the 1995 season — would come face to face with his own addiction to painkillers. Brett Favre was hooked on Vicodin.

The world would not know until May 1996, when Favre admitted his addiction in what many reports later called a "hastily arranged" press conference in Green Bay. Favre made a somber two-minute statement. He later admitted it was tremendously difficult, humbling, too. As he spoke his leg began to shake. Nearby were his fiancee, Deanna Tynes; his agent, Bus Cook; and from the Packers, head coach Mike Holmgren, general manager Ron Wolf, and associate team physician John Gray.

"It's kind of a difficult time," Favre said at the press conference. "Throughout the last couple years, playing with pain and injuries and suffering during surgeries, I possibly became dependent on medication."

The quarterback said, "I'm going into a treatment facility for however long it takes to get better so I can continue to play at the level I have and get to the Super Bowl. It's something that is very serious and something I have to take care of."

The news conference also revealed that Favre had suffered a seizure following ankle surgery at a Green Bay hospital in late February.

Gray, one of the Packer doctors, told reporters, "Any seizure is a serious medical condition. Although his life was not in danger at any time, I think it was sort of a wake-up call for Brett to say, 'I think I need to get some help.'"

It was later reported in *Sports Illustrated*, and by Favre in his autobiography, that when he came out of the surgery Gray was standing over him and said, "You've just suffered a seizure, Brett. People can die from those."

At the news conference in May, Holmgren said, "We are behind him. The entire Packers organization, his teammates, everybody involved with the Green Bay Packers will totally support him in any way we can throughout this process."

Favre would later say that by the time he had the seizure in late February, he'd already recognized he had a serious problem and stopped taking Vicodin, which is a narcotic analgesic painkiller. He said he'd flushed the last of his supply of pills down the toilet at his off-season home in Mississippi. Still, within a week of the seizure, Gray contacted Favre and suggested he accompany the doctor to Chicago for a meeting with NFL substance abuse counselors. Favre later recalled that after a few questions about painkillers, the conversation turned to his use of alcohol.

As a result of that meeting, the counselors suggested Favre check himself into the Menninger Clinic in Topeka, Kansas, for treatment of an addiction to painkillers and possibly alcohol.

Favre put up considerable resistance to entering a rehabilitation clinic. He met with another doctor who sided with the league, saying the quarterback needed treatment. Still he demurred. Then a league doctor called and said that if Brett continued to refuse treatment, the league would fine him four weeks' pay, which in Favre's situation was close to $1 million. He quit resisting.

Favre flew from Mississippi to tell Mike Holmgren about his addiction. The confidentiality clause in the league's substance abuse policy had prevented even the Packers' doctors from discussing the situation with team officials. Favre met with Holmgren, who was stunned. But the coach promised his full support, as did Wolf, who suggested going public. Word would get out soon enough anyway.

Two days after the press conference, Favre was in the Menninger Clinic. Give him high marks for candor: in his autobiography, the quarterback admits that it was a tough stay. He argued with doctors and nurses for an early release; he kept his innermost feelings to himself.

Asked in November 1997 by *Playboy* if he attended meetings at the clinic, Favre replied: "I sat there and never talked. But I did meet some good people in rehab. Bank presidents, CEOs. I learned that a lot of people who have trouble with drugs are bright. They have money and intelligence. Other people might put them on a pedestal, and they want a way to get down. To get lost. Me, maybe I wanted to hide from celebrity status. I still wasn't used to it. Maybe that's why I took pain pills and sat up all night watching TV, escaping everything. I don't know. They had a gym at the rehab center. I had nothing to do but work out, so I got in the best shape of my career."

Deanna came to visit, Holmgren too, and Frank Winters, the Packer center and one of Favre's best friends on the team.

Favre would later say that he was released (after 46 days) only after he learned to contain his anger and admit to the doctors he was a drug addict. It would be months later before he realized, truly, that they were right.

Favre was released from the clinic on June 28 and flew to Mississippi. He saw his parents, played golf for a couple of days, and then flew to Green Bay, where his first order of business was to ask Deanna to marry him. It had been a long courtship; they already had a beloved daughter; they had been through much. He had asked before and she had never been sure he was serious. This time she said yes. The wedding was nearly as hastily arranged as the press conference announcing Favre's addiction. Only six weeks had passed since then, but they'd made a profound difference in Brett Favre's life.

• • • • •

Brett and Deanna were married in Green Bay with their mothers in attendance. The honeymoon was at the beautiful American Club in Kohler because the Packer training camp was only days away. The toughest off-season of Brett Favre's life ended on a high note. Now he was ready to play football.

First, however, there would be another press conference. On the first day of training camp for the 1996 season, July 17, Favre, with Holmgren at his side, met with reporters. It generated tremendous interest — ESPN televised it live nationally. It was an unusual press conference and couldn't have been completely comfortable for Favre — though he was dressed in T-shirt, shorts, and sandals — but it had to be easier than the one two months before, when he had announced his addiction.

On July 17, he began by reading a statement: "I suffer from a dependency on painkillers. Upon completion of my in-patient treatment program, the expert on prescription medication abuse informed me and the Packers' team physician that I no longer have a dependency on Vicodin or any pain medication.

"Further, it has been rumored that my problems also involve alcoholism. The same specialist stated unequivocally that I do not have a problem in this area, namely that I am not an alcoholic.... I realize that while I am in this program, I must abstain from alcohol [under league rules, players in the program can't drink for two years]. I am aware that I have an obligation, not only to myself but also to my fans and team, to comply with the rules while in this system. Believe me when I tell you, 'This is going to be hard.' But I have faced tougher trials and have succeeded....

"Believe me when I tell you, 'This is going to be hard.' But I have faced tougher trials and succeeded . . . ."

"I also realize that during the course of the season, questions will come up regarding this particular time of my life. I hope you understand that I choose to dwell on what lies ahead for the Packers on the football field, rather than rehash the past two months of my life."

During the question-and-answer session with reporters — more than 100 were there — some of Favre's swagger returned. He was, after all, coming off a season in which he had been voted the NFL's Most Valuable Player, and now, ready to start again, he was in perhaps the best shape, both mentally and physically, of his life.

"Mentally, I'm ready to play, and that's scary," he said in response to a reporter's question. "Because if I can play as well as I did last year, the way I was.... I'm not saying I can go out and throw 50 touchdown passes this year, but I just want to win and I feel the best I ever have."

In response to another question, Favre offered this prediction on the coming season: "This year it's the Super Bowl or bust. If we don't go to the Super Bowl, then it's a disappointing year for me and my teammates."

The next day, Mike Holmgren spoke to reporters and tried to downplay — at least somewhat — his quarterback's "Super Bowl or bust" rhetoric.

"Our expectations are high as a football team," the coach said, while maintaining that talk is cheap and everyone starts a new season on level terms. "Because we made it to the championship game last year and played Dallas pretty tough [losing 38-27], that doesn't guarantee anything for this year, not one single thing. The key for me is to make sure that while we remain confident, that we know what really gets you there. And that we have the same unselfish feeling that made last season my most fun year of coaching."

The Packers opened the 1996 regular season at Tampa Bay. The Buccaneers were coming off a tough 1995 campaign in which they finished 7-9 and last in the NFC's Central Division. But they'd made a coaching change, bringing in young Tony Dungy, who would later win a Super Bowl with the Indianapolis Colts, but was now about to coach his first NFL game as a head coach.

Dungy couldn't have drawn a tougher opponent. Despite Holmgren's downplaying their favorite status, many were picking the Packers to win the Super Bowl. The cover of *Sports Illustrated,* which came out a few days before the NFL's first regular season weekend, had the Packers and Kansas City Chiefs on the cover as the magazine's picks to win their conferences and make it to the Super Bowl in New Orleans.

Brett Favre, after his opening post-rehab press conference, had enjoyed a good preseason. His weight was at 215, down 10 pounds from a year earlier. His right arm had never felt better. He would generally get ice treatments for his throwing arm during training camp when he noticed any soreness; he'd had 50 treatments in the 1995 preseason, but this past summer Favre had required just three ice treatments. He had been unable to throw at the Menninger Clinic, and the forced rest had been good for his arm.

About the only factor working in any way against the Packers was the heat. Green Bay had traditionally struggled when traveling to Tampa Bay early in the season when it was hot. The Packers were 6-1 at Tampa in games after October 15; in games prior to that date, Green Bay was 0-4.

The weather at game time for the 1996 opener was plenty hot. The temperature was 83, but the humidity was a stifling 89 percent. It was raining, too, for the hour leading up to kickoff, though by game time the rain had pretty well subsided.

Tampa got the ball first, starting from its own 20 after the Packers kicked off. The Buccaneer quarterback was 24-year-old Trent Dilfer. He was facing a Packers defense that had led the NFL in forcing three-and-outs — stopping a drive without allowing a first down — in 1995, but on a third-and-four from the 26, Dilfer hit wide receiver Courtney Hawkins on the right side for a gain of six and the game's first first down.

Dilfer quickly faced another third down, third and 10 this time from the Buccaneer 32. The Bucs lined up with four wide-outs, and on taking the snap Dilfer dropped quickly to pass. He spotted Alvin Harper momentarily open at the 40 and delivered the ball well, though Harper — perhaps because the ball was wet after all the pregame rain — couldn't hang on. He was hit hard by Packer

Favre unloads one of four touchdown passes against Tampa Bay.

corner Craig Newsome and the ball popped into the air. Packer safety Mike Prior made a diving interception at the Tampa 44, and got up and ran to the Tampa 37 before he was brought down. It was a great start for the Packers' defense, and important in that during the preseason the Packers coaches had stressed the need to generate turnovers on defense. In 1995, it had been the defense's one glaring weakness — despite making the NFC championship game, the Packers had five more turnovers than takeaways in '95, a key statistic and one they had vowed to improve.

As he brought the Packers' offense onto the field for the first time, Brett Favre may have been under a cloud related to his time in rehab and whether or not that would impact his play, but the quarterback's statistics from 1995 spoke volumes. He had hit 63 percent of his passes for 4,413 yards and 38 touchdowns. Not for nothing had he been the league's MVP.

Favre began the 1996 season with two short passes to Antonio Freeman, first to the right side of the field and then the left, completing both and picking up a first down at the Tampa Bay 25.

It was just the start he was looking for.

"Brett was throwing the ball great," Freeman said later. "It was a great over-all day. I thought he was really sharp today."

On second and seven from the 22, Favre faked a handoff to Edgar Bennett and then rolled right on a naked bootleg. It fooled everyone except Buccaneer defensive end Eric Curry, who was right in Favre's face and closing in for the kill when the quarterback lofted a short pass to tight end Mark Chmura, who caught it at the 21 and took it near the 15, about a half yard short of a first down. Dorsey Levens picked up a yard and the first down on the next play.

On first and 10 from the Tampa 15, Favre threw what would be one of his only bad passes of the day, firing incomplete between Bennett and Chmura on the right sideline; it was anybody's guess who the intended receiver was. Second-year Tampa defensive lineman Warren Sapp wrapped up Levens for no gain on second down, and then on third and 10 Favre hit Robert Brooks short on the right side, and Brooks made a nice run to the 6, but that was short of a first down. Chris Jacke came on and his 23-yard field goal put the Packers on the board first, 3-0.

Dilfer and the Buccaneers started the next drive from poor field position when a returner ill-advisedly brought the ball out from five yards deep in the end zone and made it only to the Tampa Bay 12. Still, the Bucs picked up a quick first down when Dilfer, on second and nine from the 13, stood up against a Packers' blitz and found tight end (and former Packer) Jackie Harris on the right side at the 20 yard line. Harris carried it to the 24.

All during the preseason, the Packers coaches had stressed to the defense the need for turnovers. An inability to force them had hurt the team the year before. Now in the season opener they had forced one early, and as the Bucs began moving on their second drive, with a first and 10 from the Tampa Bay 24, the Packers defense forced another. Dilfer handed to halfback Jerry Ellison, the second man in an I formation on a running play up the middle. Ellison was hit hard by Packer linebacker Brian Williams and the ball popped loose. It was recovered for the Packers by Reggie White at the 27.

The Packers nearly gave it right back. Instead, the ball bounced the right way and Green Bay almost scored. Being good and lucky never hurt anybody.

On first and 10 from the Buccaneers' 27, Favre handed the ball to his lone setback, Dorsey Levens, on a draw play up the middle. Levens was hit near the line of scrimmage, managed to spin away, and then at the 20 was really hammered by two converging Tampa Bay linebackers, Derrick Brooks and Hardy Nickerson. The hit jarred the ball loose but it was grabbed in the air at the 19 yard line by Packer receiver Antonio Freeman, who took it all the way to the Buccaneer 1 yard line before being dragged down by safety Melvin Johnson.

On first and goal from the 1, Favre faked a handoff to fullback William Henderson and then found Keith Jackson all alone in the back of the end zone for the game's first touchdown. The Packers led, 10-0.

The Bucs needed a sustained drive to both keep them in the game and give their defense a breather, and they got it. Dilfer took them on an 11-play march that ended with Michael Husted booting a 48-yard field goal to put Tampa Bay on the board, at 10-3.

The next Packer drive would not produce points, but it produced a great Brett Favre moment. On a first-and-10 from the Packer 30 (the drive had started at the 15), Favre handed off to Edgar Bennett, who started to sweep to the right side. But before Bennett could really get going, he was inadvertently knocked over by Packer guard Aaron Taylor, who was pulling and attempting to get in front of Bennett to lead the blocking. Instead he knocked his running back down. Bennett jumped to his feet and reversed direction to the left. It was a smart move because the play was flowing to the right and, with Bennett tripping, several defenders had actually overrun the play and were out of position on the right. Cornerback Charles Dimry, however, had held his position and, as Bennett ran back left, Dimry was closing for the tackle. That's when Favre threw a classic block, leaving his feet, catching Dimry around his knees and taking him completely out of the play. How many million-dollar quarterbacks would throw a body block like that? Favre's block sprang Bennett and he picked up 23 yards before Derrick Brooks pushed him out of bounds at the Tampa Bay 47.

The drive would fizzle there, however, and the Packers punted into the end zone. From the 20 off the touchback, Dilfer picked up a couple of first downs with short passes to rookie running back Mike Alstott, who was proving adept at adding on yards after making a catch. But the Bucs drive eventually stalled when blitzing linebacker Brian Williams nailed Dilfer for a six-yard loss.

The Packers, still leading 10-3, took over at the Green Bay 18 following a punt. Desmond Howard, playing his first game as a Packer, was destined to have a great year as a return man, but he had no room to run on his first opportunity. Instead, Favre took the Packers 82 yards with a masterful drive during which the quarterback utilized his running backs as receivers. He hit Bennett, Henderson, and Levens during the drive. The pass to Levens was on a first-and-10 from the Tampa Bay 48 and gained 19 yards to the 29. Levens had lost his starting job to Bennett and while not happy about that, was glad to get playing time against the Bucs.

"I didn't think I'd play as much as I did," Levens said later. "It hurts to lose your job, but I'm still contributing so I guess that's what's important."

The drive continued. On a first-and-10 from the Tampa Bay 17, Favre found Bennett over the middle for eight yards to the Buccaneer 9. The drive had lasted 11 plays and used 6:35 off the clock.

At that point a funny thing happened. On the next two plays, Favre threw two good short passes — one to Keith Jackson, the other to Freeman — and both receivers dropped the ball. Either would have been a first down. Instead, they were incomplete, and together with another couple of drops that occurred during the game, they highlight how truly re-markable Favre's performance was on this day. His final statistics would show him 20-27 in passing. The fact is only two or three of the misses were his fault; the others were dropped.

"I don't think he had anything to prove to anybody. I think if there are people who believe he had something to prove, they're living in a dream world."

After the Freeman drop, it was fourth down. Chris Jacke came on and kicked a short field goal through the uprights, but there was a flag on the play — a crucial mistake by the Buccaneers. Defensive end Regan Upshaw was flagged for holding on the field goal attempt. The Packers didn't think twice. They took the three points off the board and got a new set of downs from just inside the 5 yard line. It only took one play. Favre hit Keith Jackson, sliding into the middle of the back of the end zone, for the tight end's second touchdown reception of the game. Jacke's point after made it 17-3 with 1:40 to go in the first half.

Holmgren explained his decision-making later. "I have a lot of confidence in our red zone attack," the coach said. "And I was disappointed. We had dropped two passes prior to that and I was upset. I had a quick straw poll with my coaches. Do we take the points off the board? They all said yeah, so we did it."

Tampa brought the kickoff back to the 20. With time in the half running out, the crowd twittered when Dilfer handed off to LeRoy Thompson on first down, and Sean Jones wrapped Thompson up for a loss of two. But then Dilfer went to the air. On second down he missed Jackie Harris down the right side. Dilfer's pass had been on target, but Packer safety Mike Prior delivered a stinging hit to Harris and the ball fell incomplete.

On third down, Dilfer overthrew a long pass down the right sideline. With 1:02 to go in the first half, the Buccaneers lined up to punt. This time, Desmond Howard would strike. The former Michigan star took Tommy Barnhardt's punt — and it was a good one, 54 yards — on the Packer 27 and made the return look easy, bringing it straight up the middle of the field to the Green Bay 49, a 22-yard return.

Favre brought the Packer offense out with 49 seconds left in the half. Green Bay had no time-outs left. As the Packers huddled, the two Tampa Bay safeties conferred in the defensive backfield, but whatever was said, it was a miscom-munication. As the first-down play unfolded, neither safety would pick up Keith Jackson long down the right middle of the field, and he was not, in this game, someone to leave uncovered, as he already had two touchdown catches. Favre had dropped quickly to throw, but found himself pressured, and as he liked to do on occasion, rather than leave the pocket to his right or left, he ran forward toward the line of scrimmage. As Favre neared the line, he spotted Jackson wide open, inside the Tampa 20 on the right hash mark. Favre was still running when he unleashed a long pass in the direction of Jackson. The tight end took it in stride on the 15, dodged a tackle by Charles Dimry on the 5, and then high-stepped into the end zone for his third touchdown of the first half. With Jacke's kick the Packers had a commanding 24-3 lead.

"I just scrambled and tried to buy some time," Favre said later of the play. "The safeties seemed to be looking at me."

Of his play in general, Favre would say afterward, "I moved around real well and found the open guys. When you execute the way we did today, you're going to be successful."

Favre would pull off another forward scramble and completed long pass on the Packers' first drive after taking the second-half kickoff. The drive had started from the Green Bay 36, and it hadn't started well. Warren Sapp, the second-year defensive lineman who felt he had something to prove after a mediocre rookie year, sacked Favre on first down for a loss of four. Then on second down Sapp got into the backfield again, this time nailing Edgar Bennett for a loss of another three yards. On third and 17 from the Packers 29, Favre dropped back to pass and once again had pressure. As the pocket collapsed, Favre, just as he had done on the last touchdown pass to Jackson, ran forward, eying his receivers downfield as he did so, finally pulling up right before he crossed the line of scrimmage and this time finding Antonio Freeman, who was hugging the right sideline and made a brilliant catch, just keeping his feet in, at the Tampa Bay 44. It was a gain of 27 yards and Freeman's fourth catch of the day.

It also set a record for Favre: the completion put him over 15,000 yards passing for his career. The game was the 66th of Favre's career, tying him with Joe Namath for third place among all-time NFL quarterbacks in how quickly they reached the 15,000-yard plateau. It had taken Jim Everett 64 games; first place belonged to Dan Marino, who made it in just 56.

Favre would not throw an incomplete pass in the second half. The Packer drive eventually stalled, when on a third-and-one from the Tampa Bay 22, Favre was forced out of the pocket and tried to pick up a first down running to the left sideline. He was pushed out of bounds just short of the first-down marker and Chris Jacke came on to kick a field goal that put the Packers in front, 27-3.

The Packers' defense forced another turnover — they would extract six by game's end — on the Bucs' next series. On a third and five from the Tampa Bay 36, Dilfer hit Alvin Harper on a slant on the right side. Harper was slammed by Packers corner Craig Newsome; the ball came loose and was picked up by another Green Bay cornerback, Doug Evans, at the 49. Evans was slammed to the ground at the Tampa 45 and the ball again came loose, but the officials ruled that Evans was down, and the Packers had the ball.

By the time Favre brought the offense onto the field, all the questions from the off-season rehabilitation seemed to have been put to rest. Operating at the peak of his powers, the quarterback hit three more passes in quick succession. On first down, he hit Jackson for five yards. On second down, he found Antonio Freeman over the middle, wide open in between the short and deep coverage of the Buccaneers' zone defense. He caught the ball over the linebackers and in front of the safeties and took it to the Buccaneer 20. From there, Favre hit his other tight end, Mark Chmura, on a straight route along the right hash marks. Chmura caught it at the 5 and took it to Buccaneer 1. The next play brought a touchdown: Favre rolled right and hit Dorsey Levens in the front right corner of the end zone. The Packers now led, 34-3.

There were still a few minutes left in the third quarter, but the issue was decided. Favre to this point was 18-25 for 231 yards and four touchdowns — the most touchdown passes ever for Brett on an opening day.

Favre would hit a couple more passes during an early fourth-quarter drive that ended with Jacke pushing a 46-yard field goal attempt wide to the right. The next time Green Bay got the ball, after LeRoy Butler picked a Dilfer pass at the Packer 2 and brought it all the way back to midfield, Favre's backup, 37-year-old Jim McMahon, would come in to play quarterback.

Favre's day was done and there would be no more scoring. The first game after the difficult summer was in the books, and the Packers had won, 34-3.

Later, Favre was asked by reporters if there had been any doubt about his ability to come back and play at the highest level.

"That question has been answered," the quarterback said. "I told you guys not to bet against me."

Frank Winters, Favre's center and good friend, who had visited him at the rehab facility in Kansas, said, "I don't think he had anything to prove. What has he got to prove? The statistics show what he can do in this offense. I don't think he had anything to prove to anybody. I think if there are people who believe he had something to prove, they're living in a dream world."

Minutes earlier, walking off the field, the heat still stifling, another of Favre's close friends on the team, Mark Chmura, found himself next to the quarterback.

"Great game," Chmura said.

"I guess," Favre said, "the old Brett never left."

Carolina Panthers vs. Green Bay Packers

JANUARY 12, 1997
Lambeau Field, Green Bay, Wisconsin

Funny that the writer who would make the most profound connection between the Brett Favre-Mike Holmgren Packers of the 1990s and the fabled Bart Starr-Vince Lombardi Packers of the 1960s was a sophisticated New Yorker who had a regular table at a Manhattan restaurant called Rao's that was favored by shakers, movers, and mobsters. There wasn't a lot of fine dining in Green Bay — mobsters either — but there was history and there were stories, and Dick Schaap liked a good story even more than he liked a good meal.

Schaap came to Green Bay the first time while writing a book about Paul Hornung, the Golden Boy bon vivant who was a Lombardi favorite despite or maybe even because of his social proclivities. Schaap's visit was the beginning of a relationship between the native New Yorker and a small Midwestern city and its professional football team that eventually spanned nearly 40 years and produced six books.

Schaap had been a New York newspaperman in the 1960s, a figure in the landscape of a legendary city room at the *New York Herald Tribune*, where soon-to-be giants like Tom Wolfe and Jimmy Breslin roamed. Schaap became city editor after a stint as sports editor of *Newsweek*. It was while at *Newsweek* that Schaap began doing his first books for an imprint associated with *Sport* magazine. They were short biographies of star athletes. Mickey Mantle was first, and Schaap said later that he wrote *The Indispensable Yankee* on the train back to New York from Florida, where Mantle had let the writer hang with him during spring training. The Hornung book was next, a volume titled *Paul Hornung: Pro Football's Golden Boy*. The research brought Schaap to Wisconsin, and, he later noted wryly, nearly killed him. Schaap made the mistake of trying to keep up with Hornung's off-field training regime. In those days Hornung did not go down until the sun came up. Beneath the surface carouser of legend was a real carouser. Schaap loved every minute of it.

Schaap's real breakthrough as an author came after a magazine assignment brought him to Green Bay a second time. *The Saturday Evening Post* had asked Schaap to write a profile of the great Packer running back Jim Taylor, who was Butch Cassidy to Hornung's Sundance Kid in the Green Bay backfield. It wasn't that Schaap thought Taylor was book material. Quite the contrary — in the *Post* piece Schaap noted that Taylor emerged from four years in college "unscarred by education." But Taylor's training camp roommate was an offensive guard named Jerry Kramer and Kramer stunned Schaap when the writer went to visit Taylor one evening in his dorm room. The fullback was snoring, but his roommate, Kramer, was sitting on the room's other bed reading a book. A book! And a poetry book, at that. Schaap later recalled it was the rough-hewn, adventure verse of Robert W. Service, but still, in the NFL, reading, "The Cremation of Sam McGhee" qualified Kramer as an intellectual.

Kramer quickly became the most famous offensive lineman in football—OK, the only famous offensive lineman—as the play was rerun and rerun to the point where the co-authors decided to co-opt if for their title: Instant Replay.

Around this time, two diary-style books by a Major League Baseball pitcher named Jim Brosnan — *The Long Season* and *Pennant Race* — had drawn the attention of Schaap's book editor in New York. Pro football was not the equal of baseball, America's pastime, in the public imagination (oh, how that would change!), but the editor asked Schaap if he knew any pro football players who might do a diary similar to the Brosnan books. Schaap would ride shotgun as the "as told to" co-author.

Schaap suggested the poetry-reading Jerry Kramer, and their subsequent collaboration, titled *Instant Replay*, made history when it was published at the beginning of the 1968 football season. That's because the season Kramer's diary chronicled, 1967, was one of the most successful and dramatic in the history of the Green Bay Packers, culminating in the famous Ice Bowl game against Dallas at Lambeau Field on December 31, 1967. Schaap would later confess that when the Packers trailed, 17-14, deep in the fourth quarter, he thought the book's title would be *The Year the Clock Ran Out*. But lightning struck, for the Packers and the book. Not only did Bart Starr engineer a late drive and Packers comeback victory, the winning score came on a quarterback sneak following a block thrown by — guess who? — Jerry Kramer. Kramer quickly became the most famous offensive lineman in football — OK, the only famous offensive lineman

— as the play was rerun and rerun to the point where the co-authors decided to co-opt it for their title: *Instant Replay*. It fit the play, it fit the book's quick turnaround time and diary format, and most of all, it fit the reading public's imagination, quickly becoming the best-selling sports book of all time.

In a prolific career over the next three decades, Dick Schaap would have many successes, including book collaborations with superstars like Joe Namath and Joe Montana. He would host a successful sports talk show on ESPN. To a circle of friends so wide and accomplished as to strain credibility, Schaap would be famous for hosting lively dinner parties and dropping celebrity names with a relish that might have been off-putting had they dropped from the mouth of anyone but him. Dick Schaap, it seemed, really did know everybody.

But for all that, Schaap never experienced a professional success to rival *Instant Replay*. In part because of that, perhaps, the author found himself returning to Jerry Kramer and Vince Lombardi's Packers on numerous occasions over the years. There were books and other projects, most notably *Distant Replay*, patterned on *The Boys of Summer* and appearing in 1985. It provided readers an update on the lives of Lombardi's Packers once their football careers ended.

If Schaap had never again rung the bell quite like he did with his first Kramer collaboration in 1967, much the same could be said for the Packers. Indeed, the author fared much better professionally than did the football team. In a city and state where the Green Bay Packers are a religion, the cathedral flame had burned low for many years, if not decades. In the early to mid-1990s, of course, the arrival of Ron Wolf, Mike Holmgren, and Brett Favre changed all that.

By 1995, they were close. Holmgren's triumphant return to San Francisco and the convincing dismantling of the 49ers had advanced the Packers to the NFC title game, but there they had come up short against the Cowboys. The final score was 38-27. On the plane ride back to Wisconsin, veterans like Favre, Reggie White, and LeRoy Butler had made a point of seeking out teammates and asking how it felt, coming so close. To a man, the replies came back that it felt pretty lousy. By the time the plane touched down they had quietly set the goal for the following season — nothing less than the Super Bowl.

Dick Schaap, watching from afar, was struck by some of the similarities between Lombardi's Packers and Holmgren's Packers. Prior to the 1996 season, Schaap signed a book contract to explore those links. As the season played out, and the current edition of the Packers did its part by winning its way to the National Football Conference championship game, the author cast the first half of the book, which he called *Green Bay Replay*, against the backdrop of the Packers hosting the Carolina Panthers at Lambeau in January 1997 — a second Ice Bowl, three decades after the first one made history.

I had a chance to interview Schaap when the book came out and an author tour brought him to Madison. He was staying at the Edgewater Hotel on Lake Mendota and enjoyed having drinks on the Edgewater's pier. We spoke just days before a *Parade* magazine cover story — actually an excerpt from *Green Bay Replay* — was going to be published in Sunday newspapers around the country. Four Packers of two vintages were on the *Parade* cover: Reggie White and Brett Favre were pictured with Bart Starr and Willie Davis.

"Brett Favre and Bart Starr correspond regularly," Schaap told me when we spoke. "Willie Davis and Reggie White have a mutual admiration society."

Starr, of course, was the field general under Lombardi; Willie Davis was, like White, a ferocious pass rusher from the defensive end position.

Schaap told me that they had shot the *Parade* cover photo a month earlier at Lambeau. The author said the admiration and friendship shared by Starr and Davis all those years after their playing days was not lost on Favre. The quarterback, Schaap said, turned to White and, pointing at Starr and Davis, said, "That will be us in a few years."

Both the book's publication and the *Parade* cover were still months away when the Carolina Panthers, having upset the Dallas Cowboys in a playoff game a week earlier, came to Lambeau on January 12, 1997, for the first league championship game to be played at the stadium since the Ice Bowl.

Dick Schaap was there, too, delighting in the success of the new era's Packers. Schaap was happy because he had forged friendships with Favre, White, and a few other current Packers; he was also happy because his publisher's advance for *Green Bay Replay* gave him an extra $10,000 if the Packers made the conference championship game, $25,000 should they advance to the Super Bowl.

Lombardi-era Packers were there, as well: Starr, Davis, Paul Hornung, and Willie Wood, the great free safety. Hornung and Wood walked out onto the field prior to kickoff. Some fans were encouraging Hornung to do a Lambeau leap, but the graying Golden Boy demurred. He didn't want to wrench his back and impede his golf swing.

Starr would talk to Schaap of his admiration for Favre. "I correspond with Brett," Starr said. "I like him. I like his courage, his toughness, his ability. This young man is a complete quarterback. Truthfully, I was an overachiever. Brett's not. He's a talent."

Starr continued: "You can have all the other assets going for you, but when you're facing a great defense in a crucial game, toughness becomes paramount. The champion quarterbacks all possess it. Those that don't win somehow can't muster it."

The Packers were facing a great defense in Carolina, but it was not Starr, or even Favre, who made an emotional speech in the Packers locker room just prior to game time. It was, of all people, the receiver Andre Rison, whom the Packers had picked up off waivers after a regular season loss against Dallas.

Rison had a large talent and an ego to match; some wondered if his negative baggage exceeded his gifts. But he had played well for the Packers and there was no mistaking his ability at the receiver position. LeRoy Butler thought Rison's spark and strut positively affected the younger players, and he asked Holmgren to let Rison speak before the Carolina game. Holmgren's immediate reaction was negative, but the coach acquiesced.

Rison mentioned all the talk the Carolina defense had been getting, how their zone blitz was a wrinkle that might give the Packers trouble. "To hell with that," Rison said. "They have to stop us. We've got too many weapons. So let's go out, run our offense, and kick their ass." Butler would later describe the speech as "hip-hop Lombardi."

Two real Lombardi veterans, Hornung and Wood, stood at midfield with the current players for the toss of the coin to see which team would get the ball first. Links to the past were everywhere. Just before kickoff, the Fox field announcer, Ron Pitts, grabbed Mike Holmgren for a quick interview. Pitts' father, Elijah Pitts, had been a running back for Lombardi's Packers. What, Ron asked, did Holmgren's Packers have to do to win and give Green Bay a Super Bowl appearance for the first time since the 1960s?

"We can't turn the ball over and we have to win the field position game," Holmgren said. It was boilerplate, but true. "Both defenses are very, very strong," Holmgren continued. "Our ability to handle their zone blitz is going to play an important role."

Holmgren had let Rison speak, but obviously the coach respected the zone blitz more than the receiver did.

The weather was reminiscent of 1967, too, though not quite as bitterly cold. The air temperature for the Carolina game was three degrees above zero, compared with 13 below in 1967. The wind-chill index in 1997 was 17 below; three decades earlier it had been a dangerous minus 48. The field had been resodded from a week before and was in surprisingly good shape.

The new sod job at Lambeau inspired a banner in the stands which itself was inspired by a movie about a mystical baseball field in Iowa.

The Lambeau banner read: "If You Sod It, They Will Come."

Carolina running back Anthony Johnson would say later that the new turf had worked, that the field was not an issue. "Honestly, the conditions were pretty good out there," Johnson said.

Brett Favre, MVP of the league for the second year in a row, had one singular perk. When the Packers were on defense, Favre's helmet came off and a stocking cap went on. But Favre's helmet did not sit on the ground or the bench, getting cold. It went instead into an empty Gatorade bucket and was wrapped with heating pads plugged into a generator. The quarterback's ears would stay warm, anyway.

The Packers kicked off with the winter sun at their back, so low in the sky that Carolina's kick receivers lost the ball in the glare. Wide receiver Michael Bates finally picked it up for the Panthers, but was tackled immediately at the Carolina 15.

It wasn't the start the Panthers wanted, and it didn't get a lot better in their first series. The Panther quarterback, Kerry Collins, had played a good if not exceptional game against Dallas the week before, completing 12 of 22 passes for 100 yards and two touchdowns. The low yardage figure spoke to Collins' preference for shorter slant patterns, which his 6-foot-5 size allowed him to throw more easily than most quarterbacks.

It was a slant, to Willie Green on third down and six, that got the Panthers the game's first down at their own 25.

Carolina had scored on its opening drive nine times during the season, tying for first in the NFL in that statistic, but on this day their opener fizzled after the initial first down. On another third and six, Collins overthrew receiver Mark Carrier badly.

The Packers had developed a potent weapon in return man Desmond Howard. Carolina's attempt to punt away from Howard resulted in a poor kick that bounced out of bounds on the Green Bay 46, giving Favre and the Packers great field position for their opening drive.

As he brought the offense onto the field, Favre was a quarterback at the very peak of his powers, a big-game performer about to start his biggest game yet. Favre's career playoff statistics heading into the Carolina game told the story: 61.6 percent of his passes completed, for 1,892 yards and 14 touchdowns.

The quarterback padded those stats on his opening play, hitting Rison on the left sideline for a gain of seven. Edgar Bennett gained two on second down. Then Favre — maybe drawing on the memory of Bart Starr in the Ice Bowl — called his own number on third and one, sneaking up the middle for the first down.

Three plays later, Favre went to the quarterback sneak again, and again it worked, giving Green Bay its second first down of the game at the Carolina 31.

After a false start penalty made it first and 15, a Bennett short gain sandwiched between two Favre incompletions forced the Packers to punt. The third-down pass in particular was seriously underthrown. The cold made gripping the ball more difficult, and there was also the magnitude of the game on the line, but Favre insisted later that by kickoff time his nerves were fine.

The days leading up to the game were another matter.

"I'd never felt that way except for maybe my first game ever, back at Bay St. Louis Elementary," Favre said. "I had butterflies and my dad showed up late for the game with me in the truck. That's the last time I felt the way I felt the last couple of days. I wasn't scared, I wasn't nervous, I was just anxious and wondering. Wondering what the outcome was going to be like. Once the game finally started, I said, 'OK, finally, I can control what's going to happen.' Once the game got started, I was able to relax."

Still, it was a tough first quarter for the two-time MVP. The Packers' first drive ended in a punt. Then, after a Carolina drive stalled around midfield, the Panther punt was downed inside the Green Bay 10. On first down from the 6, looking short to Antonio Freeman, Favre missed incomplete. Then on second down came the kind of miscue Packer fans were no longer accustomed to seeing.

Favre took the snap, made a quick drop, looking right all the way. He threw in that direction, a slant pass to Don Beebe, but Panther linebacker Sam Mills had read the play, stepped in front of the receiver, and picked it off. Rison tackled Mills at the 2. Two plays later Collins found his fullback Howard Griffith all alone in the right end zone for the score.

It was 7-0, Panthers, with 5:10 to go in the first quarter.

"I wasn't so much worried as I was embarrassed," Favre said later, when asked his reaction to the early interception. "I thought I was done with those plays."

There would be one more first-half mistake — a lost fumble — but Brett Favre would no longer let adversity snowball, nor try to make up for mistakes with a gamble that might only compound the damage. He was older and wiser now.

"Back then, I probably would have thrown three or four more interceptions," Favre said. "There's no telling what I would have done. Today, more than in the past, I'm a little more patient. I take some chances, but I'm a little smarter about taking them. I knew we'd come back."

They did. On the next Green Bay drive Chris Jacke would be short on a field goal from 45 yards — the bitter cold affected kicks and passes alike — but the defense then forced a three-and-out from Carolina.

Favre and the Packers, after the punt, started from their own 27. It was worth remembering that, despite the tough start, Favre's record in the cold was eye-popping. In 18 starts up to that point, when the temperature was 35 degrees or colder, Favre's record was 18-0. He had never lost, and in those games his touchdown-to-interception ratio was 40-8. Packer fans were ready for something good to happen, and it did.

On first down Favre hit Keith Jackson with a short swing pass to the right side that picked up eight. Bennett gained a yard on second, and then on third and one from the 36 Dorsey Levens shot through a gaping hole off right tackle and picked up 35 yards to the Carolina 28. It was the end of the first quarter, and it signaled the start of a big game for Levens.

On the first play of quarter two, Favre dropped straight back, with good protection, and looked right for Levens, who had lined up in a flanker position on the right wing. Favre's pass was a bit of a jump ball between Levens and the defender, Eric Davis, in the right front corner of the end zone. Levens not only came down with it, but he managed to drag his left foot just in bounds to ensure the reception. The score tied the game at 7-7.

In the Lambeau stands, a banner unfurled that Dick Schaap and the 1960s Packers heroes could appreciate:

"VINCE IS PROUD."

The Packer defense came up big again on the next series, not allowing the Panthers a first down. After the punt, the Packers picked up a first when Favre hit Chmura over the middle for a gain of 15 to the Panther 45.

On the following first down play, Levens gained five up the middle, putting him over 100 yards rushing for the day. Favre then missed Rison high and wide on a short route to the right sideline, bringing up a third and five. Favre took the snap, dropped straight back, found nobody open, and scrambled to his left. It was then that the Packer quarterback committed his second turnover of the game, fumbling the ball — without being hit. The Panthers' Lamar Lathan pounced on it on the Packer 45.

Collins and the Panthers took quick advantage of the great field position. On first down the quarterback faked a handoff and then hit Mark Carrier on the left side for a pickup of 16 to the Packer 29. Next, Collins swung a short pass to Griffith, the fullback, who gained nine to the Green Bay 20. Collins kept in the air on the following play, hitting his tight end Wesley Walls on the left side for a first down and goal at the Packer 8. There, the Packers stiffened. Anthony Johnson ran it inside the 5 on first down, but Collins followed with two incompletions. Carolina had to settle for a John Kasay field goal that made it 10-7, Panthers. There was 8:40 to go in the first half.

After the kickoff, which Desmond Howard returned to the Green Bay 29, Favre led the Packers on a masterful drive, 15 plays that used up nearly eight minutes on the clock. Favre completed all seven of his passes on the drive, including two early third and short conversions that kept the Packers moving.

The biggest play came late in the drive after Antonio Freeman was called for an illegal chop block that left Green Bay facing a second down and 25 yards to go from the Carolina 28. Favre responded with his best throw of the day to that point. After Chmura started in motion left to right, Favre took the snap, dropped back, had good protection, then stepped up and roped the ball to Andre Rison, who caught it just outside the right hash mark at the Carolina 8, then fell forward to the 6. The Packers called a time-out with 53 seconds left in the half.

After a poor start, Favre's stats had improved to 11 of 19 for 110 yards, a touchdown, and an interception.

It was third and three from the 6. Freeman was split wide left. On the snap Freeman started right as if on a slant route, then planted his right foot and cut left toward the corner of the end zone. It's called a post-corner route and it fooled the Panthers' Tyrone Poole, who slipped when Freeman made his cut, leaving him alone and easy for Favre to find for his second touchdown pass of the day. Jacke's point made it 14-10 with less than 50 seconds remaining in the half.

"Once the game finally started, I said, 'OK, finally, I can control what's going to happen.' Once the game got started, I was able to relax."

Some might have expected the Panthers, taking over on their own 27 yard line after the kickoff, to run out the clock and go happily into halftime down just four, but they did not.

Panther coach Dom Capers said later: "I felt we had a chance to possibly go down there and get a field goal. In a game like this, I felt that was the best route to take. We had enough time and we had all three of our time-outs left. I felt if we could go out and gain 30 or 40 yards, we'd be in field goal range."

On first down Willie Green ran a streak route down the left side and Collins heaved a long ball that appeared headed over everyone's heads. But no one told Packer cornerback Tyrone Williams, a rookie out of Nebraska who played only on the most obvious passing downs. Williams launched himself at the ball, with his left arm fully extended, and made a dazzling one-handed interception.

"It was a throwaway," Williams said after the game, meaning he felt Collins had decided no one was open and was trying to launch a safe incomplete pass before regrouping.

Williams continued: "I guess the wind must have picked it up or something. I just kept running and laid out for it at the right time and pulled it in with one hand."

Williams then said something that one of Lombardi's defensive backs would not have said, and not just because the Lombardi era was pre-cable.

"I haven't seen it yet, but I'm trying to rush home and get a look at it on ESPN."

Still, Packer defensive coordinator Fritz Shurmur was plenty old school and plenty pleased with Williams. "He responds to the challenge," Shurmur said afterward. "He's been there before. He was in a lot of big games at Nebraska and we've really liked the way he has matured. Every week he's gotten better."

Better yet, Williams' pick resulted in Packer points. Favre brought his team to the line, starting from their own 38 with 35 seconds left in the half. Running out the clock was not on Favre's radar. He took the first-down snap, retreated, and was immediately chased out of the pocket. On the run to his right and toward the line of scrimmage, Favre spotted Rison open in Panther territory and hit him with a bit of a wobbly ball to the Carolina 38, a gain of 24 yards. Favre next hit Freeman running a straight route up the left sideline. There was nothing wobbly about that pass. The receiver was dragged down on the Panther 13 with 14 seconds left. Since the Packers were out of time-outs, they elected to kick a field goal.

"Too many screwy things can happen," Holmgren said later, asked why he didn't give Favre one more shot at the end zone before sending in the field goal unit.

Jacke's kick was good from 31 yards, and the Packers went into halftime leading 17-10.

Carolina was still very much in the game. When a holding call on the second-half opening kickoff brought the Packers back to their own 12, an early stop could have meant a lot. The Panthers had managed to come back and win from a halftime deficit no less than six times during the regular season. Carolina's defense had allowed the fewest second-half points of any team in the NFL.

On the other side of the ball, the Packers were thinking they needed a sustained drive, and they got it. Not for nothing had Green Bay scored the most second-half points of any team in the NFL. Favre took the Pack 73 yards in 11 plays, chewing up almost seven minutes on the clock before Chris Jacke's second field goal of the game, a 32 yarder, made it 20-10, Green Bay.

One big third-down play was typical Favre, which is to say, it was something probably no other NFL quarterback might have attempted. On third and seven from the Carolina 32, Favre dropped straight back and was quickly under pressure from the Panthers' Kevin Greene and Mark Thomas. Favre, as he did so often, ran forward rather than back, and while in the grasp of Greene he spotted Dorsey Levens open a few yards upfield. Unable to set and throw, Favre simply shoveled the ball with both hands — it resembled a pass one might make on the basketball court — to Levens, who caught it and picked up eight yards and a first down to the Carolina 24. It brought the Packers into field goal range, and a few plays later Jacke converted.

The Panthers came back with a drive of their own, 73 yards in 11 plays, but when they needed to, the Packer defense made a stop. John Kasay left-footed a 23-yard field goal with 3:23 left in the third quarter to cut the Green Bay lead to 20-13.

But that didn't last long. Taking over first and 10 on their own 26, Favre handed to Bennett, who ran up the middle for three yards.

The play of the game came next.

Holmgren, sensing a blitz, called for a screen pass to Levens. The blitz came, and Favre rolled to his right to escape it. He then lobbed a soft pass over the defenders to Levens, who caught it on the 25 yard line and started upfield. He got a great block from center Frank Winters around midfield and did the rest on his own, taking it all the way to the Carolina 4 before Tyrone Poole knocked Levens out of bounds.

Carolina linebacker Carlton Bailey said later the play took the fire out of the Panthers. "It was the perfect call," Bailey said.

Carolina might have still been dazed, because Edgar Bennett went in untouched for a touchdown on the next play. The extra point made it 27-13 with less than two minutes remaining in the third quarter.

It was still a two-score game, of course. Carolina's next drive was big and the biggest Packer of them all, defensive lineman Gilbert Brown, stepped up to shut it down.

On a first-and-10 from the Panther 40, Anthony Johnson took a handoff up the middle and appeared to have a hole. Brown, who was listed at 325 pounds but weighed significantly more — he once had a sandwich named for him at Burger King — fought off a block with his right arm and threw his left arm out as Johnson hit the hole. Brown's arm stripped the ball loose, and LeRoy Butler fell on it for the Packers at the Carolina 47.

Green Bay then managed to use up more than six minutes in an 11-play drive that ended with another Jacke field goal, from 26 yards this time, giving the Packers a 30-13 lead and, barring a miracle comeback, the game and the National Football Conference championship.

There was no miracle comeback; there was, in fact, no more scoring.

With one minute to go, Sean Jones, the Packer defensive end, snuck up on Holmgren from behind and dumped a Gatorade bucket full of ice on the coach's head.

When the game was officially over, a funny thing happened. Hardly any of the fans in Lambeau Field headed for the exit. They had been out in the freezing cold for several hours, and they wanted more. They got it. There was a trophy presentation in the middle of the field.

"This trophy is for the greatest fans in the world," Packer President Bob Harlan said to a thunderous ovation.

Former Steeler star Terry Bradshaw, now with the Fox Network, was acting as master of ceremonies. He talked to Mike Holmgren: "We're not finished yet."

He talked to Reggie White: "God has blessed this team."

And he talked to Brett Favre, who after a tough start had finished with splendid statistics: 19 of 29 passing for 292 yards and two touchdowns.

Bradshaw put his arm around Favre and asked how he felt.

"I can't even explain how I feel," the quarterback said.

Then Brett Favre said something that said it all:

"In two weeks we'll be in New Orleans."

For the first time since the 1960s, the Packers were in the Super Bowl.

Wisconsin State Journal/Joseph W. Jackson III

Favre, Reggie White, and LeRoy Butler prepare to take the Lombardi trophy home for the first time in nearly three decades.

Green Bay Packers vs. New England Patriots

JANUARY 26, 1997
Louisiana Superdome, New Orleans, Louisiana

Roy Blount, Jr. was a sportswriter before he became one of the South's foremost humorists. Blount spent the 1973 season with the Pittsburgh Steelers, and wrote a book about it called *About Three Bricks Shy of a Load: A Highly Irregular Lowdown on The Year the Steelers Were Super but Missed the Bowl.* It probably would have been better for Blount's book if they had made it to the ultimate game, but Blount himself once wrote that covering the Super Bowl, as a reporter, is impossible. The game has become too big — there is too much hype, too much extravaganza, too much everything.

"It's like trying to cover Christmas," Blount wrote.

By 1997, Blount's words seemed almost an understatement. One way to note just how crazy the whole Super Bowl experience had become was to draw some comparisons between Super Bowl XXXI, which featured the Green Bay Packers against the New England Patriots, and the first Super Bowl, which of course had also included the Packers, who played the Kansas City Chiefs of the old American Football League.

Bob Berghaus of the *Milwaukee Journal Sentinel* did a piece during the week that highlighted some significant differences. Among them:

The price of a ticket. For the first Super Bowl, the best seat in the house — the Los Angeles Coliseum — cost $12, and the game was not a sellout. For the Packers-Patriots game, the top ticket had a face value of $275 and tickets were scalped for much more than that.

The price of a 30-second television commercial during the telecast. You could buy a spot during the Packers-Chiefs game for $85,000. By the time of Super Bowl XXXI, the same buy was $1.2 million. The commercials were scrutinized almost as closely as the plays in the game itself. Advertising agencies could make or break their reputations by how their Super Bowl spots were received.

The demand for media credentials. In 1967, credentials were issued to 338 members of the media. By 1997, the number was more than 3,000. Thirty years earlier, nobody outside the United States cared about the game. By Super Bowl XXXI, 425 of the media credentials went to international press.

In the early days, Blount's colleague at *Sports Illustrated*, Dan Jenkins, had written a novel called *Semi-Tough* in which he satirized the halftime extravaganza of the Super Bowl. By 1997, a quarter century after the publication of the Jenkins novel, everything the author had projected as outrageous satire had in fact come to pass in reality. Super Bowl halftimes had fireworks and rock-and-roll shows and, as with the commercials, there were those who paid more attention to halftime than the four quarters of play.

It was, as Blount had opined, just too much. In desperation, all those thousands of media members who were, in Blount's words, trying to cover Christmas, needed an angle — some piece of Super Bowl week they could get their hands around. In the case of Super Bowl XXXI, one story jumped out at them. It concerned the Packers' two-time MVP quarterback Brett Favre and the fact that the Super Bowl was being played in New Orleans. Favre was from rural Mississippi, just up the road from New Orleans. The reporters had their angle. Santa Claus was coming home to the North Pole.

Favre would later say that the invasion started as early as Monday of Super Bowl week. On that Monday, with the game still a week away, 35 newspaper reporters and 10 TV crews showed up at the Favre house in Kiln.

The actual media day for the Super Bowl was the next day, Tuesday, and as expected Favre was a focal point. One of the 400-plus members of the international press in attendance was Lisa Olson of Australia's *Melbourne Age* newspaper, and she came away from the experience a little disgusted and a bit dazed.

"Only America," Olson wrote, "could turn something so simple and so obvious — a get-to-know-you session with football players — into something so silly and so ridiculous, it almost defies description."

Olson had just witnessed the following exchange between Brett Favre and a reporter.

Reporter: "If you were a tree, what kind of tree would it be?"

Favre: "A cactus."

Reporter: "Why is that?"

Favre: "Because then I could poke you with needles when you asked stupid-assed questions like that."

Olson also took note of Packer receiver Andre Rison, "wearing diamond Rolexes on each wrist, a diamond ring that completely covers his knuckle, and a gold cross that weighs more than some cars."

Said Rison: "I would have left all this stuff in my locker but I didn't want my teammates to steal it."

That day, Tuesday, official media day, was probably the only day of the week when much of the focus wasn't on the little town 60 miles to the northeast where Brett Favre grew up. Wednesday saw several busloads of media descend for an official tour, which also included a stop 40 miles farther north, up the road in Hattiesburg, where Favre played at the University of Southern Mississippi. Hattiesburg isn't that big, but Kiln — named for the furnace that dried out the logs for the area's large timber industry — is so small and the visiting hordes were so big that for the entire week it seemed the circus was in town.

"I was going to go over and eat with my family," Favre said at some point later in the week. "But after talking to them, I decided not to. It's crazy, kind of like Graceland. I don't why. People are paying 20 bucks to see where I went to school. That's a waste of money, really."

The buses that brought the media on Wednesday passed a big billboard at the outskirts of Kiln, population 1,260.

"Welcome to Kiln, Mississippi," the sign read. "Home of Brett Favre."

Kiln is tiny, and it is Southern. An uncharitable observer might say it is the kind of place the comedian Jonathan Winters had in mind when he said that what you often find in a town in the rural South is a filling station outside of which sit two cases of warm soda pop and a dog with an infected ear.

On Wednesday morning of Super Bowl week, media tour day, Brett Favre's father, Irvin Favre, met reporters at Rooster's Restaurant and Deli in Kiln.

The Times of London had sent a correspondent, Oliver Holt. Having arrived on the media bus (Holt referred to the visiting reporters as "pilgrims"), he offered this description:

> There are no McDonald's restaurants or Waffle Houses in Kiln, no Payless Shoe Source, no Wal-Mart, none of the usual landmarks of small-town America. Dolly's Quick Stop, a petrol station-cum-convenience store on the corner of the only crossroads in town, sells corn dogs, fried chicken and spicy sausage, and outside a furtive black dog skulks around for scraps.
>
> The pilgrims, though, head for Rooster's Restaurant and Deli a few yards farther on. A thick-set man with a crew cut and a bulging red neck is waiting inside. People are gathering around him and the camera lights are already trained on his square face, teasing beads of sweat from his forehead. He is Brett Favre's father.

On balance, though, the reporters sounded few notes of condescension — the media came away charmed by Kiln and by Brett Favre's friends and family (everyone in town is one or the other, a reporter noted). And whatever else is to be said of Kiln, it is and always will be the place that produced Brett Favre.

Holt, the English reporter, noted as much: "His statistics and achievements tell one side of the story, two consecutive most valuable player in the NFL awards, his number of touchdown throws this season that has exceeded the amount of any other quarterback save for Dan Marino, the fact the crowds mob him wherever he goes. The other side, though, is rooted here in the Deep South. This is where Brett Favre's spirit comes from, the indomitable spirit that is turning him into an American hero."

As the media prepared to leave Kiln for Hattiesburg, where they would be afforded the opportunity to interview Favre's University of Southern Mississippi roommate, Chris Ryals, and one of the Southern Miss coaches, Mark McHale, Irvin Favre offered one last word on his son. "He has got a big heart," Big Irv said. "He just won't quit."

They had worked harder than any-one, the coach said. They were the best team and they deserved it. "Now," Mike Holmgren said, "let's get out there and get after it."

What Brett Favre had, by Thursday of game week, was a cold that was beginning to feel a lot like the flu. Favre said it wasn't unusual for him to get sick upon experiencing the abrupt climate change of a plane ride from Wisconsin to Mississippi. But the stakes on this particular trip were high, as high as they could be, and by Thursday night Favre had chills and a temperature of 102. He got some antibiotics from the Packers' team doctor and by Friday morning was feeling better.

The Packers were staying in the Fairmont Hotel in New Orleans. Saturday night — to everyone's vast relief, the game was at last actually on the horizon — the team split into offensive and defensive units for some final strategizing. At the meeting of the offense, Mike Holmgren revealed the first 15 offensive plays the Packers would use, in sequence, against New England the next day. Holmgren wrote the script after conferring with his offensive assistant coaches.

The final draft for the Super Bowl featured nine passes and six runs and it was notable for being a bit more conservative than was Holmgren's norm. The coach would later explain that he felt Brett Favre would benefit from some nerve-settling basic plays at the outset. The quarterback had not had a good first quarter in the conference championship game against Carolina. Holmgren wanted to calm him down.

The first scripted play was a run to Edgar Bennett. The second play was to be a short pass in the flat to tight end Mark Chmura. Given what would transpire less than 24 hours later on the field, it pays to remember what the script called for on the Packers' second play from scrimmage — and what actually transpired.

Favre told Dick Schaap that he reviewed the game plan and was pleased to find his thoughts on attacking the Patriots on the same page with those of Mike Holmgren.

"A couple of years earlier," Favre said, "we didn't think that was possible. We're different in a lot of ways, and our philosophy of football may be a little different. But we both want the same thing, we both hate to lose and we both believe that hard work is going to get us there."

Favre's roommate at the Fairmont was his good friend and center, Frank Winters. The team curfew Saturday was 11 p.m.

Sunday morning, the team met in the hotel at 10 a.m. Holmgren again went over the first 15 plays. The players went back to their rooms and Favre said later his dad stopped by to pick up some tickets and that Bus Cook, Brett's agent, also poked his head in to wish his client good luck. The Packers had arranged for two buses, an hour apart, to take the team to the Superdome, and Favre, following a longstanding superstition, took the second bus, which departed at 2:30. The Superdome was less than a mile from the Fairmont. That still left several hours before kickoff. Favre told some jokes, made some phone calls, tried to get loose.

Right before the Packers took the field, Holmgren spoke briefly. He didn't say anything revolutionary. Words wouldn't matter much now. Holmgren said that playing this game was what they had worked for all season. They had worked harder than anyone, the coach said. They were the best team and they deserved it. "Now," Mike Holmgren said, "let's get out there and get after it."

The defenses of both teams were introduced, and then Luther Vandross sang the national anthem.

At midfield, the team's captains were joined by the six head coaches who had won previous Super Bowls in New Orleans: Mike Ditka, Tom Flores, Tom Landry, Chuck Noll, George Seifert, and Hank Stram. Stram was the senior member of the group, having led his Kansas Chiefs over the Minnesota Vikings in Super Bowl IV, so it was Stram who tossed the coin.

The toss — Stram pitched the coin some 30 feet in the air — was caught on TV by an overhead camera. The Fox Network was broadcasting the game for the first time and they were as motivated and prepared as either the Patriots or the Packers. The network utilized 29 cameras. Fox also employed 25 videotape replay machines and six more that had a super-slow-motion feature. They had several production trucks, editing suites, and electric generators. It may have been Fox's first Super Bowl, but they knew the 72,300 fans who were actually in the Superdome were peanuts. An estimated 130 million would watch on television in the United States alone, and the game was telecast in more than 100 other countries.

When Hank Stram's coin toss finally bounced on the artificial turf, New England had won the toss and elected to receive. Brett Favre, one of the Packer co-captains, grinned and shook Stram's hand, then trotted to the sideline.

Just before kickoff, a sideline reporter asked New England coach Bill Parcells what he'd told his team in the locker room.

"I told them don't worry about winning the Super Bowl," said Parcells, who had won two of them as coach of the New York Giants. "Just worry about beating the Green Bay Packers."

Across the way, a second reporter managed a word with Mike Holmgren.

"Our guys are ready," Holmgren said. The keys to the game? "Turnovers."

And then he said something that only someone who knew the long road Mike Holmgren had traveled with Brett Favre could really appreciate.

"And which quarterback plays the best today," Holmgren said. "That team's going to win."

Favre would later say his pre-kickoff practice throws on the sideline were rockets, sailing high and wide. Still, he didn't look nervous. As Craig Hentrich prepared to kick off for the Packers, Favre had his helmet off and was chatting with backup quarterback Doug Pederson.

New England brought the opening kickoff back to its own 21 yard line. The Patriots' quarterback was Drew Bledsoe, tall and rangy, not so different from Kerry Collins, whom the Packers had faced two weeks earlier. Bledsoe was a two-time Pro Bowler with a 2-1 record in the post-season, three games in which he had thrown only two touchdown passes against six interceptions.

The Patriots' first play was a run, a Bledsoe handoff to Curtis Martin, who ran right for one yard before linebacker Brian Williams brought him down.

On second and nine, Bledsoe dropped straight back and found Shawn Jefferson over the middle for 14 yards and a first down.

First down was another run by Martin, this time for no gain. The early trend of New England struggling to run the football would continue, so much so that they eventually almost stopped running altogether. But they tried again on second down in this series; a draw play, again to Martin, gained just one yard. The lack of early-down yardage was significant because the Patriots, despite winning the AFC championship, ranked just 22nd in the NFL in converting third-down chances into first downs. Now, on third and nine, Bledsoe, under pressure, threw a swing pass in the flat to his other running back, Dave Meggett, and the ball slipped through Meggett's hands incomplete.

Tom Tupa came in to punt for New England. The Packers' return specialist, Desmond Howard, was a man on a mission. For some reason, during the week more than one Patriot had felt compelled to say New England fully intended to kick the ball to Howard, despite a season of returns by the former Michigan star that had struck fear throughout the league. In the regular season Howard had returned three punts for touchdowns and then, in the Packers' first playoff game, against San Francisco, he'd had two long returns, one for a fourth touchdown. As the teams warmed up before the game, several Patriots continued to trash-talk Howard. They were whistling past the graveyard.

Maybe New England just couldn't adjust to the idea that this was a new Desmond Howard. The old one had been a bit of a bust as a pro, after winning the Heisman Trophy in Ann Arbor. He played first with the Washington Redskins. After a few years, he was picked up in the expansion draft by Jacksonville, where he lasted a year. Howard came to the Packer training camp in August 1996 after Holmgren urged Ron Wolf to sign him. His one-year, free-agent contract gave Howard a lot of incentive to have a good year in Green Bay. He didn't — he had a great year. Teams had started kicking away from him on punts and kickoffs; Howard said later he was actually offended when it became obvious the Patriots were going right at him.

It was a strategy New England would come to regret. Tupa's first punt, with a hang time of four and a half seconds, was gathered in by Howard near the left sideline at the Packer 13. Starting upfield, Howard hugged the sideline apart from one or two juke fakes to the inside; by the time he was pushed out of bounds at the Packer 45, Howard had the third-longest punt return in Super Bowl history.

Favre brought the Packer offense onto the field. Young as he was, the quarterback had already amassed some startling post-season statistics: a completion percentage of 62 percent, a total of 2,184 yards passing, and 16 touchdowns against seven interceptions.

Favre started with Holmgren's carefully crafted script. On first down Edgar Bennett ran off left tackle for a gain of one yard. Second down was scripted as a short out pattern to the tight end Mark Chmura, but as Favre brought the Packers to the line he didn't like what he was seeing out of the Patriots defense. The New England safeties were edging toward the line of scrimmage, while pretending they weren't. To Favre, that meant one thing: a blitz. The safeties were going to cover the two Packer tight ends, Chmura and Keith Jackson, and the linebackers were going to rush the quarterback. The scripted play also called for Bennett to go in motion out of the backfield, leaving the quarterback no blocking help, so that even a short drop pass could be problematic against a blitz.

In two seconds — literally — Favre had to decide whether to audible out of the script and call a new play at the line. Holmgren would later say that he'd told his quarterback that he, the coach, was fine with audibles — as long as they worked. Now Favre had to decide whether to take a gamble on the second play of the biggest game of his career, and in doing so know that he ran every risk of proving right the critics who said he got too excitable early in big games.

One last image flashed before him. Watching TV at the Fairmont that morning, killing time, Favre had happened upon a replay of Super Bowl XXIV and seen Joe Montana audible successfully in a similar situation with the San Francisco 49ers.

In that moment, Favre decided to call an audible — a deep post route to wide-out Andre Rison, who, with the safeties up, would be one on one with a cornerback.

Favre started calling signals and was nervous enough that he started calling the original play. "Shit!" he said, and then he began barking the audible, a play the Packers call 74 Razor. Favre took the snap and knew he had guessed right. The linebackers were coming. Favre retreated, planted his right foot on the Green Bay 38, and launched a pass for Rison, who had beaten corner Otis Smith and was alone at the New England 20 when the ball arrived. Rison caught it and waltzed into the end zone untouched. Back up the field, Favre had removed his helmet and was pumping it in his right hand as he ran to the sideline. It was a dream start for the Packers.

Bledsoe brought the Patriots back out, starting from their 20, after the kick-off was downed in the end zone. On first down the quarterback dropped back and, pressured, dumped a short pass to Martin, who gained only a yard. On second and nine, Bledsoe again dropped back, this time looking left for Terry Glenn along the sideline. Bledsoe threw but Packers cornerback Doug Evans stepped in front of Glenn. He appeared at first to catch the ball, then bobbled it, then tipped it back to himself with his right hand, and caught it just as he fell out of bounds for an interception.

Packers fans in the Superdome were going crazy. It had been a great start for all three Green Bay units: offense, defense, and special teams.

Now, on first down from the New England 28, Favre retreated to pass and, rolling right under pressure, was sacked by defensive end Ferric Collons for a 10-yard loss.

Dorsey Levens got five of those yards back on a draw play. Then, on third and 15, Favre made a deep drop and found Levens on a screen pass to the left side. The running back took it up the left sideline for 14 yards, to the Patriot 19, a yard shy of the first down. Packers' kicker Chris Jacke, 21 of 27 on the season, came on and booted a 37-yard field goal. It was 10-0, Packers.

Some might have sensed a blowout in the making, but it didn't happen. Instead, Bledsoe shined. A *Boston Globe* reporter would later write that the quarterback did the best play-action faking of his career in the Super Bowl, and New England's last two first-quarter drives showcased it.

The first was 79 yards in just six plays. Starting from their 21 after the Packers' kickoff, Bledsoe had his first-down pass, short to fullback Keith Byars in the left flat, swatted down by the Packers' Santana Dotson. But on second and 10, Bledsoe went right back to Byars, this time with a screen to the right side, and Byars shed a number of Packer tackles in taking the ball all the way to the Green Bay 47, a gain of 32 yards. The next play was another short toss to another back,

Curtis Martin, and Martin also slipped tackles en route to the Packer 27 and a gain of 20 yards.

"We were completely baffled," Packers safety LeRoy Butler would say later of the Pats' successful first-quarter drives. "We were missing tackles, they were flying right past us, and they were pushing us around. No one had pushed us around all year, and they were killing us, doing stuff we hadn't seen before. It was a great game plan."

The Patriots also got some help when, after incomplete passes on the next two plays, Bledsoe missed Shawn Jefferson in the Packer end zone but pass interference was whistled on Green Bay corner Craig Newsome. That made it first and goal from the one and Bledsoe took immediate advantage, faking a handoff into the line and then hitting Byars over the middle in the end zone to make it 10-7.

The Patriots tempted fate by kicking off to Howard, but he could bring it out only to the 18. From there, the Packers went three and out, with Favre missing Antonio Freeman on third down. The punt gave the Patriots good field position at their own 43, and they took full advantage. This time the drive was just four plays. On first down, following the successful formula of throwing short to his backs, Bledsoe hit Martin in the left flat for seven. Martin then carried on a run for two more to the Green Bay 48, setting up a third and short. The Packer defense was bunched tight as Bledsoe called signals. On taking the snap he faked a handoff — the play-action the Boston writer applauded — and then dropped back. The Packers had no rush, and Bledsoe, with so much time, launched a long one for Terry Glenn, who had two steps on safety Eugene Robinson on a left to right crossing route. The result was a fine catch by Glenn and a 44-yard gain to the Packer 4 yard line. The next play brought a touchdown, as Bledsoe rolled right and found tight end Ben Coates in the back of the end zone. All of a sudden it was 14-10, Patriots, and the 24 combined first-quarter points were the most in Super Bowl history, with more than two minutes still left in the quarter.

On the Packer sideline, defensive coordinator Fritz Shurmur was steaming. Bledsoe could have grilled a steak while waiting for Glenn to get open on the pass that set up the touchdown. Shurmur let his unit have it: "Enough is enough!" he screamed. "Pull your head out of your ass and do what you're supposed to do."

Shurmur singled out LeRoy Butler. "Go get Bledsoe," the coach said. "Do whatever it takes. I'll blitz you every play if I have to. Just get in his face. I want him to feel you and worry about where you are all the time."

The defense didn't have long to wait to see if they could re-energize, as Favre and the Packers went three and out after the kickoff. Favre threw an incompletion, hit a short pass to Levens, and then on third and five was sacked. Hentrich punted on fourth and the Patriots took over at their own 33 after a nice 20-yard return by Dave Meggett.

Shurmur's talk may have fired up the defense. Bledsoe threw incomplete after being forced to roll out right on first down. Martin gained five on the ground on second, but Bledsoe missed again on third, as Tyrone Williams broke up a pass intended for Jefferson. Tupa again punted to Howard, who took the ball in on the Packers 11 and brought it back to the 17. There were just three seconds left in the first quarter. Favre hit Levens for a short gain on first down and the quarter was over.

Favre's next two attempts, after the teams switched ends of the field, were incomplete. It was another three-and-out — making three in succession — for the Green Bay offense, which had started with such promise. Fortunately for the Packers, their defense had pulled itself together. Taking over on his own 42 after Hentrich's punt, Bledsoe threw three straight incomplete passes. Shurmur's stunting was paying off. Packers' corner Doug Evans blitzed on third down and under pressure, Bledsoe just threw it away out of bounds.

The question was which offense would straighten out first. It was answered after the New England punt, which Howard again could advance only three yards after taking it at the Packer 16. First and 10 Green Bay from its own 19.

For the first time since the Packers' second play from scrimmage, Favre spotted something significant as he brought his team to the line. The Packers had three wide-outs and the play called in the huddle was a pass, but Favre picked up on the Patriots' coverage that had a safety, Lawyer Milloy, one on one with Antonio Freeman, who was lined up wide right. Not only was it single coverage, but Milloy was tight up to the line, intending to bump and run with Freeman. It was a risky coverage with no help.

This time Favre's audible only called for a change in the blocking scheme. He wanted a little more time, and he was going to be looking for Freeman up the right sideline.

"I was the first read," Freeman said later, "and I was licking my chops when I saw that safety walk up. I knew all I had to do was make him stumble or move the wrong way and I had him. I gave him a hard move inside, and he took it."

As that was happening, Favre was retreating. He planted on the left hash mark and then threw across the field to the streaking Freeman, who took it in stride near midfield.

"Brett threw a great ball," Freeman said, "and the rest was just running."

It was especially sweet for the receiver, in that he had gotten a rap about not being fast enough when coming out of Virginia Tech two years earlier.

"I wasn't fast enough, I couldn't go over the middle, I didn't have 4.3 speed," Freeman said. "While I was running all I could think about was all those people who doubted me."

He went in untouched — at 81 yards, it was the longest touchdown pass in Super Bowl history. Rather than a Lambeau leap, Freeman ran to the goal post, jumped up, and spiked the ball over the crossbar.

On the sideline, Favre high-fived his backup, Jim McMahon. It was 17-14, Green Bay, with most of the second quarter still remaining.

After the kickoff, New England started from its own 24. The reinvigorated Packers' defense allowed one first down, and then on a third-and-seven from the 39, LeRoy Butler came on a blitz — Shurmur's order to get in Bledsoe's face was still ringing in Butler's ears — and, after fighting off a block by Dave Meggett, made a great one-armed sack of Bledsoe for a loss of nine.

The Patriots punted again. Maybe the fact Desmond Howard had been relatively quiet since his first punt return lulled New England a bit. But this time, when Howard fielded Tupa's punt at the Green Bay 19, he took it quickly down the sideline to the 40, where he cut inside and crossed midfield to the Patriots' 47, a 34-yard return.

The Packers cashed in on the field position. A Favre pass to Rison for 23 yards and a run up the middle by Levens for 12 brought Green Bay to the New England 11. But that's as far as they got. Bennett lost yards on a first-down run and then Favre missed Levens on an attempted screen to the right. It was a rare bad ball from Favre, landing at the running back's feet. As Favre brought the Packers up on third and 13, Mike Holmgren was motioning for a time-out from the Packer sideline. No one saw him. Favre took the snap, dropped, and fired for Rison crossing in the back of the end. Rison leaped and got his right hand on the ball, but it fell incomplete. The Packers settled for a Jacke field goal that made it 20-14. There was 8:06 left in the first half.

Starting its next drive from the 25, the Patriots appeared resigned to not having a ground game. Bledsoe went immediately to the air, hitting the tight end Coates over the middle for 19. On the drive's second play, Butler again got pressure on the blitz and hammered Bledsoe from the blind side, and the quarterback's pass for Byars fell incomplete. Bledsoe may have still been a bit wobbly from the Butler hit, but on second and 10 from the Patriot 44 the quarterback threw long over the head of a streaking Shawn Jefferson and Packer safety Mike Prior gathered it in like a centerfielder for an interception at the Green Bay 22. Jefferson hit Prior in full stride, but the safety shrugged him off and picked up a few yards on the return to the 26.

Brett Favre then engineered a beautiful nine-play drive to the Patriots' end zone. It was the first real sustained drive of the game. The key play was a first-and-10 from the Packers 44. Favre faked a handoff to Bennett, dropped, and looked long for Rison along the left sideline. Otis Smith was all over Rison. Favre had the time and composure to check away from Rison and he found Freeman open over the middle for a gain of 22 to the New England 34. From there it became evident that, unlike New England, Green Bay was not abandoning the run. Levens gained nine and then six. After Bennett picked up one, Levens struck again on second and nine from the Patriot 18, breaking an off-tackle play wide to the right and picking up eight to the New England 10. Levens gained eight more on the next play, setting up a first and goal from the 2.

It was a 99-yard kickoff return for a touchdown, the longest in Super Bowl history, and it devastated the Patriots.

At which point Favre took over. There was a little more than a minute left in the half. Out of a tight, two-running back formation, Favre dropped back and rolled to his left, looking to pass on the run. He pumped once to Keith Jackson, who was well covered in the back of the end zone. Favre then started to race for the corner end zone pylon. A Patriot linebacker, Todd Collins, had a good angle and got to Favre when the quarterback was at the 3, but Favre launched himself toward the corner. Even though Collins pushed him out of bounds short of the goal line, Favre extended the ball in front of him and to the right, and the ball crossed the corner pylon in bounds. It was a touchdown, a huge lift going into the break, and Green Bay led 27-14 at the half.

As had become the norm at Super Bowls, the halftime show was otherworldly. The Superdome went briefly dark before erupting into an extravaganza of cascading spotlights, pyrotechnics, smoke, flashing neon, motorcycles, and music from the Blues Brothers, ZZ Top, and James Brown.

In the Packers' locker room, while all that was going on outside, Mike Holmgren didn't say much. He asked the team to lock arms. "We will win this thing if we stick together," the coach said.

The Packers got the ball to start the second half. Starting from their own 25 — the Patriots had kicked to Howard again — Favre picked up a couple of first downs into New England territory. Then, on a third-and-one from the Patriot 37, Levens got nothing up the middle. On fourth, the Packers decided to go, but a handoff to Levens proved disastrous, as he lost seven yards and New England took over on its own 44.

The teams traded punts on the next two series, but the Patriots were gaining in the battle for field position. The Packers' three-and-out meant Hentrich would punt from his own end zone. He hit a good one, driving Meggett back to his own 41 to field it, but New England, starting from its 47, came up with a big drive when it really needed one.

On a third-and-five from the Green Bay 48, Bledsoe dropped, was pressured, and threw for Coates in the right flat. The ball bounced against the tight end's chest and popped in the air and then Coates gathered it in again, picking up 13 and an important first down.

It was on this drive that New England rediscovered its run game. Prior to the drive, Bledsoe had thrown 14 consecutive passes. On a third-and-one from the Green Bay 26, Martin picked up eight, and then on the very next play the give was to Martin again, right up the middle. Martin burst through a small hole at the 15, where Gilbert Brown got an arm on him, and then took it all the way in, bouncing off a LeRoy Butler tackle attempt inside the 5. All of a sudden it was 27-21, Packers. The thick smoke that still hung in the air from the halftime show wasn't the only reason Packer fans weren't breathing easy.

And then it happened. The Patriots kicked it to Desmond Howard — and this time it caught up with them.

Howard caught it at the 1 yard line in exactly the middle of the field, between the hash marks, and he stayed between those hashes all the way up to the 35, where wide receiver Hason Graham, coming from Howard's right, hit him with a glancing blow that propelled Howard toward the left side of the field. Keeping his feet, he turned back upfield and was not touched again. It was a 99-yard kickoff return for a touchdown, the longest in Super Bowl history, and it devastated the Patriots.

"Up until that point, I thought we still had an opportunity to win," said Patriots coach Bill Parcells.

Bledsoe said later, "That took the wind out of our sails."

The Packers were lining up to kick the extra point when Favre came running onto the field and startled Jacke by tapping him on the shoulder. Green Bay was calling a time-out. With the score 33-21, they were going to try for a two-point conversion. On the play, Favre rolled right, couldn't find anyone open, and then wheeled back to his left, when he spotted Chmura along the back of the end zone and hit him with a bullet for two points.

It would be the last score of the game. On New England's next series, Reggie White sacked Bledsoe twice. He would end the game with three sacks and seven hurries. Craig Newsome would record an interception. The Patriots never really recovered from the Howard return; one reason, perhaps, that Desmond Howard and not Brett Favre would get the nod for Super Bowl Most Valuable Player.

The game ended and confetti rained down. The Packers were world champions. Terry Bradshaw once again acted as master of ceremonies for the trophy presentation on the field.

Bob Harlan said, "I think it's time the Lombardi Trophy goes home to Lambeau Field, where it belongs."

Mike Holmgren said, "This is the greatest group of players I've ever been around."

Then Bradshaw put his arm around Favre, who said, "I want to thank our fans."

Later, Favre would say he felt the Packers had truly become America's team. He'd felt it all week long in New Orleans. People outside Wisconsin were pulling for them. "We have fun and people like to watch us play," the quarterback said.

It was fitting in that moment to think back to the previous summer, when Brett Favre had asked Packers fans to believe that he could bring Green Bay a world championship, a Super Bowl victory.

They did. And he did.

Green Bay Packers vs. San Francisco 49ers

JANUARY 3, 1999
3Com Park, San Francisco, California

In 1978, *Sports Illustrated* magazine named golfer Jack Nicklaus its "Sportsman of the Year," one of the most prestigious awards in the athletic world. It's given to an athlete who has had a superior year in his or her sport, but there's more to it than that. The recipient has also been judged by the magazine's editors to have behaved admirably both on and off the field of play, to have been not just a proper sportsman, but an exemplary one. It never hurts, either, if the athlete is nearing the end of a great career.

Nicklaus in 1978 was 38 years old and hadn't won a major golf championship in three years. In July 1978 he won the British Open in Scotland, at St. Andrews, the home of golf. Some thought it might be Nicklaus's last great title, and few disputed *Sports Illustrated*'s choice when it was announced that December. But Nicklaus, as it turned out, had three more majors in him, the last coming a full eight years later, in 1986, when at 46 he won The Masters for a record sixth time. His career would end with an astonishing 18 professional major wins; even more astounding to some was that he had finished second 19 times. There had been some truly heartbreaking losses — chip-ins by Tom Watson and Lee Trevino to nip him down the stretch — but Nicklaus's demeanor in defeat was wholly admirable. He was the first to shake his opponent's hand. "Well played," Jack would say.

It was interesting, though, that Nicklaus could remember little of those losses. Fans or journalists would ask about a particular shot on a particular hole and Nicklaus often couldn't summon the memory.

"You have to remember," he once said. "I don't remember the ones I win all that well, either." There had been, after all, hundreds of tournaments on hundreds of golf courses. "But when I win," Nicklaus continued, "it's much easier to remember, because people are always bringing them up."

In 2007 Brett Favre was 38 years old, Nicklaus's age in 1978, when *Sports Illustrated* magazine bestowed on Favre its "Sportsman of the Year" award. At the time the award was announced in December, Favre and the Packers were coming down the stretch in what had been an incredible season, a renaissance, as the aging quarterback defied the calendar and led the Packers, picked by many before the season to lose more often than they won, to victory after victory.

But one of the more notable aspects of the *Sports Illustrated* story announcing the award came when the magazine asked Favre the inevitable question — the favorite memory of his spectacular career — and the quarterback was quiet for a moment. Finally, when he did answer, Favre did not name one of his great wins.

"I've got so many plays running through my mind," he said. "The funny thing is, it's not only about the touchdowns and those big victories. If I were to make a list, I would include the interceptions, the sacks, the really painful losses. Those times when I've been down, when I've been kicked around, I hold on to those. In a way those are the best times I've ever had, because that's when I've found out who I am. And what I want to be."

There have been a few losses for which Favre himself was largely responsible, but more often he has played well in defeat. There are, of course, many ways to lose, and the Green Bay Packers, in the years after their glorious Super Bowl triumph in New Orleans in January 1997, discovered most of them. Only one team out of more than 30 is all smiles at the end of each season.

A year after that Super Bowl win, this time facing Denver at Qualcomm Stadium in San Diego, Favre and the Packers were forced to swallow the bitter pill of making it all the way to the ultimate game — and coming up short. They had been heavily favored — by 11 ½ points — to beat the Broncos that day, having already earned playoff wins against Tampa Bay (21-7) and San Francisco (23-10). Favre once again had enjoyed an outstanding year. He became the first player to win the NFL's Most Valuable Player award three years in a row. Favre had 35 touchdown passes during the regular season while leading the Packers to a 13-3 record.

The game started well for Favre and the Packers. Green Bay returned the opening kickoff to its own 24 and from there, Favre engineered a scoring drive that culminated with a 22-yard strike to Antonio Freeman. (It was only the third time in Super Bowl history a team had scored a touchdown after receiving the opening kickoff.)

It would be a second straight strong Super Bowl performance for Favre, who ended the game with 25 completions in 42 attempts, for 256 yards and three touchdowns, against one interception. His statistics were actually much better than those of Denver quarterback John Elway (who was 12 of 23 for 123 yards, an interception, and no touchdowns), but as the old saying has it, the only stat that truly matters is the final score, and the Broncos prevailed, 31-24.

Favre had driven the Packers into Denver territory, to the 35 yard line with a little over a minute to go, but there the drive stalled. Favre's fourth-down pass intended for Mark Chmura was broken up by Denver linebacker John Mobley, and the game was over.

Favre would have many tough losses over his long career. By the 1999 regular season, even the Packers' invincibility at Lambeau Field had vanished. They lost two in a row at home for the first time since 1991 when the arch rival Bears visited on Nov. 7, 1999. A week earlier, Seattle — under former Green Bay coach Mike Holmgren — had drubbed the Packers, now coached by Ray Rhodes, 27-7. The Bear game was closer, heartbreakingly so. The Packers trailed 14-13 when they got the ball back on their own 17 yard line with a little over three minutes left to play. Favre worked the clock masterfully, driving the Packers deep into Bears territory as the seconds wound down. They reached the Chicago 10 yard line with time left for one play. Ryan Longwell came on for the game-winning field goal attempt. It was from just 28 yards but the snap was low and so was Longwell's kick, low enough that the Bears' 6-foot, 4-inch defensive lineman Bryan Robinson blocked it. The game ended 14-13, Bears, and Favre and the Packers were gutted.

"I'm sort of numb, I guess," the quarterback said afterward.

A month later brought another crushing loss at home, a game in which Favre once again played well. Carolina came to Lambeau and, despite putting up 31 points behind a 26-for-38 passing performance by Favre (for 302 yards and two touchdowns), the Packers fell short. The final was 33-31. It was particularly wrenching for Favre because there should have been an opportunity for the Packers to get the ball back with around 40 or 45 seconds left. The Panthers had a fourth and goal at the Packers' 5, trailing Green Bay 31-27. Quarterback Steve Beuerlein had made a short completion on third down, setting up what would be Carolina's last play, fourth and goal from the 5. For some reason Packer coach Ray Rhodes neglected to call a time-out. The clock wound all the way down to five seconds, at which point Beuerlein scored on a quarterback draw as time ran out. "I should have called time-out," Rhodes said later. Favre said only, "I would have liked to have had another chance."

Perhaps the most devastating loss of Favre's career came four years after that forgettable 1999 season, when the Packers had fought their way back to the playoffs under a new coach, Mike Sherman, and in a divisional playoff game had the top-seeded Eagles on the ropes.

Green Bay jumped out to a 14-0 lead in the game, played January 11, 2004 at Philadelphia's Lincoln Financial Field. They might have taken a 17-7 lead into halftime, but Sherman elected to gamble on fourth and one at the goal line with time running out in the second quarter. The Packers didn't make it and their halftime lead was just a touchdown.

Still, Green Bay led, 17-14, late in the game, and Philadelphia was down to its last chance, in its own territory and facing a fourth down and 26 yards to go, after Eagle quarterback Donovan McNabb had been sacked for a 10-yard loss. Philadelphia had one last, desperate chance. Incredibly, McNabb found Freddie Mitchell somehow open in the Packers' seven-deep prevent defense, and Mitchell gained 28 yards, two more than he needed, saving the season for the Eagles. A short time later they kicked a field goal to send the game into overtime. In the extra period, the Packers stopped the Eagles on their first drive. Now a score would win it for Green Bay. But Favre overthrew Javon Walker and the pass was intercepted by Philadelphia's Brian Dawkins, who returned it to the Packers' 34. A field goal ended the game and the Packers' season, 20-17.

How badly it hurt Brett Favre could be seen in his refusal to speak to reporters afterward. They could count on one hand the number of times the quarterback had opted out of post-game interviews over a 12-year career.

While Favre insists that he wants to remember all those stinging losses along with his victories, one suspects that the losses he will reflect on most often are those in which both teams played well, with a lot on the line. There have been a few such games in Favre's career, when the season was in the balance and both sides dug deep and neither deserved to lose. Perhaps the single best example of such a game came when the Packers traveled to San Francisco to play the 49ers in the 1998 NFC wild card playoff game.

The date of the game was January 3, 1999. The two previous seasons had seen the Packers make it to the Super Bowl and win it once. Now as 1998 turned into 1999 and the season wound down, there was a sense of things changing in Green Bay. An era might be ending.

The feeling was inescapable. Reggie White, their heroic defensive lineman, had announced this would be his final campaign. Even more important, the buzz around the league was that this could also be head coach Mike Holmgren's last hurrah on the Packer sideline. Holmgren felt he had done most of what he could as a head coach alone; he wanted a situation in which he could be both coach and general manager, with the final say on personnel decisions. The Packers had their own mastermind of a general manager in Ron Wolf. It looked like Holmgren was headed out of Green Bay.

The swan songs of Holmgren and White would have been enough to make the game extra special, but there was more. The 49ers' head coach was now Steve Mariucci, who had been so instrumental in Brett Favre's development when Mariucci was the quarterbacks' coach of the Packers. In one version of a famous story from Favre's second or third year, it was Mariucci who had convinced Holmgren not to bench Favre when the head coach had wearied of the quarterback's sometimes reckless play. Plenty of mutual respect and affection remained between the men, but Mariucci was feeling tremendous pressure to get a win against his old team. While both the Packers and 49ers had enjoyed successful runs over the past decade — at least one or the other had played in nine of the last 10 NFC championship games — the Packers had held the upper hand lately. Going into the January game, the Packers had defeated San Francisco five straight times, including three straight in the playoffs. If there was a sense of pending change in Green Bay, there was a sense of urgency in the City by the Bay. Mariucci, at home, needed a win.

"Those times when I've been down, when I've been kicked around, I hold on to those. In a way those are the best times I've ever had, because that's when I've found out who I am. And what I want to be."

The weather at game time was ideal, 61 and sunny.

The 49ers brought the opening kickoff back to their own 28 yard line, and Steve Young, the gifted left-handed quarterback, brought the offense onto the field. Young might have felt as much under the gun as his coach, since the quarterback had a personal eight-game losing streak against the Packers, dating back to when Young played for Tampa Bay. So far, Young's 1998 season had been superb — he had passed for more than 4,000 yards and 36 touchdowns. But the question lingered: could he do it in the playoffs, and against the Packers?

The game's first big play came early, on the third play from scrimmage. Facing third and three from his own 35, Young dropped back to pass and was immediately set upon by Packers strong safety LeRoy Butler. Butler had blitzed with great success in earlier match-ups between the teams, so it was no surprise to see him coming. What was surprising, given the 49ers' stated goal of stopping him, was that Butler arrived in the 49ers backfield untouched and should have sacked Young. He had the quarterback in a bear hug at the 30, but Young somehow slipped loose, took a step to his left, and hit wide receiver Terrell Owens with a pass at the San Francisco 41, which would have been a first down. But Owens was hit hard by Packers' safety Darren Sharper; the ball came loose and was recovered by still a third Packers' safety, Pat Terrell, in the game on a passing situation.

The early fumble accentuated an incredible statistic in the recent Packers-49ers rivalry: in the last three playoff games between the two teams, San Francisco had turned the ball over 12 times, the Packers only once.

Favre brought the Packers on. They had scored on six opening drives during the past season, and they would score on this one. Mixing handoffs to William Henderson and Dorsey Levens with passes to those same running backs (the two accounted for all the Packer yardage in the drive), Favre took Green Bay to the 49ers 5 yard line before the drive stalled. Ryan Longwell's 23-yard field goal put the Packers on the board first.

The next 49ers drive ended with a punt into the Packers end zone. Favre missed Chmura on first down from the 20. On second down the quarterback handed the ball to Levens on a slow-to-develop run off right tackle. Levens was hit behind the line by safety Tim McDonald and then the other 49ers safety, Merton Hanks, slammed his right hand into the ball and forced it from Levens' grasp. The fumble was recovered by 49ers end Chris Doleman at the Green Bay 19. It was only the second Packers' turnover in the last five-plus games against the 49ers.

San Francisco took quick advantage. Two runs by Terry Kirby gave the 49ers a second-and-goal from the Packer one. From there, Young hit tight end Greg Clark in the end zone to put the 49ers ahead, 7-3.

The next Packers drive started from their 38, after a nice runback by their Pro Bowl-bound return specialist, Roell Preston. It would be a nice drive, too, unusual in that the Packers, who had one of the league's top-rated passing attacks but only a mediocre ground game, ran the ball successfully. Levens gained 18 yards on one play early in the drive. The run was there because in many of its defensive formations San Francisco was employing its safeties to double-team the Packers' wide receivers, especially Antonio Freeman. Once a running back cleared the line of scrimmage, the chance for a big gain presented itself.

Later in the drive, on a crucial fourth-and-one from the San Francisco 24, Levens took Favre's handoff, started around right end, then cut suddenly back toward the middle, where he popped through a hole and carried the ball all the way to the 49ers' 2 yard line, as the first quarter ended. On the first play of the second quarter, after the teams switched sides of the field, Favre hit Antonio Freeman crossing from the right side in the back of the end zone, and the Packers regained the lead, 10-7.

The 49ers brought the ball inside Packer territory on their next possession, but the drive ended on a first-and-10 from the Green Bay 46. Young took the snap, dropped back, and never took his eyes from his wide left receiver, J.J. Stokes, who was running a straight go pattern down the sideline. Tyrone Williams had good coverage for the Packers, but Young lofted it high anyway. Williams and Stokes went up for the ball together; neither came down with it. Instead, Williams batted the ball into the air as they fell, and Darren Sharper, arriving from his safety position in the middle of the field, grabbed it for the interception and rolled out of bounds at the Green Bay 18.

The Packers, however, did not take advantage, going three and out, which gave San Francisco good field position at the Green Bay 47. From there, the 49ers, mostly utilizing running back Garrison Hearst, drove to the Packers' 16 before stalling. It's worth noting that, up to this point, not only had San Francisco's great receiver Jerry Rice not made a catch, but Young hadn't yet thrown a ball in his direction.

Wade Richey's field goal tied it, 10-10, with 6:53 to go in the first half.

Despite a 47-yard completion from Favre to Freeman that took Green Bay to the 49ers' 30, the Packers came away with no points on their next drive. Longwell pushed a 50-yard field goal attempt wide right.

The teams would then swap turnovers. Taking over on their 40 after Longwell's miss, the 49ers went three and out, but Reggie Roby's punt was bobbled and then dropped by Preston at the Packers' 18. It took the officials nearly two minutes to untangle the pile; once they did, it was San Francisco's football. But then, after Hearst gained a yard on first down, Young gave it right back to the Packers. Rolling right and under pressure, Young's second-down pass to Hearst in the flat was intercepted by a diving Packers' linebacker, George Koonce.

The Packers, with help from the 49ers and the officials, would take advantage this time. On first and 10 from his 17, Favre hit tight end Tyrone Davis at the Green Bay 35, but Davis dropped the pass. A flag also dropped, back near Brett Favre, who was struggling to regain his feet after a late hit by end Chris Doleman. The flag infuriated the 49ers' other end, Roy Barker, who for his protests was called for an unsportsmanlike conduct penalty by the same official who had whistled Doleman. With his flag already on the field, the official threw down his hat to signal the Barker penalty. It was 30 yards, all told, and the two penalties gave the Packers a first down at their own 47.

From there Favre hit Robert Brooks down to the San Francisco 27. After a couple of short gains and the two-minute warning, Favre and Levens teamed up on a deft screen pass that the running back took all the way to the San Francisco 2 yard line. It was fitting that Levens then got the call on the next play, a run to the right side, resulting in a touchdown that gave the Packers the halftime lead, 17-10.

It had been a fairly good first half for Brett Favre and the Packers; the third quarter would be less so. Favre's stats for the first half showed him completing 11 of 17 passes for 136 yards and a touchdown. He had thrown no interceptions, but that would soon change.

The Packers started a nice drive after receiving the second half kickoff and moved into 49ers territory but a holding penalty against guard Marco Rivera made it a first-and-20 from the Green Bay 43. On second down, after Levens lost a yard running right, Favre dropped back to pass. His protection, good at the outset of the play, began to break down when the quarterback could find no one open. San Francisco lineman Charles Haley, activated just before the game, finally beat tackle Ross Verba and was in Favre's face when he threw the ball over the middle, where it was picked off at midfield by linebacker Lee Woodall and returned to the Green Bay 34. As the play ended, Favre and 49ers' defensive lineman Gabe Wilkins began to scuffle. They were jawing at each other and Favre actually threw a half-punch/shove in Wilkins' direction before they were broken up. The suspicion is that Wilkins, who had played with the Packers before leaving for the 49ers in the previous off-season, did most of the trash-talking. He kept it up even after the final whistle, in the 49ers' locker room. "You can come home and kick the dog every day," Wilkins told reporters, "but sooner or later he's going to bite you."

Woodall's interception would turn into points for the 49ers. Two nice runs by Garrison Hearst brought the ball to the Packers' 11. Kirby picked up three on first down, and then on second, Young picked up on a Packers' blitz and threw to the right end zone where Terrell Owens was wide open after making a great inside fake that fooled Craig Newsome. Young's pass hit Owens in the hands — and he dropped it. The sun had been directly in his eyes but it was still an embarrassing miscue. With his first-quarter fumble and at least two other dropped balls, it had not been a good game for Owens. Fortunately for Owens and the 49ers, on the following play Young found tight end Greg Clark in the end zone for a score that tied the game at 17.

Behind, on the road, facing a fired-up defense and a frenzied crowd, coming off a terrible turnover in his last possession, Favre brought his offense to the line. What happened over the next few minutes was magical.

There were still nine minutes left in the third quarter of a game that was beginning to feel like a barnburner.

The Packers failed to get a first down on their next series, after Preston had made a good return of the kickoff to the Green Bay 33. Favre was sacked while trying to pass on second down. On the sideline, the future Hall of Famer Jerry Rice, who still had yet to catch a ball that day, was exhorting the San Francisco crowd to make noise. They did, and it only escalated after the 49ers got the ball back. On first down from their 23, Garrison Hearst carried off left tackle on a run that featured several missed tackles — most notably one by Darren Sharper, who had a clean shot at the 49ers' 30. Still on his feet at the San Francisco 40, Hearst stiff-armed Packer safety LeRoy Butler, who eventually ran Hearst out of bounds at the 46 after fighting off the stiff-arm. The crowd noise was deafening and the play ended with Butler in a shoving match with 49ers' receivers Terrell Owns and J.J. Stokes.

San Francisco's drive would stall — Owens had another drop — but a 48-yard field goal by Richey gave the 49ers back the lead, 20-17, with just over two minutes left in the third quarter.

What followed was a big drive for the Packers. They needed something to slow down the 49er momentum and quiet the crowd. What they got was a well-engineered 11-play drive to tie the game. One key play came on a first down from their own 34, when Favre hit fullback William Henderson over the middle at the 45 and Henderson scampered for more than 20 after-catch yards. He leaped right over 49ers safety Tim McDonald at the San Francisco 42 and made it to the 33 before finally going down. The Packers would eventually get a first and goal at the 49er 10, but Marco Rivera was again called for holding and Green Bay settled for a Ryan Longwell field goal of 37 yards to tie the game.

It was 20-20, with 11:51 to go. It had been a great game, and it was a long way from over.

The 49ers came back with a 10-play drive of their own. Young came up clutch time and again, first hitting J.J. Stokes for a first down on a third-and-seven from the San Francisco 30, then scrambling out of the pocket and picking up 10 and another first at midfield. On the next play Terrell Owens began to redeem himself. He ran a go route straight down the left sideline and Young put the ball up where Owens could fight for it with corner Tyrone Williams, who had good coverage. Owens simply out-battled the Packer and caught the pass. It was a gain of 34 to the Green Bay 16. There the Packer defense toughened and Richey kicked another field goal, 40 yards this time, putting San Francisco back on top, 23-20.

There was 6:20 to go in the game — and for one of the teams in the season.

Green Bay's next possession started from its 21, and it started disastrously. Brett Favre threw one of his worst passes of the day and perhaps, given the stakes, one of the worst of his career, seriously under-throwing a ball lofted for tight end Tyrone Davis on the right sideline. Darnell Walker made an easy interception for the 49ers and returned it to the Green Bay 40.

Here, the Packer defense came up big, but it had help from Owens, who dropped yet another pass on a big third-and-10. Young's throw hit Owens at the 30, just enough for the first, but the receiver could not hang on. The 49ers had to punt.

Favre and the Packers took over on their own 11, with 4:19 to go. Behind, on the road, facing a fired-up defense and a frenzied crowd, coming off a terrible turnover in his last possession, Favre brought his offense to the line. What happened over the next few minutes was magical.

The drive began with a short pass to Tyrone Davis that gained nine. Henderson then dropped a short pass on second down. On third, Favre missed Robert Brooks. All of a sudden, the season was in the balance with a fourth-and-one from the 20. Levens gained two off right tackle to keep the season alive.

But the clock was now winding down toward the three-minute mark and the Packers were going without a huddle. Favre called the play at the line. He took the snap, dropped, and down the right sideline saw a rookie receiver, Corey

Bradford, running a fly route with a step on his defender. Favre's pass was perfect. Bradford caught it and tumbled down at the San Francisco 31.

The Packers hurried up to the line, and Favre hit Bradford again, short this time, a gain of six to the 25. The Packers called time out, with 2:34 left.

Favre's stats to this point: 19 of 33 passing, for 277 yards and a touchdown.

On second and four, Tyrone Davis dropped a short ball from Favre. On third down, Favre handed off to Levens, who started right and, as he had done earlier in the game, cut it back to the middle, where he found an opening and 10 crucial yards to the San Francisco 15.

The two-minute warning gave the Packers another chance to confer. On the sideline, Holmgren called for another sweep right to Levens. Favre trotted to the Packers' huddle. He called the play, but as he looked around at his teammates' faces, Favre mentioned the possibility of an audible, depending on what they encountered from the 49ers' defense. His likely audible, Favre said, was something he called a "sprint out and go" — a route in which the receiver starts one way, as if on a short slant route, then cuts straight up field toward the end zone. As the Packers approached the line, Favre could tell a run right was not the play. The 49ers were giving every indication of a blitz. He began to audible. Out wide right, Antonio Freeman looked back toward his quarterback.

"He just gave me a little wink," Freeman said later.

Favre took the snap and rolled right against the blitz, which he had forecast correctly. The Packers' line picked up the rushers and Darnell Walker bit on Freeman's fake. Favre lofted the ball toward the end zone and Freeman gathered it in easily. "Free ran a good route and I just laid it up," Favre said afterward.

The Packers were in front, 27-23. There was 1:56 to go.

Now it was the 49ers turn to make magic.

They started from their 24 after the kickoff, and Young quickly hit J.J. Stokes with a couple of passes that brought the ball to midfield. Nice gains, but Stokes had not been able to get out of bounds, and the clock had run.

With a first-and-10 from the Green Bay 47 and 50 seconds remaining, Young called signals on what would be the second-most important play of this last drive. Young dropped to pass and found Jerry Rice short over the middle. It was the great receiver's first catch of the day — giving him receptions in 22 straight playoff games, tying the record of Cowboys star Drew Pearson. But when Rice was tackled, in bounds, at the Green Bay 41, he appeared to fumble the ball. The official ruled him down before the ball came loose.

"It could have been a fumble, but I thought I was down," Rice said later.

It was a fumble. The television replays would leave no doubt, but the replays were not then being utilized by the officials. America saw a fumble, but it wasn't a fumble, not where it counted, on the field at 3Com Park.

Twenty-seven seconds left.

Young hit Kirby out of the backfield for a gain of nine to the Packers 32, where Kirby got out of bounds.

Twenty seconds.

On first down Young hit Hearst over the middle with a short pass to the Green Bay 25, where the 49ers called their last time-out.

Twelve seconds.

Young dropped back to pass, had pressure, and threw for Stokes down the right side. Almost intercepted by Craig Newsome, the pass fell incomplete.

Eight seconds.

The Packers decided against a blitz, opting instead for a three-man rush and eight pass defenders.

Young dropped back, slipped, and regained his footing. As soon as he did, Young stepped up and threw hard and long over the middle for Terrell Owens, coming over the middle at the goal line. The pass needed to be perfect, and it was. Owens caught it and was hammered almost simultaneously by Packers' safeties Darren Sharper and Pat Terrell. Owens, who had dropped so many easy balls on this day, hung onto this one. It all happened in an instant, and then it was over. Touchdown, San Francisco. The 49ers had won, 30-27.

The Packers appeared stunned. It was the end of something. Just five days later, Mike Holmgren would resign from the team and be named executive vice president of football operations, general manager, and head coach of the Seattle Seahawks.

In the immediate aftermath of Owens' unlikely touchdown, as 3Com Park exploded around him, Brett Favre stood alone on the Packers' sideline. Beneath a beige baseball cap that said PACKERS in green letters above the bill, Favre's face was void of expression. He stood staring into the middle distance. He was, it would appear, remembering.

The Packers' four-point win over the Raiders was a classic Favre heart-stopper.

Oakland Raiders vs. Green Bay Packers

SEPTEMBER 12, 1999
Lambeau Field, Green Bay, Wisconsin

Brett Favre's growing legend was fueled many ways. The quarterback's consecutive-start streak and his ability to always win in cold weather were two. A third, and one that would be called on several times over the first month of the 1999 season, was Favre's uncanny ability to rally his team when they were most in need — to bring them from behind, to somehow *will* a big play with time running out, to wrest victory from defeat. Many quarterbacks have a few fourth-quarter comebacks in them. By the end of the 2006 season, Brett Favre had brought the Packers to victory from behind in the fourth quarter more than 20 times. On nearly as many occasions, he had fashioned a Packers victory after a fourth-quarter tie. It was like a champion golfer who can somehow raise his game on the back nine on Sunday of a Masters or U.S. Open. Favre once put it this way: "Anybody can throw a touchdown in the second quarter."

Favre's last-second magic was never more tested than early in the 1999 season, when the team was trying to win without Mike Holmgren, the coach who brought the Titletown mantle back to Green Bay, but who had decamped for Seattle the previous January.

Packers GM Ron Wolf's choice to replace Holmgren, former Packers assistant Ray Rhodes, was not without controversy. There might have been considerably more questioning had Wolf not had such an enviable track record as a talent scout. Who wanted to doubt the man who had brought Mike Holmgren and Brett Favre to Wisconsin?

Ray Rhodes was famous for his drive and intensity, but in the previous season, his fourth as head coach of the Philadelphia Eagles, the fire had died. Two 10-6 seasons were followed by a disappointing 6-9-1 1997 season. The next year the bottom dropped out. The Eagles limped to the end of the 1998 season with a 3-13 record.

Writing in the *Philadelphia Daily News,* sports columnist Bill Conlon described it like this: "The fire that burned so brightly inside him his first two seasons was a lifeless ember as this wretched season unfolded. If he knew during the exhibitions that he was gone at the end of the season, Rhodes taught a clinic in the art of mailing it in."

Clearly Ron Wolf saw beyond the disastrous end in Philadelphia. He had, in fact, suspected for much of the 1998 season that Mike Holmgren would be leaving. So, although Rhodes was hired within days of Holmgren's announced departure, it wasn't as rushed as all that. Wolf had mentioned Rhodes to Bob Harlan in the middle of the 1998 season, if only as someone who might "some day" steer the Packers. Rhodes in January 1999 was 48 years old, a defensive specialist whose long tenure as defensive coordinator for the San Francisco 49ers had secured his reputation.

". . . The most important thing was to be able to sit down and talk with him and let him know exactly what I expect from him. I will hound the team and I will hound him."

In the days following Holmgren's resignation, Wolf and Rhodes spoke by phone. Then on January 7, a Thursday, Wolf traveled to Philadelphia and met with Rhodes at a hotel in the city. The meeting was not announced to the media. It went well enough that by the weekend, Rhodes' agent was involved in the negotiation. It was finalized Monday, January 11, 1999. The deal was reported to be $4 million over four years. Late that afternoon, at 4 p.m., Wolf introduced the team's 12th head coach to the media gathered at Packers headquarters.

The second question of the news conference addressed the fact that Rhodes had left the Packers five seasons before.

"Ray, why did you leave here the first time?"

It had been said that Rhodes wasn't crazy about the climate, but who is? Rhodes said it had more to do with his having daughters who had liked San Francisco much more than a small, cold city in Wisconsin.

Now, at the news conference, he said: "The first time I left here you know, I had a couple of teen-age daughters that had come from the Bay Area, and things were a little different for them."

He continued: "Maybe it's more my fault not being a stricter parent and shutting them up each day. But they have since grown and are out of school. One's finishing up in college, so I don't have that problem anymore. They're not coming back home, so they won't be living with me. When they get a certain age, everyone knows it's time to leave."

Of the job itself, Rhodes said he knew taking over for Holmgren put him on the "hot seat," but he also said he knew he was inheriting a good football team, not something many newly hired coaches can say.

"There's a standard that's been set here and it's a standard that I want to make sure that we maintain," Rhodes said. "You're looking at a football team that's not broke. I don't want to come here and feel the engine needs repair, and this part of the car needs fixing. I think right now what you do is pull the spark plugs out, you wipe them off and make sure you keep the car fine-tuned."

Rhodes had spoken with Brett Favre prior to the news conference and told the reporters: "Brett's a very big part of this football team, and the most important thing was to be able to sit down and talk with him and let him know exactly what I expect from him. I will hound the team and I will hound him. I will be firm, but I'm going to be fair."

At the press conference, Ron Wolf reiterated that he'd had his eye on Rhodes for some time. (Team president Bob Harlan confirmed that, saying that with the probable departure of Homgren, Harlan and Wolf discussed the coaching situation daily during the 1998 season. "Ray Rhodes was mentioned right from day one," Harlan said. "Ray was still working, but he was the kind of person who appealed to Ron.")

Wolf said: "He's been a former head coach, he understands what winning is all about, he's been in exciting and big games, and the bigger the game, the better his team has performed. All of those things, all of those characteristics more or less make this, as far as I'm concerned, a very, very easy decision for me. I think we needed a specific type of individual to come in here because of the aura and the giant shadow Mike Holmgren cast here. We needed somebody that can carry the mantle, and I think this is the perfect person for that."

In the end, Ray Rhodes wasn't that person. He lasted just one season in Green Bay, producing an 8-8 record that could have been significantly worse without the comeback heroics of his quarterback.

In three of the Packers' first four games in that 1999 season — the other being a loss to the Lions in Detroit — Brett Favre rallied the Packers with late fourth-quarter drives when all appeared lost. It was the most impressive string of improbable comebacks in his storied career.

The last in the string came October 10, 1999, at Lambeau against the Tampa Bay Buccaneers. It was the least dramatic of the three, yet still dramatic enough. Trailing the Bucs, 23-19, with less than two minutes to go in the game, Favre engineered a 73-yard drive for the winning touchdown. It took him less than a minute to do so. The clincher came from the Tampa Bay 21, with the Buccaneers in a blitz. Favre found Antonio Freeman for the game winner, breaking the Bucs' hearts. The final was 26-23, Green Bay.

The great Tampa Bay tackle Warren Sapp said: "I would have bet my life we would have stopped them on that last drive."

After the game, Packer coach Ray Rhodes called Favre "the ultimate warrior."

He'd been that, too, in the Packers' game that preceded the Tampa Bay comeback. When Green Bay hosted the hated Vikings on September 26, 1999, they were staring a loss squarely in the face, trailing 20-16 with less than two minutes to go. The good news was the Packers had the ball. The bad news was they were on their own 23 yard line.

Favre took them down the field in impressive style, first hitting Corey Bradford for 22 yards, immediately making the impossible seem possible. He almost made it look easy, until the drive threatened to stall with a fourth-and-one at the Viking 23. Less than half a minute remained. The Packers were out of time-outs. Getting a first down and staying in bounds would run the clock down dangerously low. A field goal would not help. A touchdown was required, and that is what Brett Favre produced, finding Bradford for the 23-yard score and moving *Chicago Tribune* pro football writer Don Pierson to compare Favre to the very greatest comeback artists to ever play in the NFL. "This was Unitas and Layne and Graham and Elway and Staubach at their best, taking command of a game when all looked lost," Pierson noted.

The best comeback of them all, however, may have come in the season opener. It was a critical game — as any first game sets the tone for the season. But when the Oakland Raiders came to Lambeau on September 12, 1999, there was even more on the line than usual. It was the first game of the Ray Rhodes era, but perhaps more important, it was the Packers' first test in the post-Mike Holmgren era. Fans, media — everyone — wondered whether the Packers could stay among the NFL's elite or whether the magic had left town with Holmgren.

One big positive for the Packers' hopes was that Rhodes had convinced the offensive coordinator under Holmgren, Sherm Lewis, to stay in Green Bay. Lewis may have felt he deserved the head job himself, but he was a close friend of Rhodes, tight enough to swallow his pride and stay on to run the offense.

In the week leading up to the 1999 opener, Favre announced himself thrilled that Lewis was still around.

"It meant a great deal for him to stay," Favre said. "I talked to Ray several times in that process, and I know he was trying his best to keep Sherm. I know Sherm was exploring some other avenues. I talked to Sherm a couple of times at his house and just keep reiterating how much I would love to have him back."

It was cloudy with a chance of rain when the Packers and Raiders took the field at Lambeau to start the 1999 regular season. The Oakland head coach, Jon Gruden, was himself a former Holmgren assistant. He'd led the Raiders to an

8-8 mark in 1998 and now had a new quarterback, Rich Gannon, who had come over from the Chiefs for a four-year, $16-million contract.

The Packers received the opening kickoff, but went three and out. On a second-and-12 from the Packers 18, Favre had thrown up the right middle for his tight end, Mark Chmura, who got his hands on the ball but couldn't make the catch. Chmura had sat out the entire pre-season with a painful disc injury in his back. He figured to be rusty.

Packers' punter Chris Hanson hit a short one from the Green Bay 8, and the Raiders' Darrien Gordon, who averaged 13 yards a punt return on his career, had to run forward to try to field it. It came down at his feet at the Raiders' 49 and Gordon was unable to make a catch, kicking it instead. A couple of Packers — most notably long snapper Rob Davis — had great chances to recover the ball for Green Bay, but missed. Davis rolled right over it. In the end, it was the Raiders' ball on the Green Bay 45.

Oakland's first play was a handoff to running back Napoleon Kaufman and he, too, appeared to fumble. (It would be a sloppy game in terms of penalities and turnovers.) Kaufman, on being hit at the line of scrimmage by LeRoy Butler, lost the ball, but it bounced into the hands of Raiders wide-out Tim Brown, who ran it all the way to the Packers 34 before being pushed out of bounds. But the officials ruled Kaufman had been down by contact — no fumble. It was a break for the Packers.

The Raiders would eventually advance the ball as far as the Green Bay 25 on their opening drive, but it finally stalled. Then Raider kicker Michael Husted was wide left — barely missing — on a 48-yard field goal try.

Favre and the Packers took over on their own 38. The quarterback hit Freeman for a quick 10 on the drive's opening play, and then Favre settled into a mix of runs and short passes that quickly took them down the field. On two occasions he found Chmura, consecutive plays of 12 and 16 yards, which indicated the big tight end had shaken off the rust. The seriousness of his disc injury should not be discounted. Chmura had suffered considerable upper-body numbness and there had even been talk of retirement. Instead, he was again one of Favre's favorite targets and his second grab of the drive gave the Packers a first down at the Raiders' 11.

On first down, Favre dropped, faked a handoff to Dorsey Levens, found no one open, and began drifting forward. It was another instance of Favre vacating the pocket by running *toward* the line of scrimmage, rather than sideways or even backwards as most quarterbacks do. As he neared the line, Favre shuttled the ball forward to Levens, who caught it at the 7 and advanced it to the 4.

On the next play, Favre threw a slant to Bill Schroeder for the Packers' first touchdown of the 1999 season, and Green Bay led, 7-0.

The Raiders came back with a field goal on their next possession, the key play coming right after the kickoff. On first and 10 from the Oakland 17, Kaufman took a quick pitch from Gannon and turned the corner on the left side, spinning and leaving a befuddled Darren Sharper in his wake. LeRoy Butler missed on a diving tackle as well and Kaufman turned the simple quick sweep into a gain of 48 to the Packers' 35. The Raiders eventually settled for a 41-yard Husted field goal, making it 7-3, Packers.

Oakland would quickly get the ball back. After the kickoff, on a third-and-nine from the Packer 32, Favre dropped, was blitzed, and got off a good, hard pass to Corey Bradford coming over the middle from the left on a crossing route. The ball hit Bradford in the hands, but he couldn't grab it; instead, it skipped high in the air behind the receiver, where the Raiders' Darrien Gordon intercepted. Oakland had a first down at the Green Bay 32.

There was considerable muttering from the crowd at Lambeau, and not just because it had begun to drizzle.

It would not be the last miscue of the game for the Packers. Afterwards, Ray Rhodes was shaking his head.

"We went out and did all the things we talked about that we couldn't do," the coach said. "Turn the football over, give up big plays, dropped balls, balls bouncing off guys, holding penalities, defensively giving up big plays down the field, third-down situations, things that we have tried to stress and work on. All those things happened today."

Oakland took quick advantage of the interception. On a third-and-eight from the Green Bay 20, Gannon caught the Packers in a blitz and threw while backpedaling down the left sideline for Tim Brown, the great wide-out coming off his sixth straight season with 1,000 or more yards receiving. Tyrone Williams actually had decent coverage on Brown, but never looked back for the ball. Brown caught it and was forced out of bounds at the 2 yard line. Two plays later, running back Randy Jordan took it over the goal line off right guard, and the Raiders led, 10-7.

That's how the first half ended. The Packers had one more good drive in the second quarter derailed by a turnover, an interception that once again was not Brett Favre's fault.

This time, on a third-and-seven from the Oakland 27, Favre threw for Chmura on the left side. The ball slid through the tight end's hands and was kept alive by Oakland corner Eric Allen, who batted it into the air, where it was picked off by linebacker Greg Biekert and returned to the Oakland 37. The Raiders eventually had to punt and the half ended.

Two of the game's most significant plays occurred not long after the second-half kickoff. The Raiders had received and picked up a couple of first downs, but then were forced to punt. Green Bay took over on its own 12 yard line. On second and nine from the 13, Favre took the snap from center, made a quick drop, and released the ball while backpedaling, looking for Bill Schroeder on a slant from the left. The ball was too far in front of Schroeder and fell incomplete, but the drama was back behind the line of scrimmage, where Favre was bent over in obvious pain.

In a preseason game against Denver, Favre had jammed the thumb on his throwing hand; now he had aggravated it, and quite severely. As Favre followed through on his pass for Schroeder, his right hand clipped Raider tackle Russell Maryland and his thumb was bent backward. The pain was intense, but Favre huddled and called another play. Incredibly, fate was not yet done with Favre and his thumb. He took the snap — it was now third and nine from the Oakland 13 — and, after a long drop, Favre set at the 6 and, ignoring the pain, threw a long, beautiful pass over the middle for Antonio Freeman, who caught it at the Packers' 27, spun to shake defender Charles Woodson, and then ran to the right sideline and up the field all the way to the Oakland 36, a gain of 51 yards.

It was a great play, but for the second pass in a row, Favre on his follow-through had clipped a defender. This time it was Lance Johnstone, and Favre's already aching thumb was jammed hard. As the quarterback ran up the field after Freeman's long gain, he was shaking his right hand and grimacing. Yet he stayed in the game, further testimony to his legendary grit.

"At one point, I almost came out," Favre said afterward. "I didn't even mention it to the coaches or anything. I was actually sort of scared to throw the ball downfield. I didn't know if I could put anything on it."

LeRoy Butler would say the thumb looked like it had been driven over by an automobile.

A few plays after Freeman's 51-yard reception put the Packers in business in Raider territory, the receiver Favre called "Free" garnered another, this time on a second-and-10 from the Raiders' 26. The call was a delayed slant from the left side, and Freeman took it for 11 yards to the Oakland 15.

Just two plays later, on a second-and-seven from the 12, Favre went again for Freeman, who was open just outside the right hash mark near the goal line. The catch was good for a touchdown, and the Packers went up 14-10 with 6:32 to go in the third quarter. After delivering the pass, Favre pumped his fist — his left, not his throwing hand — and then sank to his knees in pain, grasping his right hand in his left.

Still he stayed in the game. Following an Oakland punt that resulted in a touchback, the Packers started from their 20, but a holding penalty against tackle Ross Verba pushed them back 10 yards, making it first and 20 from the 10. On the next snap, Favre found William Henderson for five yards to the 15. Then, on second and 15, disaster struck. As Favre dropped to pass, a Raider linebacker named K.D. Williams was lurking, screened from the quarterback's vision by other players. Williams had only recently joined the Raiders as the unlikeliest of free agents; just eight months before, he had been working as a sky captain at the Tampa International Airport.

Now Williams interrupted the flight of Favre's pass, intended over the middle for Dorsey Levens at the Packer 20. Williams stepped in front of Levens at the 19, intercepted, and returned it to the Packers' 5. It was Favre's third interception of the game, but the first one that was really his mistake. As the quarterback walked off the field, he was motioning to an official that he felt Levens had been held. The official ignored him, no doubt making Favre's thumb throb even more.

It took Oakland just one play to take advantage of the turnover. Gannon handed the ball off left tackle to Tyrone Wheatley, who bumped it outside and went into the end zone standing up, making it 17-14 with a little more than two minutes remaining in the third quarter.

It appeared the tide may have turned to the visitors, an impression strengthened after Favre took a bad sack and the Packers were forced to punt to end the third quarter. The nervous twitters at Lambeau were growing louder—and they must have shifted to outright concern when the Raiders began the fourth quarter by mounting an impressive eight-play, 68-yard drive, culminating in Randy Jordan's one-yard touchdown run. The key play in the drive was on third and nine from the Packers' 44. Gannon had set the Raiders, but didn't like what he saw from the Packers' defense; he called time-out and ran over to the Oakland bench. Back under center, Gannon made a quick drop as his linemen tried to hold off a six-man Packer rush. Before they could get to Gannon, the quarterback lofted a pass down the right sideline for James Jett, who had a step on rookie Packers' defensive back Fred Vinson. Jett caught it at the 12 and was knocked out of bounds by Vinson on the 1. Jordan scored on the next play and the Packers, trailing 24-14, with 10:52 to go in the game, were in danger of losing their opener at home and the first game of the Ray Rhodes era.

Aching thumb and all, Brett Favre was determined that wasn't going to happen. After the kickoff, Favre engineered an eight-play, 68-yard drive that brought the Packers within three with a little over seven minutes to go.

Big plays on the drive included a first-and-10 from the Packers' 37 in which Favre found tight end Tyrone Davis — who had started all the pre-season games due to Chmura's injury — open down the middle at the Oakland 42, and Davis took it to the Raiders' 30 for a pick up of 33 yards.

Then, on a second-and-11 from the 31, Favre was chased right out of the pocket. Sprinting straight sideways toward the right sideline, Favre spotted Davis again. Favre threw just before going out of bounds and Davis made a dive for the ball at the Oakland 14. The official on the play ruled it incomplete, but the Packers challenged the call — instant replay review had been reinstated — and it was ruled that Davis had indeed made the catch. It was a Green Bay first down. Two plays later, Favre found Corey Bradford in the end zone for a touchdown. Green Bay now trailed 24-21, with 7:20 to go in the fourth quarter.

The Packers needed the defense to come up big, but Gannon and the Raiders picked up a first down after the kickoff, and then another, when the quarterback appeared to miss on a third down pass but Packers' defender Mike McKenzie was called for interference. The Raiders now had a first-and-10 at their 49 yard line. It was here the Green Bay defense toughened. Facing a fourth and short from the Packers' 42, the Raiders chose to punt. It was a touchback.

The game almost ended on a third-and-10 for the Packers from their own 20. After two straight incompletions, Favre dropped back and threw, but the ball was batted high into the air by Raiders tackle Chuck Osborne. Favre, angry at having his pass deflected, saw that the ball was coming down from on high in the direction of Raider defender Lance Johnstone, who was primed for an interception, which would have effectively sealed the game for the Raiders. Favre rushed toward Johnstone and hit him head on just as the ball arrived, converting an interception into an incomplete pass and giving Green Bay a chance to punt the ball into better field position.

The last-gasp Packers drive would start from their own 18, with 1:51 to go and no time-outs remaining. It would prove to be one of the most glorious drives of Brett Favre's career.

Still, it looked bleak. The Raiders took over on the Oakland 37, with 2:19 left in the game. Oakland ran twice for little gain, but the Packers were forced to use their last two time-outs. On third down Gannon missed on a pass and the Raiders punted. Green Bay was called for an illegal block on the return, so the last-gasp Packers drive would start from their own 18, with 1:51 to go and no time-outs remaining.

It would prove one of the most glorious drives of Brett Favre's career.

It started with a short pass to Levens over the middle. He caught the ball at the Packer 20 and then did the rest himself, getting all the way to the Green Bay 40 before being brought down, in bounds.

Favre rushed the Packers to the line. There was no huddle. He took the snap with 1:26 showing on the clock and threw short to Freeman on the right hash mark, for a gain of six to the Packer 46.

By the time the Packers could snap the ball again, just 1:06 remained. This time, they gambled with a running play. Favre handed off to Levens over right tackle and it worked beautifully; a big hole was opened and Levens took it to the Raiders' 42 before being tackled.

Favre sprinted the Packers up to the line, took a quick snap, and spiked the ball, stopping the clock.

There was now 54 seconds remaining. The Packers trailed by three.

On the next play, Favre hit Bill Schroeder on the left side for a gain of 10 to the Oakland 32, though Schroeder was tackled in bounds.

Favre's stats now showed him 25 of 40 for 302 yards and three touchdowns.

He quickly added another incompletion, however, after spiking the ball to stop the clock. Now 38 seconds remained.

On second and 10 from the Oakland 32, Favre threw incomplete for Levens near the left sideline. The play only used six seconds on the clock, but it was now third and 10.

Favre took the snap, dropped, set himself on the left hash mark at the 38 yard line, and threw across to the right side for Schroeder, who made the catch at the Raiders' 21, tried to wheel free of a defender, and was brought down, in bounds, at the 20.

The clock ticked as Favre rushed the offense to the line and quickly spiked the ball.

Twenty seconds to go.

On second and 10 from the Raiders' 20, Favre dropped back, set, and threw a high lofted spiral to the right side, where Corey Bradford was running with two Raider defenders, Charles Woodson and Eric Turner. Bradford made a great catch and was pushed out at the 1 yard line.

Fourteen seconds left.

The Packers brought out a new formation, with three tight ends. Jeff Thomason was in at that position for the first time all game. Favre took the snap, made a quick drop, looked right, dropped a bit farther back, and floated a pass to the right middle of the end zone, where Thomason had shaken himself loose and where he made the catch for the game-winning touchdown. The extra point made it 28-24, Packers, and Lambeau Field was going crazy.

Favre was emotional, even in a bit of a daze, after the game.

His coach, Ray Rhodes, was effusive in his praise: "A storybook drive. You've seen Joe Montana do it. You've seen Elway do it a number of times. That's why Brett is one of the best quarterbacks in football. That's a perfect drive."

Thomason, who caught the winning touchdown pass, said of his quarterback: "You could tell he was tired and beat up, but he just kept fighting. He was just awesome. You admire a guy like that so much for the way he played that game and the way he finished, because I knew he was, emotionally, just completely worn out. That just shows you what he's capable of doing as far as fighting and pushing himself to extreme limits. He did it today."

Just how truly spent he was could be seen at his own abbreviated news conference after the game.

Favre was asked how bad he was hurting.

"I'm not sure," he said quietly. "Which part?"

"Your thumb," somebody said.

"It's sore," the quarterback said. "I can't believe I played."

Did the injury impact his throwing?

"I could hardly feel the ball, but we won the game, so…" Favre's voice drifted off.

He was asked how much the victory meant.

"I don't know," he said. "I'm so drained right now."

And Brett Favre began to softly cry. No one knew what to say. The tears continued for close to a half minute before Favre stood and walked out of the press conference.

Offensive coordinator Sherm Lewis said it was as emotional as he'd ever seen Favre.

Earlier, the quarterback had been asked one brief question about whether the thumb injury might keep him out of the next week's game, against the Detroit Lions.

"I haven't thought about it," Favre said. "I don't want to think about it."

To the surprise of no one, he played.

Wisconsin State Journal/Steve Apps

"Brett loves to run around": Scrambling against the Ravens' defense.

Baltimore Ravens vs. Green Bay Packers

OCTOBER 14, 2001
Lambeau Field, Green Bay, Wisconsin

The summer of 2000 was the first time it was prominently suggested in print that Brett Favre might be over the hill. It wouldn't be the last. With success comes scrutiny, and few athletes have ever had more success or been more highly scrutinized than Favre. But could the tide turn that fast? The summer of 2000? Favre's three straight MVP seasons remained fresh in memory. Still, that didn't stop the Associated Press from visiting the Green Bay training camp in August and sending out on the wire a story that in at least one Canadian newspaper carried this headline:

"Is Favre finished?"

The secondary headline read: "Former MVP battling injuries, slump."

It was true that the 1999 season, following the Packers' devastating last-second loss at San Francisco in the wild card playoff game, had been disastrous by recent Packer standards.

Green Bay finished 8-8, tied for third in their division with the Detroit Lions, behind both Minnesota and Tampa Bay. Every loss is painful in its way, but for the Packers there seemed to be an inordinate number of close games in which they were defeated in the end by a bad decision on the field or on the sideline. There were also blow outs, perhaps none more humiliating than an October visit to Denver in which the Broncos crushed the Packers 31-10 in a game that was even more lopsided than the score indicated.

The odds had actually seemed to favor the Packers going into the game. The Broncos were the two-time defending Super Bowl champion but were without their own superstar quarterback, John Elway, who had retired. They'd lost two other offensive stars to injury — tight end Shannon Sharpe and running back Terrell Davis — as well as their best defender, linebacker John Mobley.

The Broncos were 1-4 when the Packers came to Mile High Stadium on October 17, 1999. The final score was bad enough, but the statistics were worse, especially for the offense. The Packers managed just 133 total yards on 35 plays from scrimmage. Only 12 plays gained yards. Favre's personal numbers were equally poor. He hit just seven of 23 passes and had three interceptions. Favre's numbers on the season were the worst of his career. He played all of 1999 with a thumb on his throwing hand that never healed from an injury in the pre-season, but he had problems beyond his thumb. Favre had more interceptions than touchdown passes in 1999 (23-22) and a quarterback rating that placed him 25th among the league's passers.

"So much has been made of playing with the thumb injury last year," Favre told the Associated Press in the summer of 2000. "This is football. You play with injuries. Your teammates count on you, the coaches count on you, the fans count on you."

He also said this: "Football is a job now, and it wasn't always like that. I knew it was a business, but it's a lot of work now. I still enjoy it, and I wouldn't want to do anything else, but it's not like it used to be."

It's a lot more fun to win.

Toward that end, the Green Bay management — notably GM Ron Wolf— was quick to bite the bullet after the disappointing 1999 season and announced the firing of Ray Rhodes, the head coach Wolf had hired only a few days after Mike Holmgren had announced his departure for Seattle. Wolf liked Rhodes' toughness and never really looked seriously at another candidate. He was equally quick to send Rhodes packing when it didn't work out. Wolf called Bob Harlan, the Packers president, on the Sunday morning before the last game of the 1999 season and said he was going let Rhodes go when the season was over.

"Do what you need to do," Harlan said.

A little later, when Harlan learned from Wolf that one of the people Wolf was considering to replace Rhodes was former Holmgren assistant Mike Sherman, Harlan put in a positive word for Sherman. He remembered that when Sherman, who had been the Packers' tight ends coach, decided to follow Holmgren to Seattle, Sherman had made a point of stopping by Harlan's office to say how much he had enjoyed Green Bay and the high esteem in which he held the Packer organization.

Harlan later recalled that he told Wolf, "This place is very important to Mike Sherman."

Sherman got the Packers head job on January 18, 2000. It was his first head coaching job anywhere, and if it was a great opportunity, it also carried plenty of risk. Sherman had earned wide praise for his competence, but there was no preparing for the fishbowl of being head coach of the Packers in Green Bay. It's one of a handful of the most pressurized jobs in professional sports. Green Bay fans turn out to shovel the stadium seats for minimum wage when it snows before a game; their devotion doesn't subside just because the team is losing. A Packers head coach is a celebrity and a lightning rod. Sherman, who had enjoyed Green Bay as an obscure tight ends coach a few years earlier, was assuming center stage, like it or not.

He had no history as a headliner. Born and raised in Massachusetts, Sherman played football well enough in high school to get a scholarship to Central Connecticut State University. He played both ways — tackle on offense, end on defense — and was considered solid but not a star. He majored in English and parlayed that and his athletic resume into a couple of early jobs teaching high school English while serving as an assistant football coach. His first college job was at the University of Pittsburgh, and that led to subsequent positions at Tulane, Holy Cross, and Texas A&M.

Sherman's specialty was the offensive line. When Mike Holmgren brought him to Green Bay in 1997, it was to coach the line and the tight ends. When Holmgren left Green Bay after the 1998 season, he invited Sherman to join him in Seattle as his offensive coordinator. He was there a year later when Ray Rhodes was fired in Green Bay and the Packers came calling.

The other name in the mix to replace Rhodes was Marty Schottenheimer, who had been a head coach in the league and would have been a more conventional choice than Sherman. Ron Wolf went back and forth and finally chose Sherman's enthusiasm over Schottenheimer's experience.

In retrospect, Sherman's first season as head coach of the Packers, 2000, would be viewed as on-the-job training. The Packers lost their first two games, and were a glum 5-7 with four games to go, when something clicked. It may have been as simple as the coach and players attaining a comfort level with one another, but whatever it was, the Packers won their last four games to finish 9-7 on the year.

Brett Favre, the veteran quarterback and forever the straw that stirred the drink in Green Bay, came out publicly in praise of Sherman. The team liked him, played hard for him. It was a good vibe. Packer CEO Bob Harlan was impressed enough that when Ron Wolf stepped down as general manager before the 2001 season, Harlan asked Sherman to assume the general manager duties in addition to being head coach.

"I think Brett said it best when the season was over last year," Harlan said later, "when he said it was the best chemistry he had seen in the nine years he had been here. That was a huge statement."

The next season, 2001, started better, with three decisive wins.

"We're all more comfortable with each other," Sherman said in the middle of that year. "They know me, and I know them. As you develop your chemistry and people become more familiar with each other and you have your certain characters and comics on the team, the team does have tendency to loosen up a little bit."

Even Sherman, with his reputation for great intensity, had become comfortable enough in the limelight that an occasional joke wasn't out of the question. It had produced an atmosphere in which Brett Favre was having fun playing football again.

"I think you have to have fun at your job because it's a long season," Favre said. "If it's just grind, grind, grind, it can get tough. So there has to be times of levity, and then you have to be able to flip the switch and go back to work."

The Packers were definitely in work mode when the Baltimore Ravens came to Lambeau on October 14, 2001. After their stellar, three-victory start to the season, the Packers had laid an egg in Tampa, losing 14-10 to the Buccaneers. Brett Favre had thrown three interceptions in that game.

"He told me, 'We're going to get 400 yards on this team.' I kind of said, 'OK, you're right, Tom.' I was thinking, 'This guy's crazy.'"

Some in Green Bay wondered what an offense that could muster only 10 points against Tampa and a quarterback who threw three picks in that game would do against the Baltimore Ravens' defense, which more than a few experts were calling the best of all time.

The Ravens had gone 12-4 during the 2000 season and then won Super Bowl XXXV without much of an offense. The Ravens' defense was that good. It was epitomized by middle linebacker Ray Lewis, a terror on and (on occasion) off the field who was defensive player of the year in the NFL. In the Super Bowl, the Ravens' defense crushed the New York Giants, with Baltimore prevailing, 34-7. The Ravens' defense had four sacks, forced five turnovers, and didn't give up a touchdown. (The Giants scored on a kickoff return.)

Early in the 2001 season, the defending champions' defense was as intimidating as ever. As the Ravens came to Green Bay to face the Packers, the longest scoring drive they'd surrendered thus far was 34 yards. Brett Favre, who was having fun again but was not all that far removed from the forgettable 1999 season and whispers of his decline, would have to produce something magical if the Packers were to beat the Ravens.

The Packers' offensive coordinator, Tom Rossley, may have been in the minority, but he thought it could happen. He developed a game plan that would put Favre in the shotgun formation — several yards back from center — with an extra receiver split wide. It was an aggressive, attacking strategy, one that if successful might neutralize Ray Lewis in the middle.

Early in the week of the Ravens game, Favre came into the Packer offices to watch film, and Rossley told him the defense could be had.

"He told me, 'We're going to get 400 yards on this team,'" Favre recalled later. "I kind of said, 'OK, you're right, Tom.' I was thinking: 'This guy's crazy. He must be drinking.'" That was Tuesday. As the week went on, Favre became more of a believer.

Favre also found it necessary to go to bat for his favorite receiver, Antonio Freeman, who had been quoted in the press complaining about not getting the ball enough. When he was asked about it, Favre insisted Freeman was just a little frustrated, wanted to be involved and make a contribution. That, the quarterback said, was a good thing.

Sunday morning in Green Bay, it almost felt like a playoff game. The weather was excellent — 56 and sunny, though there was a bit of wind, 12 mph — and the anticipation was high.

Packers' trainer Curt Fielder had tried to give Favre some added incentive before he taped him Sunday morning. Lewis, during the week, had said nice things about the Packer quarterback — "he's a 60-minute player with a linebacker's mentality" — but he had also left no doubt in his belief that the Ravens could shut down the Packer offense. Fielder seized on that.

"First thing before he tapes me he wants to show me the quote Ray Lewis said during the week," Favre said afterward. "Curt's ready to fight before the game — I'm trying to relax and not think about how great their defense is."

Fielder said, "Can you believe they said that?"

Favre, remembering later, described his reaction. "I said, 'Hell, they won the Super Bowl. They have a great defense.' But in the back of my mind I was thinking I'm pretty good too. Our team's pretty good."

Favre, who had turned 32 during the week, was making his 146th straight start for the Packers.

As the Packers huddled after returning the opening kickoff to their own 23, Favre looked around at the faces of his offensive linemen and gave them a quick pep talk. Running on Baltimore would be very difficult. The Packers were going to pass, and Favre needed time in the pocket. The shotgun would help, but the linemen needed to step up.

"I told them in the huddle before we ran our first play, 'You guys up front will be the difference in the ball game,'" Favre recalled later. "'There's a challenge in front of you and let's see how you handle it.'"

Favre didn't waste any time trying to get Freeman involved. The quarterback took the shotgun snap, rolled right, and threw back against his body for Freeman, who was well covered in the middle of the field. The pass was incomplete, but the Packers picked up a first down two plays later when a short pass to Bill Schroeder was followed by a five-yard-run by Dorsey Levens.

The Packers picked up another first down on a slant pass from Favre to Schroeder that moved the ball to the Packer 48.

On the next play, Favre, again in the shotgun, handed off on a draw to Ahman Green, who broke right through a good hole. But even as he ran to the right, Green had the ball cradled in his left arm, an idiosyncrasy that would cost him. Most backs switch the ball to the arm away from the defensive pursuit. Green did not, and it left the football more exposed. He'd been subject to fumbling throughout his career and now on this run, as he reached the Ravens' 46 and was popped by two defenders, the ball shook loose and was recovered at the Ravens' 37 by Baltimore safety Corey Harris. From there, it took only four plays for the Ravens to score, with the touchdown coming on an 18-yard Elvis Grbac to Travis Taylor pass. Packers corner Mike McKenzie had tried to bump and run with Taylor from the line of scrimmage, but McKenzie slipped and fell and Taylor was wide open in the right end zone.

That quick, it was 7-0, Ravens.

Favre would say later: "In a game like this, at our place, the one thing you don't want to have happen is to turn the ball over early, and have them go right down and score. I'm thinking on the sideline, 'This is the spark they needed.' The last thing we wanted to do was give them an edge. I didn't know what to expect."

The Packers picked up a first down after returning the kickoff to their 30. Then on a second and 11 from the 40, Favre, not in the shotgun but over center, took the snap, dropped back, and threw an excellent pass down the right middle of the field that hit Freeman in stride. The receiver, however, may have sensed a hit coming — and it did come. Freeman was hammered by Harris, who'd recovered the earlier fumble — and Freeman dropped the ball. The fans booed, not a common occurrence in Lambeau. Favre figured they were getting on Freeman for his comments to reporters about not seeing enough balls thrown in his direction.

"I don't know if that came across in a negative way to our fans," Favre said later. "It didn't to me and it didn't to our team."

The Packers had to punt. The Ravens were in the process of putting a second good drive together when, on second and nine from the Green Bay 40, Grbac handed the ball to fullback Obafemi Ayanbadejo. The fullback, running left, was hit by Packers tackle Santana Dotson; then Ravens' receiver Travis Taylor, trying to block LeRoy Butler, inadvertently popped the ball out of Ayanbadejo's grasp with his helmet. Cletidus Hunt recovered for the Packers on their 41. It was a timely break for the Packers.

Favre came out throwing. He went to Freeman first, for a gain of eight on the left side. After a run to Green was stuffed, Favre found Bill Schroeder running a shallow crossing route and Schroeder, the fastest Packer receiver, took the ball all the way to the Ravens' 37 for a first down. After another short pass to Schroeder, Favre next went back to Freeman, who made a nice catch at the Baltimore 13.

The Ravens had given up only five touchdowns in their first four games. If the Packers could continue into the end zone, it would be the longest touchdown drive of the year — 59 yards — against the Baltimore defense.

The Packers made it four plays later, with the touchdown coming on a first-and-goal from the 2. It was a short pass from Favre, who had rolled out right, to tight end Bubba Franks in the back of the end zone.

That made it 7-7, with just under 14 minutes to go in the second quarter.

One interesting sidelight to the game was the presence in the Lambeau stands of Harry and Pauline Sharper, who had two of their sons playing, one on each team. Darren Sharper was a Packers' safety and Jamie Sharper was a Ravens' linebacker; Harry Sharper was wearing Ravens' colors while his wife was clad in the Packers' green and gold. They were sitting next to one another in the stands and whatever happened, they were going to get a good meal out of the game, because Darren and Jamie had made a bet that whichever of them made the biggest play, the other would take the family out for dinner.

After the Packers' touchdown, the Ravens went three and out. Favre, on getting the ball back, stayed aggressive. On first down after the punt, he faked a run to Green, and then tried to hit Schroeder on a fly pattern down the left sideline. The Ravens corner, Chris McAllister, beaten on the play, reached out with his right arm and grabbed Schroeder before the ball arrived. A pass interference penalty gave the Packers a first down at the Baltimore 31.

The Packer drive stalled a few plays later after Levens lost five on a screen pass, but Ryan Longwell made his field goal attempt and Green Bay took its first lead of the game, 10-7.

Baltimore made a couple of first downs on its ensuing drive before being forced to punt. Kyle Richardson's boot was a beauty, pinning the Packers on their 2 yard line, from where they went three and out, with Josh Bidwell's punt from the Green Bay end zone traveling only to the Packers' 31 — great field position for the Ravens.

The defending Super Bowl champions did not, however, take advantage. They did pick up one first down, but on first and 10 from the Packers' 19, Grbac dropped back to pass and could find no open receivers. He was hit by Packers' lineman Santana Dotson and the ball came loose, bouncing on the turf where Packers' end Vonnie Holliday bent down to pick it up. He struggled to get a handle on the ball and it finally came to rest under a pile at the Green Bay 36.

It took a moment but the officials finally ruled — Packer ball. Ravens' coach Brian Billick threw a challenge flag, hoping that a replay might show that Grbac had forward motion and the play was an incomplete pass rather than a fumble, but the challenge was overruled.

Again, Favre came out firing. The Packers were displaying the kind of confidence no one was supposed to have against the Ravens' defense. From the shotgun, Favre dropped and threw deep over the middle for Donald Driver, who dove for the ball and made a great catch at the Ravens' 36. Driver was horizontal to the ground when he made the grab, a fact not lost on his quarterback.

"Brett loves to run around. If his legs don't beat you, his arm will. Once he gets out of the pocket, it's backyard football."

"When you throw the ball downfield," Favre said later, "you have to make plays and those guys made some phenomenal catches today."

Longwell would eventually miss a field goal to end that drive, but the Packers got the ball right back when Mike McKenzie picked off a Grbac pass intended for Travis Taylor at the Green Bay 26.

This time, though only 1:19 remained in the first half, the Packers would take advantage. On first and 10 from the 26, Favre, out of the shotgun, unleashed a deep pass to Corey Bradford, who was running a fly pattern down the left sideline. Bradford's arms were completely outstretched when the ball arrived at the Ravens' 30. He caught it, stumbling as he did, and went down at the 27. It was a sensational catch of a beautiful pass. Favre' s statistics to that point were staggering, considering the opponent. He'd hit 15 of 19 passes for 172 yards and a touchdown.

Time was now an issue. There was 1:01 left in the half when Favre handed off to Green out of the shotgun on first down from the 27. Green could manage only a yard and the clocked ticked down to 43 seconds. Favre took the second-down shotgun snap and fired to his right side, where Freeman came up with the ball in traffic at the Ravens' 13. The Packers took time out.

Next play, 31 seconds remaining, Favre took the snap out of the shotgun and hit Ahman Green to his left for a gain of five to the Ravens' 8. The clock was running. Favre got the next snap with 12 seconds left and threw incomplete for Schroeder in the end zone.

Eight seconds left in the half.

Favre called time out, even though the incompletion had stopped the clock. He went over to talk to Sherman and, even as he did, Schroeder, who had been banged up trying for the catch on the last play, collapsed as he came off the field. He was OK, but wouldn't return to the game.

Favre and Sherman, meanwhile, decided that eight seconds was enough time to throw a pass into the end zone and still kick a field goal if it was incomplete.

It became a moot point when Favre took the shotgun snap, rolled right, pumped once under pressure, drifted even farther right, and then threw on the run into the front right corner of the end zone, where Freeman had shaken himself open. It was a touchdown and the Packers went into halftime leading the defending champions, 17-7.

The play was vintage Favre, and it put the Ravens behind at halftime for the first time that season.

"Brett loves to run around," Ravens' safety Rod Woodson would say later. "If his legs don't beat you, his arm will. He is going to run around and throw the football. Once he gets out of the pocket, it's backyard football. Those receivers are going everywhere, and you've got to plaster up. But we weren't plastering up in the secondary or with the linebackers."

Chris McAllister, the Ravens' corner, was more blunt.

"I'm shocked about this," he said afterward. "Favre did exactly he needed to do whenever he had to."

The Ravens got what appeared to be a boost on the second-half kickoff, when Jermaine Lewis returned it almost to the 50 yard line, but a holding call brought it back and Baltimore started from its own 21.

They launched a nice drive from there, advancing the ball all the way inside the Packers' 30. Then on a third and three from the 29, Grbac, under pressure from Packers' tackle Jim Flanigan, threw a sideline pass intended for Qadry Ismail (brother of "Rocket" Ismail) that was intercepted by Darren Sharper, giving Green Bay the ball back at its own 28. From there the Packers went three and out. Bidwell's punt was taken by Lewis at the Ravens' 29 and returned all the way down the right sideline to the Green Bay 35. There were no flags. Matt Stover eventually kicked a 28-yard field goal to bring the Ravens back within a touchdown at 17-10. (The kick gave Stover field goals in 31 straight games, tying an NFL record.)

Now the Ravens, who hadn't allowed a long touchdown drive all year until the first half, needed a defensive stop. They didn't get it. The kickoff was a touchback, giving the Packers the ball at the 20. From there Brett Favre led them on a masterful drive.

Later, the quarterback would be asked if he could explain why he looked so comfortable while up against the league's fiercest defense.

"No," Favre replied. "I'd love to sit up here after the fact and tell you we knew it was going to be a piece of cake. But I'm not going to do that. They have a great defense. Maybe the best defense to ever play. But it says we're good too."

They were better than good. On the first play after the kickoff, Favre hit Freeman over the middle for 14. Then on a third-and-10 from the Packers' 34,

Favre took the shotgun snap, dropped back, had plenty of time, and led Driver perfectly on a pass the receiver gathered in at the Ravens' 40 and took an additional 10 yards to the 30.

Two plays later, facing a third-and-eight from the 28, Favre took the snap in the shotgun and handed on a draw to Ahman Green, who danced and then raced all the way to the Ravens' 9, setting up a first-and-goal.

Mike Sherman said later the Packers utilized "a lot of new type of runs out of the shotgun that we haven't employed very much lately."

An interference call near the goal line on second down gave the Packers a first at the 1 yard line, and from there Green punched it over. Nine plays, 80 yards, 24-10 Packers.

As the third quarter ended, the sunny skies that had begun the game gave way to clouds and hail, then light rain.

Baltimore picked up one first down after the Packers' touchdown, but then had to punt, after which the teams exchanged three-and-outs. The Packers were left with the ball on their own 17 yard line.

From there, incredibly, Favre engineered yet another long drive. It was a mix of successful passes and runs and the key play was a bit of both. On a second-and-six from the Ravens' 48, Favre took the shotgun snap and hit Freeman short in the right flat, on the Baltimore 45. Freeman took off across the field to the left, making it all the way to the Ravens' 2 yard line before he was stopped.

On the very next play, Favre hit Bubba Franks in the back of the end zone and the Packers now had a three-touchdown lead, 31-10, with seven minutes left in the game. It was the most points the Ravens had allowed in a game in more than three years.

When the Ravens got the ball back, their quarterback was not Grbac but Randall Cunningham, a 38-year-old veteran. It was not a capitulation by the Ravens, but rather a recognition by Grbac that he'd been hurt worse than he thought on a sack by Santana Dotson in the second quarter. Indeed, the Ravens' starting quarterback had a mild concussion.

"As the game went on," Grbac said later, "it was like my body just wanted to go to sleep. Then it was my mind shutting down. I was just trying to hang in there and make some plays."

As it turned out, Cunningham produced more plays in seven minutes than Grbac had managed in three and a half quarters. It could be that the Packer defense lost its fire. In any case Cunningham took the Ravens down the field for atouchdown that made it 31-17, and then Baltimore scored again after recovering an on side kick. A failed two-point conversion made it 31-23, Packers, with just 37 seconds left. The next on side kick was recovered, fittingly, by Antonio Freeman, and the game was over.

Freeman had played a great game, and his quarterback had been better yet. In the days that followed, people would speak in awe of what Brett Favre had done against the Ravens. His final stats were 27 of 34 passes for 337 yards, three touchdowns, and no interceptions. He got the ball to nine receivers, and nine times to Freeman alone. Favre's quarterback rating for the game was the highest against the Ravens' defense since the first game of 1997.

Packers' general manager Ron Wolf said: "Consider who he was playing. The talk at the beginning of the year was that this was greatest defense ever in any form of football. When you consider what he did to it? Pretty impressive performance."

Coach Mike Sherman: "It was special. The way he played the game was special. He made plays with his arm and with his feet and with his head. He hit every aspect of being a quarterback in that game. . . . When you take into account the nature of their defense, I thought he was the best he ever played."

Favre himself, in the locker room after: "I'm a confident person but I'm amazed at what we did."

No doubt there were many Favre fans, if not the man himself, who wished there was a way to seek out the headline writer who a little more than a year before had raised the question of whether Brett Favre might be finished as a top quarterback.

Since that wasn't possible, the rainbow that appeared over Lambeau as the Ravens game ended would have to suffice.

Wisconsin State Journal/Steve Apps

"The best eulogy possible": Favre brings a smile, and a victory, out of loss.

Green Bay Packers vs. Oakland Raiders

DECEMBER 22, 2003
Network Associates Coliseum, Oakland, California

Brett Favre was on a golf course near the Packers' hotel in Berkeley, California when the call came. The Packers were in the Bay Area to play the Oakland Raiders on *Monday Night Football* in the second-to-last game of the 2003 regular season, a game that had playoff implications for Green Bay. The Sunday afternoon of a Monday night game is down time for the players, so Favre and three others — backup quarterback Doug Pederson, punter Josh Bidwell, and placekicker Ryan Longwell — decided to tee it up at a club not far from their hotel. Favre is an avid golfer and plays to a single-digit handicap.

They were on the course when Pederson's cell phone rang. Favre would later remember he heard Pederson say, "Hi, Deanna," and a few seconds later the look on Pederson's face was such that Brett knew the news his wife was calling with wasn't good.

In that moment, he thought of his father. Irvin Favre had always lived large, but by December 2003 he had reached an age — 58— when it was time to slow down and begin taking care of himself. Lately his son had been telling him as much. Lose some weight, Brett had said. Get to the doctor for a physical.

Now Doug Pederson confirmed the worst: Brett's father had died. It appeared to have been a heart attack.

Late that Sunday afternoon in Mississippi, Irv Favre had walked out of the family-owned restaurant, Favre's on the Bayou, in Kiln, and started up his pickup truck. A few minutes later he was driving on Mississippi Highway 603 when the pickup left the road, winding up in a ditch. It was just before 5:30 p.m. Mississippi time.

Mississippi State Highway Patrol Sgt. Joe Gazzo told reporters the following: "It didn't appear that the accident was serious enough to cause him to be unconscious, so that leads us to believe that a medical condition was what caused him to go off the road."

Gazzo continued: "First the witnesses, then the ambulance, and then at the hospital they tried to revive him."

Irv Favre never regained consciousness. He was pronounced dead at 6:15 p.m. at the Hancock Medical Center. It would be determined later that he had suffered a massive heart attack.

"It's going to be a great loss to the community," Gazzo said. "He was a great guy."

Hundreds of miles away, on a golf course in California, Irv's famous son began to digest the news. Grief can manifest itself in many ways. In the immediate moment, people can feel they are moving in slow motion or may even feel outside of their own bodies, as if they are observing themselves react. Brett would recall that it was several moments before he could take the phone from Pederson and talk to Deanna. Even then, he couldn't find many words. He asked his wife to come to California as soon as she could, and she promised she would. He told her he loved her and he hung up.

Meanwhile, word was racing through the Packers organization— or maybe it is better to say the Packers family, given what would transpire over the next 36 hours. That may sound sentimental, but it was never truer. Brett Favre's close friend and agent, Bus Cook, called Packers' vice president of player finance Andrew Brandt, who in turn relayed the news to head coach Mike Sherman.

Back at the team hotel, Brett Favre met with Sherman. The game was the following night and Sherman made it immediately clear that whatever Brett decided, whether to play against the Raiders or return immediately to Mississippi, the team would support the decision.

Once people inside and outside the Packers' organization absorbed the news, most wondered whether the quarterback would play Monday night.

Packer safety Darren Sharper said, "I don't know if he's going to play. I don't know if I could. I just don't know. His dad was a coach, so maybe he'd want him to play."

Bus Cook, Favre's friend and agent, said, "Knowing Irvin and how much he loved football and enjoyed watching his boy play, and as much as he bragged on him, Irvin would not only want but would have insisted that Brett play. I think — no, I know — that he would want him to play."

Working through his feelings, Brett came to the decision that he wanted to play the game. That's what he told Mike Sherman. He knew everyone would have an opinion on the "right" course of action, but in the end both his head and his heart told him what the opinion would be of the one who right then mattered most. Bus Cook had it right. Irv Favre would have wanted his son to play.

Of course he would. Brett's father loved football so much that even when he retired from high school coaching after almost 30 years, to farm and raise the black angus cattle his famous son had purchased, he couldn't stay away. "I catch a lot of airplanes to watch that boy of mine play," Irv said, but it was more than that. In 2001 he had volunteered to coach a minor league semi-pro team, the Mississippi Fire Dogs, who played indoors in the Mississippi Coast Coliseum in Biloxi. The players got $200 a game but they also, thanks to their charismatic coach, got a title. Irv Favre led the Fire Dogs to a 17-1 record and the National Indoor Football League title in 2001.

He had taught his son to play the game and to love the game. That Sunday night in California, the son could hear the father saying he owed it to his teammates to play.

Brett told them as much at an emotional team meeting at the hotel around 9 p.m. that night. He would recall saying: "I'm with you, and if you ever wondered before, you don't have to wonder now." He mostly avoided the subject of the game itself, refraining from any "win one for the Gipper" dramatics, but he spoke directly, from the heart.

Several teammates would say later that when the meeting broke up, they called their own fathers. Defensive end Chukie Nwokorie recalled: "I called him and just told him to stop smoking and take care of himself. I don't know what's going on in Brett's head, but he's a stronger person than me. Because I don't think I'd be able to play."

Some days later, Packers' receivers coach Ray Sherman remembered Favre's talk to the team: "I think everybody felt his pain," Sherman said. "It was very emotional for him. He wanted to let the guys know that he's going to be there for them. He's got their backs. He said he loves the game, he loved his dad. I've got to tip my hat off to him for wanting to play. He's a strong man, very strong."

Not so strong that he wasn't nervous, even a little scared, as game time approached. The Monday night game is pro football's biggest stage. Stepping upon it a day after receiving such shocking news would be uncharted territory for anyone, and that included Brett Favre.

Down in Kiln, some 15 members of the Favre family gathered at Bonita's house to watch the game. It was Brett's older brother Scott's birthday. The gathering provided a few hours' respite from their grief. Bonita's mom, Izell French, spoke to a reporter from the *Biloxi Sun Herald*, and said, "I sure hope Brett can win this game for his daddy."

Out in California, it had been a strange day. Al Michaels, who would announce the game for ABC-TV, had been doing an interview with a New York radio station around 11:15 California time Monday morning when the host sensed something and asked Michaels what was going on.

"We're having an earthquake," Michaels replied.

It was serious — 6.5 on the Richter scale — but its center was in central California, far enough south of Oakland that there was little or no damage in the Bay Area.

Brett Favre, whose own world had been rocked the day before the quake, had a difficult Monday.

There had been an early afternoon phone conversation between Brett and his sister, Brandi, who was at the Favre home in Mississippi. Brandi later described the conversation as terribly difficult. "Brett lost it," she said. "And then I started to cry. It's just so hard."

Doug Pederson, Favre's friend and backup, told John Madden, the ABC commentator, that Brett got better Monday as the day went on. Pederson went from wondering if his friend could even play to thinking that he would not only play, but play well.

Favre would later say that his warm-up throws—which he conceded were poor—were the least of it. The quarterback was having trouble even breathing. His hands had a tremor.

The quarterback himself was still uncertain. Favre's normal routine was to come out on the field early, loosen up a bit, return to the locker room, and then come out again an hour or so before kickoff. That Monday in Oakland, he first appeared on the field about 45 minutes prior to the start. His warm-up didn't go well. His practice passes missed their mark. Favre would say later his warm-up throws — which he conceded were poor — were the least of it. The quarterback was having trouble even breathing. His hands had a tremor.

Deanna Favre had arrived in California before dawn on Monday morning. She had been down on the field earlier, but as game time approached she watched from behind glass in a private box provided by the Raiders. No one was seated immediately next to her, but the Packers' team chaplain, Father Jim Baraniak, was in the box as well. Deanna's face showed her concern.

It may have helped Brett that Raider fans, not known for their hospitality to visiting players, gave him a warm ovation when he was introduced.

A woman in the stands wearing a Raiders Christmas stocking cap and the number 81 jersey of Oakland wide receiver Tim Brown held a sign:

"TO BRETT: OUR HEARTS ARE WITH YOU. THE RAIDER NATION."

Another fan's sign said:

"OUR PRAYERS ARE WITH YOU BRETT."

Raider fans were considerably less kind to their own team, which had struggled for much of the 2003 season after making the Super Bowl a year before. Oakland had lost big in that one — 48-21 to the Tampa Bay Buccaneers — and some traced the beginning of their decline back to that deep disappointment. In any case, the Raiders were on their way to a 4-12 record for the 2003 season, almost unthinkable for a team that had played for pro football's ultimate prize just 11 months earlier.

The Packers, meanwhile, were not a lock to make the playoffs. Their defense had struggled early in the year and at one point Green Bay's record was 3-4, but they had rallied and with a victory over the Raiders would pull even with the Minnesota Vikings at 9-6, tied for the lead in the NFC's North Division.

The Raiders received the opening kickoff and returned Ryan Longwell's kick to their own 32 yard line.

The Raiders' quarterback from their Super Bowl season a year earlier, Rich Gannon, was sidelined with an injury, and the starter was Rick Mirer out of Notre Dame.

On first down Mirer threw a quick out to the right side to Jerry Rice, who made the catch and was brought down after a 12-yard gain by Michael Hawthorne, playing corner for the Packers in place of the injured Mike McKenzie. Rice, the certain Hall of Famer, was making an incredible 44th appearance in a *Monday Night Football* game. In those Monday games alone, Rice had caught passes totaling more than 3,700 yards. He'd scored 35 touchdowns and had 12 games with more than 100 yards receiving. What would have been a good career for some wide receivers Jerry Rice had managed solely on Monday nights.

"I still enjoy the game," Rice said in the days leading up to the Packer game. "I'm still hungry. I know I can still play."

On the Raiders' next play, however, the veteran Rice was called for a holding penalty after Mirer hit the other Oakland wide-out, Tim Brown, with a swing pass to the left that would have been a first down but for Rice's hold.

The penalty led to a Raider punt, after Mirer was sacked on a third-and-seven pass attempt by Packer lineman Kabeer Gbaja-Biamila. Shane Lechier's punt went into the end zone, so Favre and the Packers would start from their 20.

Statistically, the Packers' quarterback was having an excellent year. Favre was hitting 65.4 percent of his passes coming into the Monday night game, with 27 touchdowns and close to 3,000 yards passing. He did have 20 interceptions, but considering that the thumb on his throwing hand had been fractured during the season, Favre's year had been remarkable. Now as he brought the offense to the line for the first time in Oakland, he was about to write a new chapter.

Stepping into the huddle, Favre said: "Hey, we need this game. Here we go."

Ahman Green, who was having a Pro Bowl year for the Packers, gained 10 up the middle after taking Favre's handoff on first down.

On first and 10 from the 30, Favre swung a pass to tight end David Martin on the right side. Martin caught it but was tackled for a two-yard loss. Second and 12 became second and 17 after tackle Mark Tauscher was called for a false start. Green got six back on another run into the interior of the line, but that brought up a third and 11 from the Packers' 29.

Favre took the snap out of the shotgun and looked first for Donald Driver on a crossing route across the middle. Raider corner Charles Woodson — later to be a Packer — had Driver covered, and in that instant Favre also noticed the Raider safety shading the middle. The quarterback looked right, where Robert Ferguson was to have run a down-and-back route, faking the fly and coming back toward the line of scrimmage. Ferguson, though, had breezed past Raider corner Phillip Buchanon on the fly part of the pattern and then just kept going in hopes that Favre might adjust. He did. In that split-second Favre slung the ball up the right sideline and it was perfect, hitting Ferguson right in stride at the Raiders' 30. He was tackled at the 24, a gain of 47 yards.

Favre would later recall that play as the moment when he thought the night was going to go OK.

From the 24, Green picked up two on a first-down run. The next play produced a pass that Brett Favre said later was one of the best of his career. He took the snap over center and faked an inside reverse handoff to tight end David Martin. Favre then rolled to his left, never easy for a right-handed passer, and spotted tight end Wesley Walls with a step on Raiders' safety Derrick Gibson in the left end zone. Favre threw on the run from the 30, a soft, lofted pass that looked for a moment like it might be batted down or picked by Gibson, whose outstretched right hand barely missed the ball. It settled instead into the arms of Walls in the back left corner of the end zone. It was a nice catch of a perfect pass, and with Longwell's kick it put the Packers ahead, 7-0. Walls would hang onto the ball after the game was over. It was his first touchdown pass from Favre

"If it's a ball in the air that we can catch, we'll try to go for it. That's why we're here. We're here to make plays for Brett Favre."

and the 342nd touchdown pass of Favre's career, which tied him for second all time with Fran Tarkenton, behind Dan Marino.

A nice kickoff return by the Raiders was negated by a holding penalty, and Oakland took over on its own 22. They picked up one first down on a short pass interference penalty, but after that it was three plays and out. Antonio Chatman made a nice return of the punt for the Packers, fielding it at the Green Bay 33 and bringing it out to the Packers' 47.

Favre brought the Packers' offense out for a second time. A first-down holding call on a run to Green moved them back 10 yards to their 37. After a couple of short gains, Favre took the snap on third and 12 and dumped a short screen pass over the middle to running back Tony Fisher, who broke a tackle at the Oakland 48 and took it all the way down to the Raiders' 23, a gain of 32 yards.

The next play called was designed as a short pass in the flat to tight end Bubba Franks, who was supposed to start the play by faking a run block before drifting out for the short reception. As it played out, however, the left corner for the Raiders took Franks to the ground right after the ball was snapped. Favre, after faking a handoff, rolled right and saw that Franks was not where he was supposed to be. But Javon Walker, split wide right, had seen the corner assigned to him drop off, leaving only a safety to beat. Walker freelanced a sprint to the right corner of the end zone. He beat the safety and Favre found him with another perfect pass. That put the Packers up, 14-0.

Favre had started the game six for six passing, for 128 yards and two touchdowns.

Walker, who caught the second TD ball, said later, "For him to come out and throw the ball the way he did, we just wanted to make plays."

Walker added, "If it's a ball in the air that we can catch, we'll try to go for it. That's why we're here. We're here to make plays for Brett Favre."

But after the second Packers' touchdown, the Raiders came right back. Doug Gabriel returned the kickoff to the Oakland 39. From there Raiders halfback Charlie Garner did most the work, catching a 14-yard pass from Mirer and then, on the sixth and final play of the drive, running 25 yards through the Packer defense for the first Raider touchdown of the game. The point after made it 14-7 with 2:03 remaining in the first quarter.

Favre and the Packers went to work after the kickoff. On a third-and-eight from the Green Bay 38, Favre hit Walker on a down and out route to the right sideline that picked up 11. As the first quarter ended, Favre was seven for seven for 139 yards, the second-most first-quarter yards of his long career, in a game when many doubted he would be able to play at all, let alone perform at his best.

He hit his next pass, too, on the first play of the second quarter, short to Robert Ferguson. After a sack and facing a third-and-12 from his own 49, Favre took the snap out of the shotgun. The Raiders blitzed but the Packer blockers handled it well, and Favre threw down the field over the middle for Donald Driver, who grabbed it at the Raider 31 and took it to the 19 for a gain of 32 yards.

Favre was now nine for nine, for 183 yards and two touchdowns. He had utilized seven receivers.

Driver, who had caught the last pass, said afterward, "For him to come out and play this game, he's a better man than most of us on this team. We knew that we had to go out and get him everything that he wanted. He wanted this game as bad as we did, and we did it for his dad."

Two runs by Green left the Packers with a third-down-and-four from the Raiders' 13. Favre took the snap over center with no running backs, rolled right, and under pressure from Raiders end Lorenzo Bromell, who had an arm on the quarterback, lofted the ball out of bounds incomplete, his first missed pass of the game.

Ryan Longwell came in and kicked a 31-yard field goal to put the Packers up 17-7. A week earlier, Longwell had passed the great Packer receiver Don Hutson as the leading scorer in team history.

After the kickoff, the Raiders went three and out, though a booming punt put the Packers back on their own 11 to start their fourth offensive drive of the game.

It was a long way to go — and it took all of five plays.

Favre handed to Green on first down and Green scampered up the middle all the way to the 30, a pick up of 19. The Raider game was a comeback of sorts for Green, who'd had three straight games under 100 yards rushing. Against Oakland, he would gain 127 yards on 24 carries, behind an offensive line that took a lot of pride in their back's performance. All five starters on the Green Bay offensive line had started every game that season for the Packers.

On first and 10 from the 25 — after a false start call on Bubba Franks — Favre was heavily pressured by blitzing linebacker Napoleon Harris, but Favre managed to dump a short pass to fullback William Henderson for no gain. Green then picked up five on a quick pitch to the right side.

On third and 10 from the 30, Favre found Robert Ferguson running a straight route down the right sideline. The receiver walked a tightrope to stay in bounds while making the catch, again beating the Raider cornerback Buchanon, who was not having a good night. It was a gain of 27 to the Oakland 43 and it came right in front of the Raider bench.

Raiders' coach Bill Callahan threw his challenge flag just before the next snap. Callahan got his challenge but didn't win it — the replay showed Ferguson had caught the ball in bounds.

On first and 10 from the 43, Favre struck again. This time he faked a hand off to Najeh Davenport, then drifted right, looking downfield for Javon Walker in the middle of the field near the goal line. Raider linebacker Napoleon Harris was closing in on Favre when he planted and threw for Walker, even though the receiver looked to be blanketed by two Oakland defenders, the twice-burned Phillip Buchanon along with Anthony Dorsett. Sometimes it comes down to who is paying the best attention to where the ball is at any given moment. As this pass played out, the two Raider defenders actually overran the ball and it cost them, because Walker zeroed in on it and caught it in front of them on the goal line.

Favre was run over by Harris and heard a strange kind of roar from the crowd that he couldn't immediately interpret. Was it a touchdown or an interception? It was a touchdown. It wasn't Favre's best throw of the night by any means, but it was a touchdown, and it put the Packers up 24-7. Favre was 12 for 13 for 254 yards and three scores.

"Adversity strikes all of us," head coach Mike Sherman said afterward of his quarterback. "It's not the adversity that affects you, it's how you handle it. And he handles it extremely well. His focus and concentration on this football game this evening was extraordinary. When he puts his mind to anything, even off the field, he can accomplish anything he wants to accomplish."

The teams next traded punts — each ran three plays and had to punt — but the exchange favored the Raiders for field position, as they took over on the Green Bay 47. After two incomplete passes, Mirer hit Rice for nine to the 38, setting up a fourth-and-one with 3:21 to go in the first half. The Raiders elected to try for the first down. Mirer faked a handoff and threw short for Tim Brown, but the pass was broken up by Darren Sharper. Green Bay ball.

Would the Packers play conservatively, settling for a 17- point halftime lead? Not on this night. Green gained nine on first down, but then on second another Favre handoff to Green resulted in a loss when Raiders' end Chris Cooper came into the backfield unblocked — a guard had pulled out early — and grabbed Green in a bear hug, tossing him backward almost like he was discarding at gin rummy. The running back tumbled to the ground at the 43 and the Packers had a third-and-five as the two-minute warning was given.

Favre took the third-down snap over center and Cooper was again in the backfield almost immediately. Favre avoided him by spinning to his left. The quarterback then hit Driver with a short pass. The receiver got what looked to be a favorable spot and — after an official review in the booth upstairs — a first down.

The Packers' next play was a called roll-out to the right. Favre planted his right foot on the Packers' 38 and threw long into traffic for Walker, who went up among three Raiders on the Oakland 6 yard line and came down with the ball. It was a great catch and evidence of the Raiders again not paying attention to the football.

Now there was a minute left in the half and the Packers had first and goal to go. Favre took the snap on a play that looked designed to go left but was in fact a kind of trap, as the quarterback looked against traffic to the right and found tight end David Martin pretty much alone at the 5 yard line. Favre delivered the ball and Martin took it into the end zone, completing an astonishing first half that left the Packers ahead 31-7, with Favre having completed 15 of 18 passes for 311 yards (his most ever to that point in a first half) and four touchdowns.

"I've never seen a first half like that," Favre said afterward. "I think that everyone who watched the game saw what took place. I'd like to take credit for a lot of it, but when you make catches like those guys did and block the way our guys did, I don't know if I've ever seen an effort quite like that before."

Favre might not have come right out and said he felt his father's presence on the field, but given the circumstances and the quarterback's performance, it seems fair to say it was a bad half for atheists.

Among other things it was also Brett Favre's 24th straight game throwing at least one touchdown pass. The record was held by Johnny Unitas, who accomplished it in a remarkable 47 consecutive games.

With the issue not really in doubt, the second half loomed as potentially anticlimactic. Favre, however, nearly took up where he'd left off before the break. There had been a nice moment coming down the shared tunnel after halftime when a couple of Raiders — Tyrone Wheatley and Tim Brown — made a point of approaching Favre and expressing condolences. But then Najeh Davenport returned the second-half opening kickoff all the way to the Raiders' 30, and on first down Favre lofted a perfect pass right over David Martin's head in the end zone. It hit the tight end in stride and in the hands — and he dropped it. The Packers wound up settling for a 27-yard Longwell field goal, pushing the lead to 34-7.

There would be only one more score on the night. It came in the fourth quarter, after the Packers got the ball on their own 23 after the Raiders were unsuccessful on a fourth-down pass. A new quarterback, Rob Johnson, had replaced Mirer for Oakland.

Favre was still in for the Packers and he brought them out with a little over nine minutes remaining in the game. A run to Green gained two, and then on second down Favre threw one of his only poor balls of the night, a low pass that bounced in front of Ferguson in the left flat.

On third and eight, Favre and Donald Driver connected on a long pass up the left sideline, which the receiver caught between two defenders while falling backward to the Raiders' 34. It was a 41-yard gain. The next several plays were runs and brought Green Bay a first down at the Oakland 23. Then, on third and nine from the 22, Favre took the snap over center, dropped back, and found Antonio Freeman — his 12th receiver of the night — at the Oakland 7 for a gain of 15 and a first down. On the next play, Green took a handoff around left end into the end zone untouched. Longwell's kick made it 41-7, Packers, and word circulated that Brett Favre was done for the night.

Teammates and coaches took turns coming up to Favre and giving him a hug or a high five. His wife, Deanna, had made her way to the sideline from the private box and she, too, gave Brett a hug.

The next few days would not be easy for the quarterback or his family, but the miracle — would any less a word really do? — of what happened on this Monday night may have helped. The funeral was in Mississippi on Wednesday and one of the first things that the Rev. John Ford did at the Mass was recall what had happened less than 48 hours earlier at a football stadium in California.

"I do not come to give a eulogy for Big Irv, folks," Ford said. "If you want to hear and see a eulogy for Big Irv, go back to the game his son played on Monday night. That was the best possible eulogy."

The service was held in the church where Irv and Bonita had been married 38 years earlier. Some 500 people attended, including Chris Havel, the Green Bay sportswriter who had collaborated with Favre on the quarterback's autobiography and who filed a heartfelt story from the funeral. Brett's sister Brandi spoke for the family. "While clearly fighting back her emotions," Havel noted, "she spoke with a humor, affection and sadness that had the assembly crying and laughing, often at the same sentence."

Several Packer players and executives were in attendance. One of them, vice president of player finance Andrew Brandt, told Havel that once again, in a totally different arena, Brett Favre had excelled.

"It was the first time," Brandt said, "that I've seen Brett as a brother, as a son, as a friend, as a hometown boy. I'd never seen that side of him before, and it was touching."

Brett himself did not speak at the funeral Mass. He had not said a great deal either after the game in Oakland, though he did stop to speak with ABC sideline reporter Lisa Guerrero just as the game ended. She asked him about the game.

"I knew my dad would want me to play," Brett said. "I love him so much. . . And love this game. It's meant a great deal to me, to my dad, and to my family."

Here his voice broke a bit. "I didn't expect this kind of performance. . . .But I knew he was watching tonight."

Guerrero asked if he might describe his father.

"He meant a great deal to me," Brett said. "I loved him dearly. I've got two brothers and a sister and I know they feel the same way. He coached me growing up, in baseball and football, and coached my brothers."

He paused. "I don't wish it upon anyone." With that he left the field.

What remains to be said? One might simply choose to recall Ernest Hemingway's definition of courage: grace under pressure.

Sudden death: Only an overtime miracle could save the Packers' playoff hopes.

Wisconsin State Journal/Steve Apps

Seattle Seahawks vs. Green Bay Packers

JANUARY 4, 2004
Lambeau Field, Green Bay, Wisconsin

In retrospect, Brett Favre may have been insisting a bit too much that Mike Holmgren's first game back in Lambeau Field, coaching a team other than the Packers, was no big deal.

This was week seven of the 1999 season and Holmgren was bringing his Seattle Seahawks to Green Bay for a Monday night game with the Packers. This coach was the coach who had helped mold Brett Favre into a superstar, who had nursed and cursed his prodigiously talented but occasionally reckless quarterback through the first half of the 1990s as together they climbed the mountain to NFL supremacy.

At the end of the 1998 season, after a wrenching last second loss in San Francisco (which had itself been a homecoming of another kind for Holmgren), the coach and the quarterback split up. Holmgren signed a deal with the Seahawks that published reports put at a mind-boggling $32 million over four years. The most important thing for Holmgren was that the deal in Seattle gave him control over player personnel. The Seahawk gig allowed him to be Ron Wolf, too. Somebody said a good chef eventually wants a say in buying the groceries.

Given the speed with which the deal was consummated (Holmgren signed with Seattle less than a week after the Packers' season ended in San Franciscso), it's doubtful anyone on either side had looked seven games into the next season to see the match-up that was already on the schedule. Seattle vs. Green Bay, at Lambeau. Holmgren comes home, in a hurry.

Even when the realization dawned, both teams tried to downplay it. They said it was just another game, but of course it was not. The memories were too fresh. Still, they tried, Brett Favre maybe most of all. The quarterback said it was important only in that both teams were 4-2 on the season and a win would set the table for a playoff run. A loss meant digging out of a hole to keep the season from getting away.

"It's a great match-up and people are going to try to make more of it than it really is," Favre said during the week. "It's us against Seattle. It's not Mike Holmgren against Brett Favre. But people are going to try to make it that way. We both need to win this game, for obvious reasons, not for personal satisfaction."

Well, it was a big enough deal that the *Green Bay Press-Gazette* felt obligated to offer readers of its editorial page that Monday a four-step program for dealing with the emotional crisis of having a beloved former coach return to Lambeau as the enemy.

"What's a loyal Packers fan to do Monday night," the editorial began, "when Mike Holmgren is introduced at Lambeau Field as coach of the Seattle Seahawks?"

The newspaper offered a four-pronged response, beginning with this: "Applaud Holmgren warmly to remember what he did for the Packers in his seven years as head coach." The next three steps included feeling a bit short-changed because Holmgren had departed so quickly, understanding that pro football is a business and the coach left for a better deal, and finally, cheering hard for the Packers to win the game.

As it turned out, the game — Seattle's first Monday night appearance in more than seven years — was a debacle for the Packers. Mike Holmgren was cheered (a warm ovation when he was introduced) and Brett Favre was booed. That reaction seemed unthinkable right up until the game started and everything went sideways for the Packers' offense. Favre threw four interceptions, fumbled twice, and was benched in the middle of the fourth quarter. He hit just 14 of 35 passes. It was a nightmare performance.

In the opposing team locker room, Holmgren was elated. "It's a very emotional night for me," he said. "To come and play the Packers this way, it's hard to put into words. I'm happy for the guys in this locker room. They really earned it."

By October 2003 and Seattle's next visit to Lambeau Field, the relationship between the two franchises had become even more intertwined.

There was still the Holmgren-Favre angle, of course — whenever they were on the same field that would always be a big story line. But now there was more. Ray Rhodes, who had been head coach of Green Bay the first time Holmgren brought the Seahawks to Lambeau, had been fired at the end of his one and only season in the top job and was now in Seattle as Holmgren's defensive coordinator. Meanwhile, a former Holmgren assistant in Seattle, Mike Sherman, was now the head coach of the Packers. Green Bay's top running back, off to a brilliant start in 2003, was Ahman Green, whom the Packers had acquired in a trade with the Seahawks. Finally, Matt Hasselbeck, the quarterback who had come in for Favre when Favre was benched in the 1999 Seahawks-Packers game, was now the starter for Seattle.

It was a good thing the teams wore different colored uniforms.

The October 5, 2003 game was a vindication for Favre, though the quarterback insisted he didn't see it that way. After the debacle against the Seahawks in 1999, the quarterback repeatedly said he'd just had a bad night and hadn't been pressing to have a big game against his mentor. Others weren't so sure, though in the run-up to this second meeting both Favre and Holmgren were typically gracious in talking about the other.

Favre spoke at his mid-week press conference about how he'd told Hasselbeck, after Hasselbeck was traded to Seattle, to expect some harsh criticism from Holmgren and to take it, because in the end it would make him a better quarterback. Favre had learned that lesson the hard way.

Holmgren, when asked before the game about Favre, was full of praise: "He still is one of the best quarterbacks in football, and as long as he's playing for the Packers, you guys can be very optimistic you have a chance to go to the Super Bowl."

Holmgren was proven right as the game unfolded. Favre completed 19 of 25 passes for two touchdowns and led the Packers to a convincing 35-13 win over the previously unbeaten Seahawks.

Hasselbeck, the vanquished rival, was impressed. "He was awesome," Hasselbeck said of Favre. "He was fun to watch."

The teams didn't know it at the time, but another meeting was just three months away, and the stakes would be higher still. Again Lambeau Field was the meeting place, only this time, it was the first round of the playoffs, and for both teams everything was on the line.

For a time as the 2003 season wound down it looked unlikely either the Seahawks or the Packers would make it into the post-season. The October loss in Green Bay had triggered a road losing streak for the Seahawks, but they righted their ship and beat San Francisco in the regular season finale. Coupled with a New Orleans upset of Dallas, the win put Seattle into the playoffs as a wild card team.

Green Bay, meanwhile, trailed Minnesota in the NFC North, but closed strong. First came the emotional win in Oakland — Favre's magical performance the night after his dad died — and then, in the regular season closer, the Packers stuffed the Denver Broncos 31-3. Still, it didn't look good for Green Bay because they still needed a Minnesota loss.

The Vikings, after trailing 6-0 at halftime, ran up a 17-6 lead on the Arizona Cardinals. Packers' fans throughout Wisconsin grew despondent as the score stayed 17-6 deep into the fourth quarter.

Then, with 1:54 to play, Arizona quarterback Josh McCown found Steve Bush with a do-or-die fourth-and-goal touchdown pass from the 2 yard line. The Cardinals then went for a two-point conversion to try to cut the deficit to a field goal, but Emmitt Smith was stopped shy of the goal line after catching a short pass from McCown.

Arizona, down 17-12, then rolled the dice with an on side kickoff, which the Cardinals' Damien Anderson recovered.

A long pass interference call got the Cardinals to the Vikings' 31. They eventually made it to the Minnesota 13, but then McCown was sacked on consecutive plays, and it appeared almost hopeless for the Cardinals — and the Packers. It was fourth and 25 with four seconds to play and the ball on the Viking 28. McCown somehow found receiver Nathan Poole in the back of the Vikings' end zone. Poole made the catch as he was falling out of the end zone and it took an official review to determine he'd made the reception in bounds and been pushed out by Vikings defenders.

It was a touchdown, an unlikely victory for the Cardinals, and the Packers were in the playoffs.

It was a noon start at Lambeau, January 4, 2004, a wild card playoff game with the winner traveling to Philadelphia to meet the Eagles.

Naturally all the entangling alliances between the Packers and Seahawks were once again a big storyline in the week leading up to the game. It may have been talked about a little less since it was the teams' second match-up at Lambeau in just three months.

It was cold, but not crazy cold for Green Bay in January. At kickoff the temperature was 20 degrees, and there was a bit of a wind, pushing the wind chill index down to just 8.

Brett Favre had his right thumb in a splint. He had broken it on his second pass in a loss to the St. Louis Rams in October. It remained a nagging concern the rest of the season. The thumb would seem to be getting better and then Favre would ding it again. It was never bad enough to keep him out of a game, but it hurt and it was, after all, on his throwing hand.

He had practiced without the splint during the week and told the coaches Saturday he probably wouldn't wear it. Saturday night, he changed his mind.

"For whatever reason," Favre said after the game, "when I got to the hotel last night and was watching TV, I said, 'I think I'm going to wear the splint.' I don't know if it's old age or what, but I'm getting soft."

Nobody believed that, and splint or no splint, the injury had not prevented Favre from throwing 34 touchdown passes during the regular season, which led the NFL.

Holmgren, who had never lost a playoff game in Lambeau (his record was a perfect 5-0), told the Seahawks in the locker room before the game that it was time to step up.

"We didn't bleed and sweat and cry and all that stuff this season to come in here and lose this game," Holmgren said.

He repeated what he had told the team to a sideline reporter just before kick-off. Then the reporter asked how the Seahawks intended to contain Brett Favre.

"First of all we have to stop Ahman Green," Holmgren said. "Tackle him. And then we have to make Brett more uncomfortable than he was in the first game. He kind of had his own way."

Favre and Holmgren exchanged a warm handshake on the field before the game, smiling and chatting.

By kickoff, the smiles were gone. The Packers received the kick and started the first series from their own 27. The crowd was loud, as it always is at Lambeau. Packers' coach Mike Sherman had prepared the team for the crowd noise: he brought in an official referee to the team's scrimmages during the week, closely monitoring off sides and false starts to help his team avoid them during the game.

Favre started with a handoff to Green that gained two. On second and eight Favre took a quick drop and found Bubba Franks on the right side for nine and a first down at the 38. Green got a yard and then on second and nine lineman Mike Wahle moved before the snap — so much for the special scrimmage. The penalty pushed the Packers back and their opening drive ended three plays later with a Josh Bidwell punt that Bobby Engram fielded on the Seahawk 15 and returned to the 31.

It was Bidwell's first punt of the game and his last good one. The punter struggled with the cold weather and wind and was booed by the Packers' crowd later in the game.

"Terrible conditions," Bidwell said. "It was really not supposed to be very windy and it wound up being one of the windier days I've played in out there. Freezing. Just made the balls miserable to kick. If you didn't hit the sweet spot you didn't have a chance."

Matt Hasselbeck, in his first post-season start, brought the Seahawks to the line at the 31. Seattle had led the league in producing touchdowns on opening drives, with seven during the regular season. Hasselbeck's first drive as a playoff quarterback did not produce a touchdown, but it was a good one nevertheless. He came out throwing, hitting Koren Robinson for 11 on a crossing route on first down and returning to Robinson on the very next play, a straight route along the right sideline that gained 15 to the Green Bay 43. They had called Hassel-beck "Mr. August" during his years with the Packers because he played well during the preseason. But given Favre's durability, that was the only time he played. His time was now.

On first down Hasselbeck handed to running back Shawn Alexander up the middle for two. On second down, Alexander was stopped for no gain. Then Hasselbeck took the snap on third down, bootlegged left, and hit tight end Itula Mili for nine and another first down.

Then it was back to Alexander, with a quick pitch right; Alexander took it and then cut back inside, slashing all the way to the Packers' 9 for a pickup of 17. There the Packers dug in. Alexander was hammered at the line on two running plays. Then on third and 12 Hasselbeck looked to have halfback Maurice Morris open in the back right corner of the end zone. Morris had a step on Mike McKenzie, but after catching Hasselbeck's pass with his left foot planted in the end zone, Morris made a mistake. Instead of dragging his right foot as a veteran receiver might do to keep it in bounds, Morris took a full step and his second foot came down out of the end zone, resulting in an incomplete pass. The Seahawks settled for a 30-yard Josh Brown field goal to take the lead, 3-0.

An illegal block penalty on the kickoff return meant the Packers started their second drive of the day from the 16. On first down, out of the I formation, Favre pitched to Ahman Green, who gained eight around right end.

Green had enjoyed a tremendous year, rushing for a team record 1,883 yards, accumulating 2,250 total yards, and scoring 20 touchdowns. All three were Packer records. The ball went to Green again on second and two and he picked up a first down at the 26.

On second and nine, Favre hit Donald Driver on a down and out to the left sideline that gained 18 yards and a first down. A couple of runs by Najeh Davenport — who was averaging more than five yards a carry — netted only two yards. Facing third and eight, Favre called signals from the shotgun. It was during the snap count on this play that Favre showed his veteran wiles. Seahawk linebacker D. D. Lewis had approached the line and appeared to have found a gap through which he could blitz. Favre deliberately slowed his count, allowing his linemen to adjust their blocking assignments. When the snap came, the blitz was picked up and Favre had time to throw a beautiful pass over the middle to Antonio Freeman. It hit Freeman right on the numbers. Shockingly, he dropped it. Bidwell came on to punt.

"We didn't bleed and sweat and cry and all that stuff this season to come in here and lose this game," Holmgren said.

The Seahawks then went three and out, and a poor punt by Tom Rouen gave the Packers the ball at their own 45 yard line. On first down Favre hit Wesley Walls over the middle in traffic for a gain of five, and that was the end of the first quarter.

After the teams switched sides, Favre brought the Packers to the line. The quarterback had his hands in the belt pack that was strapped around his waist.

Inside were a bunch of "hot bags," heating pad warmers, the kind golfers use to keep feeling in their hands on cold days. A quarterback needs just as much touch as a golfer and the wind chill temperature in Lambeau wasn't much above zero. Favre would go through up to 30 of the "hot bags" in the course of the game.

The Packers started the second quarter with a handoff up the middle to Green that gained nothing, but on third and five Favre made a nice throw while rolling right and hit Javon Walker for 10 yards and a first down at the Seattle 40. Walker would catch five balls on the day for more than 100 yards, a crucial performance for the Packers in that Driver was hobbled by a bad ankle and Robert Ferguson had a sore Achilles tendon.

Walker's one run from scrimmage, however, didn't work out so well. After Walker's first-down catch and then a Favre-to-Driver short toss that gained five, the Packers had a second-and-five from the Seattle 35. Favre took the snap over center and pitched left to Green on what looked like a sweep. Green ran left but then handed the ball to Walker, who was passing him coming right on a reverse. The highlight of the play was probably the fine block that Favre put on Seahawk lineman Lamar King. Unfortunately for the Packers, nobody blocked Seattle corner Shawn Springs, who tripped up Walker well behind the line of scrimmage, a loss of eight yards.

On third and 13 from the Seattle 43, Favre took the snap out of the shotgun and then lofted a dangerous pass down the middle in traffic for tight end David Martin. The ball fell incomplete, and Bidwell came on for already his third punt of the day, which carried into the end zone for a touchback.

The Seahawks had another three-and-out and lost field position when Hassebeck was called for grounding on third and eight from the 22. Rouen's punt, not a good one, gave the Packers the ball at midfield.

It would be their first scoring drive of the day. The big play of the drive was the first one, as Favre rolled right and hit fullback William Henderson for 29 yards to the Seattle 21. The Packers had to settle for a field goal after Favre's third down pass for Bubba Franks was batted down by Seahawk linebacker Anthony Simmons. Ryan Longwell's 31-yarder tied the game at 3-3.

Seattle came right back with another field goal of their own. The big play was a first-down pass from the Seahawks' 44 in which Hasselbeck found Bobby Engram down the right sideline in front of Darren Sharper for a gain of 28 and a first down at the Green Bay 28. The other important play in the drive was on a second-and-10 from the Packers 17, when Hasselbeck dropped back, looked to his left, pumped the ball as if to pass, and then appeared to try to stop his motion. The ball came out of his hand and the Packers' rookie linebacker Nick Barnett scooped it up at the 16 and returned it untouched 84 yards for a touchdown. Seahawks' coach Mike Holmgren immediately threw his challenge flag and a review overturned the ruling on the field: it was an incomplete pass, not a fumble. Two plays later, Josh Brown gave the Seahawks back the lead with a 35-yard field goal that made it 6-3.

Favre brought the Packers storming back. On first and 10 from the 20 following the kickoff, Favre faked a handoff to Green and made a deep drop to pass. The Seahawk defense went for the run fake and in any case was playing an eight- or nine-man front, determined to stop Green and almost daring Favre to pass. (In fact they did a good job on Green — the Pro Bowler averaged less than three yards a carry for the game, with 66 yards on 23 carries.) But Favre took the dare. He spotted Javon Walker one on one with Shawn Springs on the right side and lofted a long throw that Walker grabbed for a gain of 44 to the Seattle 36.

"It's the excitement," Walker said later about his good play in the high tension of a playoff game. "I know what kind of player I am. If I want people to see what I can do, what better time to do it than in the playoffs?"

After Favre overthrew Driver on first down from the 36, he next dumped a screen pass to Green (who had five receptions in the game) on the left side and Green, behind a good block by guard Mike Wahle, picked up 13 to the Seattle 23.

Next came a handoff to Green that went nowhere. Then, on second and 10 from the 23, Favre took the snap over center, dropped and looked right, where a screen pass to fullback William Henderson was developing. Favre pumped in Henderson's direction, but rather than throw, Favre pulled the ball back, planted his right foot on the 30 yard line, and fired a pass down the middle, where Bubba Franks had beaten Seahawk safety Damien Robinson at the goal line. Robinson's desperation dive only landed him at Franks' feet as the tight end took Favre's pass right in stride for the touchdown that put the Packers up 10-6, with 4:37 left in the first half. It was Favre's 14 consecutive playoff game with a touchdown pass, an NFL record.

The Seahawks next went three and out and were lucky to do it. Hasselbeck's attempt to pass on first down from the Seattle 24 almost ended disastrously as the ball was stripped by a Packer defender and bounced all the way back to the Seahawk 10, where center Robbie Tobeck fell on it. The Seahawks wound up facing a fourth-and-28 from their 6. Tom Rouen's punt traveled only to the Seattle 39 and the Packers had great field position with 2:18 to go in the half.

It looked for a moment like the Packers might cash in. On second and six from the 35, Favre dropped back and was immediately confronted with a blitzing Seahawk linebacker, Randall Godfrey, who hit the quarterback when he threw what turned out to be a floater down the left sideline for Driver that the Seattle defenders actually overran. Driver, by keeping his eye on the ball, was able to gather it in at the 12 yard line. But after a false start penalty on first down, the Packers stalled and ended the half with a Longwell field goal that sent them in up 13-6.

Seattle came out smoking in the second half. They not only tied the Packers in the third quarter; they took the lead. Hasselbeck, who had hung in there in the first half when his receivers suffered through a lot of drops (the cold made the ball hard and slippery), had a great third quarter.

Favre would say later, "He played a hell of a game." Packer coach Mike Sherman concurred: "He certainly played a great football game."

Hasselbeck engineered two fine drives in the quarter. The first, starting from the Seahawks' 26, began with a quick pass to Darrell Jackson coming over the middle. The receiver then cut it to the outside, ending with a gain of 25 to the Green Bay 49. Hasselbeck next hit tight end Itula Mili on a couple of passes that took the Seahawks to the Green Bay 9, where they had first and goal.

After an incomplete pass and a Shaun Alexander three-yard run, Seattle had a third down from the 6. The following play was as strange as it was important.

Hasselbeck dropped back and looked right. No one was open, but the Packers were only rushing three linemen so Hasselbeck had time to look elsewhere. He looked to the center of the field, thought he spotted Engram open in the end zone, and threw one of his worst passes of the day. Hasselbeck had somehow missed seeing Packer linebacker Hannibal Navies, who didn't have to move to have the ball thump him directly in the chest. The startled Navies didn't catch it, however. Instead it bounced into the air where it was grabbed — legally — by Seahawk left guard Steve Hutchinson at the 5 yard line, and Hutchinson made it to the 1 before he was tackled. It was a huge play for Seattle, and interesting in that Hutchinson was acquired by the Seahawks in a trade with Green Bay — a swapping of draft choices in 2001 after which the Packers took Jamal Reynolds and the Seahawks took Hutchinson. Most observers felt Seattle got the best of that exchange.

They also got a touchdown after Hutchinson's unlikely reception, when Alexander carried it in from the 1 on the following play, which was a critical fourth-and-goal. Now the game was knotted at 13.

After the kickoff Favre and the Packers took over on their 33. It had been a good first half for the Green Bay quarterback; he'd hit on 15 of 20 passes for 190 yards and a touchdown. He started the second half off strong, too, hitting Walker for 20 on first down to take the ball into Seahawk territory. But the drive ended quickly after that, with Favre missing Freeman over the middle on third and 5, the ball skidding on the ground at Freeman's feet. The quarterback-receiver timing was off on the play and some thought Freeman had been held, but the officials were calling the game loosely, especially defensive holding.

Mike Holmgren, who rarely missed an angle, had approached the officials prior to the start of the game and asked that if they were going to let the Packers' cornerbacks use their hands, something Holmgren felt sure would happen —

he'd seen them get away with it on film. He wanted to make sure the Seahawks' corners had that same leeway. As a result, it was a very physical game for the wide receivers on both sides.

After the incomplete pass intended for Freeman, Bidwell came in to punt for the Packers and got off another poor one, resulting in boos from the home crowd when the ball was downed at the Seahawk 23.

From there, Hasselbeck engineered his second impressive drive in a row. One of its biggest plays came early, on a third and three from the 29. It was a play to remind people that Hasselbeck had understudied Brett Favre. Taking the snap, Hasselbeck faked a handoff to Alexander, rolled to his left, and slipped, almost completely losing his footing. But the quarterback quickly got back to his feet and threw a sidearm pass down the middle for Koren Robinson, who caught it at the Green Bay 46 and ran it all way to the Packers' 19, where he was pushed out of bounds by Darren Sharper.

It was Hasselbeck channeling classic Favre: not giving up on the play, turning a near disaster into a big gain.

As the chains moved, Hasselbeck ran to the Seattle sideline, where he used a brush to try to clean his cleats, like a golfer before going into the clubhouse.

Hasselbeck's numbers were now 16 of 25 for 208 yards.

Starting from the Packer 19, Hasselbeck connected on three passes in the next four plays, two to Mili and one to Darrell Jackson, that combined gave the Seahawks a second-and-goal from the Packer 1. Hasselbeck threw into the end zone incomplete, but then on third and goal Alexander took it over for the touchdown. The extra point made it 20-13, Seattle.

Favre, who had just watched Hasselbeck engineer two long scoring drives, was in serious need of one of his own. The Packers started in good field position, their own 40, and 11 plays later, they scored the tying touchdown. It was a mix of runs and short passes. In the middle of the drive, with the ball on the Seattle 42, the Packers ran the exact same play twice in a row. It was a fake handoff to Green after which Favre passed to Green in the middle of the field between the coverages. The first time it gained 13 to the Seahawk 29 and on the following play Green got seven to the 22.

Another big play came on third and one from the 20. Najeh Davenport gained eight up the middle, a driving run in which he seemed to push a pile of blockers and defenders ahead for several extra yards. On second and nine from the 11, Favre used his left hand to shovel a short inside pass to running back Tony Fisher, who took it to the Seahawks' 3. It brought up a third and 1 for the Packers. The call was a no-brainer: Every time Ahman Green had carried on a third-and-one situation that season, he had made the first down. Now Favre handed to Green on the biggest third and one all year. He didn't make it! The Seahawks stacked up the line and then it was fourth and inches from the 3.

The Packers were going for it. Favre called signals over center. He took the snap and handed to Green running left. The back was immediately set upon in the Packers backfield by Seattle linebacker Randall Godfrey. Green somehow slipped Godfrey's tackle, ran wide to the left, picked up two yards and the first down at the 1. It was a huge play by Green. On the next play he took it over for the tying touchdown.

The game was knotted at 20, with 10:01 to go.

It was here the Packers' defense stepped up. Having given up two consecutive drives to Hasselbeck, now they forced him into three consecutive incompletions, and Seattle right away had to give the ball back to the Packers. Antonio Chatman made a nice return of the punt for the Packers, who started from their 49. Green ran for three on first down and caught a Favre pass for six on second, making it third and one from the Seahawk 42. This time it was Najeh Davenport who failed to pick up the first down, giving the Packers their second fourth-down- and-one situation in the last few minutes. Josh Bidwell and the punting team came on for the Packers. At that point the officials decided to measure to be certain Davenport hadn't made the first down.

On the Packers sideline, Brett Favre slowly shook his head. It was going into overtime.

He hadn't, but in the time it took to measure Mike Sherman changed his mind and the Packers decided to go again on fourth down. Favre handed to Green off right guard and he gained two, but the play ended in controversy when Green, struggling in a pile-up for every inch, lost the ball. The officials ruled he had made the first down and was stopped before the fumble. Holmgren was livid. He said afterward Green's legs were still moving forward when he fumbled. The more Holmgren complained on the field, the louder the crowd booed — the Holmgren-Green Bay separation was complete.

Given that break, the Packers cashed in. Favre hit Walker for 11 to the Seattle 29. After that it was mostly Ahman Green running behind the Packers' punishing offensive line. The drive was 12 plays. Fittingly it was Green who took it in for the score, on a second-and-goal from the 1 with just 2:44 left in the game.

The Packers led, 27-20.

Hasselbeck, with the game on the line, brought the Seahawks back. The biggest play was a second-and-10 from the Packers' 43. Hasselbeck dropped straight back and threw a perfect pass down the middle of the field for Engram, who was pretty well covered by Nick Barnett. The ball just cleared Barnett; Engram gathered it in at the 12 and fell forward to the Packers' 8. On third and goal from the 6, Barnett was called for interference in the end zone, giving the Seahawks a first-and-goal from the 1. Alexander then punched it in with less than a minute to go in regulation time.

The Packers had a chance to win it in regulation. Starting on his own 29 with 45 seconds left, Favre quickly hit three straight passes, the third and longest going to Walker over the middle. He caught it at the Seattle 38 and took it to the 30. The Packers, with one time-out left, sprinted up to the line of scrimmage and Favre spiked the ball, stopping the clock with 12 seconds left. He next handed it off to Green, who gained a yard to the 29, at which point the Packers called their last time-out.

Five seconds remained. Ryan Longwell lined up for 47-yard field goal try to win it for Green Bay.

Seattle called time-out, trying to ice Longwell.

Now the snap came and Doug Pederson placed the ball and Longwell kicked it true. The ball sailed just to the inside of the right upright — but short! The cold weather had taken a yard or two off the kick and it came up just that short. Back at the 37 yard line, Pederson gave Longwell a consolatory hug. On the Packers' sideline, Brett Favre slowly shook his head. It was going to overtime.

The Seahawks' and Packers' captains came to mid-field for the coin flip to see who would get the ball to start the overtime.

The referee said, "This is a whole new ballgame. We're starting all over from scratch. Who's going to call it?"

The Seahawks, as visitors, would get to call. Their defensive tackle John Randall pointed at Hasselbeck and said: "He'll call it."

The referee said, "What do you call?"

Hasselbeck said, "I'd like to call heads."

The referee flipped the coin, examined it and said, "Seattle has won the toss."

Hasselbeck said, "We want the ball and we're going to score."

Those words, heard over the public address system at Lambeau, would come back to haunt the Seahawks quarterback.

The Seahawks did not score in their first playoff possession, but neither did the Packers. With their seasons on the line, the teams exchanged punts.

Seattle got the ball for the second time at its own 34. Hasselbeck hit a couple of short passes to give the Seahawks a first down at their 45. He pitched to Alexander, who was stopped for no gain on the right side. Hasselbeck then overthrew Jackson down the middle on second down, bringing up a third and 10 from the Seattle 45. The Packers took a time-out to set their defense.

Hasselbeck, over center, appeared to audible. On taking the snap, he dropped quickly back and looked immediately to his left, where Alex Bannister appeared for the moment to be open. Hasselbeck threw but Bannister wasn't open. Cornerback Al Harris had been lurking, anticipating the pass, and Harris cut in front of Bannister and intercepted the pass on the Green Bay 48. Harris sprinted down the sideline. The one Seahawk with a chance at him was Hasselbeck, who had an angle and dove, to no avail, at the Seattle 8 yard line. Harris ran into the end zone and kept going all the way to the end zone seats, where he handed the ball to a fan. The Packers had won and Lambeau was going wild.

Harris said later, "I was just praying that he did throw the ball, because I was going to gamble on that play."

Hasselbeck, who later confirmed he had audibled in anticipation of a Packer blitz, was in shock. At midfield, Brett Favre put his arm around his one-time back up and whispered some words of encouragement.

In the locker room, Packers' coach Mike Sherman would say he felt Favre had a great game, even better than the Monday night against the Raiders a few weeks earlier in Oakland.

"One of the best games he's had," Sherman said, "especially since I've been here."

Mike Holmgren, in the other locker room, was honest in defeat.

"I'm dying inside," he said.

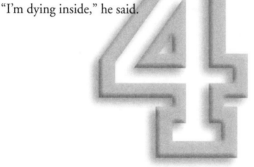

Favre made his 200th game a thrilling one for the fans at Lambeau.

Wisconsin State Journal/Steve Apps

St. Louis Rams vs. Green Bay Packers

NOVEMBER 29, 2004
Lambeau Field, Green Bay, Wisconsin

Wisconsin Governor Jim Doyle could have found any number of reasons over the years to declare an official Brett Favre Day in the state. It's certain no athlete and likely no human being has been as universally beloved in Wisconsin as Brett Favre was by late November 2004, when Doyle made it official by named November 29 in honor of the longtime Packer quarterback.

The occasion was Favre's 200th consecutive regular-season start as quarterback for the Packers, dating back to early 1992, when, following his come-from-behind heroics in a game against the Cincinnati Bengals, Favre started September 27 against the Pittsburgh Steelers. Defying all odds, he'd started every Packer game since.

"On Monday," Doyle said in a statement, "Brett Favre will mark yet another milestone in a remarkable career with the Green Bay Packers." Indeed the game and Favre's feat would be played out on ABC's *Monday Night Football.* "The streak of 200 straight starts," the governor continued, "is a testament to the determination and perseverance that Brett Favre shows both on and off the field." Doyle also made note of Favre's charity work both in Wisconsin and Mississippi.

Doyle had been an athlete at Madison West High School, a basketball player who kept playing serious pickup games well into middle age. He was a golfer, a sports fan, and a great admirer of the state's most famous athlete. When a reporter asked the governor why it was important to honor Favre with his own day, Doyle elaborated.

"Every day is Brett Favre Day," the governor said. "What's really remarkable about him, and we've seen it here in the state and people have seen it across the country, is how hard he works. In many of those 200 consecutive games, I'm sure he could have said he was too banged up to start. But he does it without complaining and he does a superlative job. Another one of his great qualities is his ability to work with young players and bring them into the system. When a young player sees a superstar like Favre working harder than anyone else, it sets the tone for the whole organization."

It could, as Doyle said, have been just about any day, but the governor's choice of the 200th consecutive start for Brett Favre Day was a good one. Favre had been consistent in his insistence that he had never played football to set records. But of all the marks that Favre had in his possession or was still chasing, the one he most often mentioned, the one that seemed to resonate most, was the consecutive starts. It made all the others possible, certainly, but it was more than that. It spoke to his toughness, of course, and also to his luck, his tenacity, and the way he played the game and lived his life.

In September, prior to the start of the 2004 season — and before the incessant talk about his 200th start had become tiresome — Favre had sat with reporter Rob Demovsky in the lounge area of the Packers' Lambeau Field locker room and talked quietly about the streak. Demovsky later recounted the conversation in the Madison *Capital Times*.

"It really is starting to impress me," Favre said. "Deanna and I were joking that if you're a truck driver or pilot, over time, the odds are leaning in your favor of you getting in a wreck or something. It's amazing that I've been lucky enough — not that I haven't been injured — to come back every time, but that's kind of how my career has been."

By the week of the Rams game in late November, Favre appeared to have wearied of all the talk about his streak. When the game was over, in his press conference, Favre said: "I wouldn't have talked about it had it not been for you guys," meaning the reporters.

In the run-up to the game, at his mid-week meeting with reporters, Favre seemed to go back and forth on the significance of the number-200 milestone.

"It means a lot," he said, though he added, "But I treat this game no differently than I've treated other games. The fact that I'm still here, and playing, I think speaks for itself. I'm fortunate in a lot of ways to be able to do this. To overcome injuries, adversity, and still be able to play at a high enough level that the Packers still want me around."

He concluded that thought by saying, "It does mean something."

A minute or two later in the same press conference, Favre said, "I treat this as just another game. I know it has been a long time, a lot of games, a lot of consecutive starts. I'm aware of that. But it's another game that we've got to win."

One can assume Favre was not quite as pleased with having made 200 consecutive mid-week press conferences. Indeed he probably missed a few over the years. But it was hard to blame anyone — reporter, governor, or ordinary fan — for making a big deal about the consecutive start streak.

His coach, Mike Sherman, commented on it a few days before the Rams game. Sherman suggested the streak probably meant more to Favre than the quarterback was letting on.

"Of all the awards he's won," Sherman said, "and all the accomplishments he's attained, I don't know if there's one that he's more proud of than the consecutive starts. Because that embodies his character, and I think that's what he's really all about."

The streak, remarkable on the surface, is even more so when you look at some of the particulars, the games when Brett Favre probably had no business being in the starting line up.

There are plenty of them. The mental toughness it took to not only play but play at the highest level the day after his father died in December 2003 is a good place to start. The fact he also had a broken thumb on his throwing hand that night — for most of the 2003 season — barely gets mentioned.

One of the earliest games that spoke to Favre's toughness was in his first year with the Packers, when a hit by his future teammate, Reggie White, separated Favre's left shoulder. Not only did Favre stay in the game and lead the Packers to a come-from-behind 24-21 win over the Philadelphia Eagles, he started the next week in Chicago and led the Packers to a 17-3 win over the Bears. White would later say the grit Favre showed by staying in the Eagles game after being body-slammed helped convince Reggie to become a Packer himself.

Others point to the Chicago Bears game in November 1995, when Favre couldn't practice in the week leading up to the game due to a severely sprained left ankle. He'd hurt it the week before in a loss to the Giants. Many doubted Favre would play. In an interview for this book, I had a chance to ask LeRoy Butler if he thought Favre would play that week against Chicago.

"Deanna and I were joking that if you're a truck driver, or a pilot, over time the odds are leaning in your favor of you getting in a wreck or something."

"I saw his ankle," Butler said. "I wanted to see it for myself. I knew that to beat Chicago we had to have him. But when I saw the ankle I didn't think there was any way he could play. It was blue and green and looked like a rainbow."

Butler recalled giving his friend a questioning look. "Brett just said, 'It's not my arm.' So I figured he would play."

He did — throwing five touchdown passes to beat the Bears 35-28. Butler intercepted a Bears' pass in the end zone to ice the victory.

Six weeks later, in a Christmas Eve game at Lambeau against the Pittsburgh Steelers, with the Packers in the hunt for their first division title in 23 years,

Favre took a fourth-quarter hit that broke a blood vessel in his esophagus. He'd been sandwiched between three Steelers and, as he came to the sideline to confer with Mike Holmgren during a time-out, the quarterback was coughing up blood. Favre not only stayed in the game, but he threw the game-winning touchdown pass to Mark Chmura on the next play.

More? During a Monday night game against the Buccaneers at Tampa Bay in November 2000, Favre absorbed a vicious third-quarter sack from Warren Sapp that had him clawing at his left foot and removing his shoe before he could hobble off the field. It was diagnosed as a mid-foot sprain, and it was serious.

Coach Mike Sherman said early the following week: "He cannot walk at the present time. It's too early to tell, but I anticipate that he'll miss next week's game and maybe longer."

Of course, he didn't even miss the next game, which was against the Colts at Lambeau. Favre led the Packers to a 26-24 victory, throwing for two touchdowns and more than 300 yards.

There were others, including a 2002 game against the Washington Redskins when Favre tore a ligament in his left knee after a sack by linebacker LaVar Arrington. Favre left the game and it no doubt helped that the Packers had a bye the following weekend. Still, it was just 15 days after tearing the ligament when Favre started the Packers' next game, a 24-10 Monday night win over the Miami Dolphins.

In fact, less than two months before Brett Favre Day, the quarterback suffered a concussion in a game against the New York Giants. He had to leave the game, but returned the following week against the Tennessee Titans.

Favre started that Titans game, a Monday night match at Lambeau, but he didn't play well and the Packers were badly beaten. It was Green Bay's fourth straight loss after opening the season with a win. Then, just when the season seemed on the brink of collapse, the Packers turned it around, winning five straight to bring their record to 6-4 coming into the Brett Favre Day game November 29 at Lambeau, another *Monday Night Football* extravaganza.

The Monday night stage still belonged to ABC at the time, and the network made a huge deal of Favre's 200th straight start, securing taped tributes from all-time great quarterbacks like Joe Namath, Steve Young, and John Elway — and even baseball ironman Cal Ripken, Jr.

The most meaningful tribute came when legendary Packer quarterback Bart Starr was asked what he thought his coach, Vince Lombardi, would have thought of Brett Favre.

Starr didn't hesitate. "Coach Lombardi would have loved him," Starr said, "because he embodies, I think, the great points which Coach Lombardi constantly stressed — the mental toughness, the preparation, the discipline, the commitment, all of those words. Brett is is right out front telling you about them because of the way he leads. As a result Coach Lombardi would have loved the opportunity of working with him."

Some hours before the game, ABC commentator John Madden was eating a bratwurst outside one of the television production trucks when some Packers' fans approached him and suggested he put Favre's photo up on the side of the truck. That was a reference to a Monday night tradition in which the ABC crew, after the game, selects the game's top player and mounts his photo on the truck, which Madden had dubbed the "horse trailer." The catch was the Packer fans wanted Favre's photo up before the game.

Madden waved his brat at them and said he'd think about it. The odds, Madden figured, were that Favre's photo would be going up on the horse trailer, along side the other Monday night heroes from the 2004 season. They'd wait until after the game, but the photo would likely be Favre. (In 2005, an ABC production assistant told *The Sporting News*, "Brett Favre is always the most kissed man on the trailer.")

The Rams game was a big one for Green Bay, and not only because the governor had designated it Brett Favre Day. Having turned their season around with five straight wins after the Monday night debacle against Tennessee (Packer fans actually started leaving that game in the third quarter — unthinkable), the Packers were now in a position where a win over the Rams would put them at 7-4 and in a tie with the Minnesota Vikings for first in their division. (The Packers also were ahead on the tiebreaker as well, having defeated the Vikings earlier in the year.)

The Packers were dinged up, as most teams are 11 games into the season. The most significant injury was to running back Ahman Green, who would miss the game due to sore ribs. His back up, Najeh Davenport, had a sore right hamstring, but would play, making his first career start. He had been coming into the Packer practice facilities early all week, at 6 a.m., for physical therapy — ice, heat, and massage. When he wasn't on the field during the game, the Packers had arranged for Davenport to employ a heating pad for the hamstring on the bench. All the hard work and preparation would pay off for Davenport against the Rams.

The Packers received the opening kickoff, but couldn't do much with it. On a third and seven from their 36, Favre missed Javon Walker running a down-and- out to the right sideline, and Bryan Barker came on to punt for Green Bay.

The Rams and quarterback Mark Bulger took over at the St. Louis 27 and went right to the air. On first down Bulger faked a handoff to Steven Jackson, then threw long down the right side intended for Isaac Bruce, but the ball fell incomplete. On second, Bulger handed off to Marshall Faulk, a great running back in his 11th year who was not having a great season by his standards (just 681 yards rushing coming into the game). Faulk picked up five off left guard.

On third and five from the 32, disaster struck the Rams. Bulger, under center with four wide-outs, took the snap and dropped straight back. Bruce was on the right side and had run a curl route, faking the straight fly, then quickly stopping and turning back toward the quarterback. Bulger delivered the ball at the 36. Bruce caught it and fell forward toward the 37 and a possible first down. Bruce's fall was caused by Packers rookie cornerback Joey Thomas, who came over Bruce's back and stripped the ball. It bounced on the 39, where it was scooped up by another rookie, Packers' corner Ahmad Carroll, who took it all the way down the sideline untouched for a Green Bay touchdown. As Lambeau went crazy, Ryan Longwell added the extra point and the Packers led, 7-0.

It was time for Favre, who had not had a great first quarter, to do something on Brett Favre Day.

Bulger brought the Rams right back. He hit a couple of nice passes on the second St. Louis possession, including a long one over the middle to Bruce, which gave the Rams a first down at the Green Bay 32. They would get as far as the 20, but then a holding call and a sack of Bulger left them facing a fourth and long. Jeff Wilkins came in to try a 42-yard field goal. Wilkins had hit 12 of 15 on the season, but this time he pulled it left, and the Packers got the ball back, still leading 7-0.

They made one first down, on a nifty Favre to Robert Ferguson pass for 13 yards, and then a run by Davenport that took them into Ram territory. But a false start penalty helped kill the Packers' drive and Barker punted out of bounds on the Ram 10.

From there, Bulger engineered a long, 14-play drive that carried over into the second quarter but did not result in a touchdown. The Packers' defense stiffened just as the Rams threatened the red zone. This time Wilkins was good on a 37-yard field goal. It was 7-3, Packers, with 12:47 left in the first half.

Green Bay took over following the kickoff on its own 25. It was time for Favre, who had not had a great first quarter, to do something on Brett Favre Day. He did, leading them on a 12-play scoring drive, though it did not begin auspiciously.

On the drive's first play, Favre looked for Driver on a crossing route over the middle and badly underthrew. The Rams' defenders were overplaying the Packers' receivers with an eye toward the sideline — leaving the middle of the field more open — because statistics on the season had shown Favre almost twice as effective when throwing to the outside.

"There was a lot of pressure to peform," Favre conceded at his post-game press conference. The game was crucial for the Packers regardless, the quarterback said, so the 200th start and Brett Favre Day only added to expectations.

"I didn't need all the added attention and pressure," Favre said.

One thing that had often worked for the Packers when the offense was struggling was the screen pass. On second and 10 Favre took the snap over center, dropped back, and dumped a screen to Tony Fisher on the left side, and Fisher picked up 11 yards and a first down to the 36.

The play seemed to lift the Packers. Davenport next got seven off right tackle and then Favre hit William Henderson on the right side for five more and a first down at the Packer 48. Luck, too, proved to be with them. On first down, Favre handed off to Antonio Chatman coming from his split wide position on an end around run to the left. Chatman had just turned the corner upfield when he was hit and fumbled, but the ball squirted forward out of bounds, and the Packers retained possession. Two plays later, Favre hit Driver for 12 yards and a first at the Rams' 28.

After Fisher picked up four off left tackle on first down, Favre next threw a beautiful ball down the right side that hit backup tight end Ben Steele in the fingertips at the goal line. It was one of those passes that would have been a very good catch if he'd made it, yet it was catchable, so Packers fans groaned when it fell incomplete.

On third and 11 from the Rams' 29 after a false start penalty, Favre dropped straight back and, with plenty of time, fired over the middle for Driver who caught it at the 19, stumbled, regained his footing, and took it to the 11 for a gain of 18.

On first down Davenport got four around right end. Then on second and seven, Favre took the snap over center, rolled back and right to the 15 yard line, pumped once toward the right corner, and then looked back toward the middle of the field, where he spotted tight end Bubba Franks at the 2. Favre delivered the ball and Franks caught it, falling into the end zone for a Packers touchdown. Longwell's point after made it 14-3, Green Bay.

It set another record for Brett Favre: the most consecutive seasons with 20 or more touchdown passes. Dan Marino had held it with 10; Favre now had 11.

The Rams started the next drive from good field position, their own 36. Bulger completed a pass for a first down in Packers' territory. From there, however, Aaron Kampman sacked Bulger and St. Louis had to punt for the first time in the game. That brought onto the field Kevin Stemke, a left-footed punter just signed by the Rams, who had grown up in Green Bay and played college football at the University of Wisconsin-Madison. Out of college he'd had an unsuccessful tryout with the Packers. Now he was back, with the visiting team, and Stemke's parents, who still lived in the city, were in the crowd.

"It was a lot of fun," Stemke said afterward. "When I was here in 2001, it was my first experience of being on Lambeau Field. But to be here in the regular season, on *Monday Night Football,* and in the hunt for the playoffs, what a thrill."

Antonio Chatman made a fair catch on Stemke's punt at the Packers' 17.

Favre and the Packers picked up where they'd left off a few minutes earlier. After Davenport picked up one on a run up the middle, Favre hit Driver short in the right flat and the receiver turned it upfield for a gain of 11 to the Green Bay 30, where he was pushed out of bounds.

Next play, Favre pitched left to Davenport, who was having the game of his career. On this play he got a great block from fullback William Henderson, who led through the hole and took out Rams' safety Antuan Edwards with a hard block. Davenport burst past, turned upfield, and rumbled all the way to the Rams' 39 before he was brought down. It was a gain of 31 yards.

Two plays later, and the Packers had another touchdown. Favre first threw long over the middle for Bubba Franks, who had a step on Antuan Edwards and caught it right in stride at the 16. Edwards eventually pulled him down at the 10.

Favre went right to the air again on first down, this time finding Javon Walker at the 3, and Walker took it in for the touchdown. The Packers led, 21-3, with less than three minutes to go in the first half.

It might have signaled a rout, but St. Louis refused to quit. Taking over after the kickoff at his 22, Bulger brought the Rams down the field with a series of key completions. (For the game, Bulger would attempt an astonishing 53 passes, completing 35 for 448 yards, a record for an opposition quarterback at Lambeau. Still, the Rams' success in the air was offset by their inefficiency on the ground. At one point in the second half, Marshall Faulk's statistics showed seven carries for six yards.)

Bulger hit Shaun McDonald for 22 yards to start the drive. Then, on a third and 10 Bulger hit Kevin Curtis on a short pass that Curtis, with a sleek move, converted into 13 yards and a first down. Isaac Bruce contributed a 16-yard reception. Then, with 30 seconds left in the half, Bulger again found Bruce for a four-yard touchdown pass. The Rams went into halftime still in the game, down 21-10.

St. Louis got the second-half kickoff, and Bulger came right out throwing. On first and 10 from the St. Louis 32, he hit Bruce over the middle near midfield, but the veteran dropped the pass. Unfazed, Bulger took the next snap, dropped back, and hit Brandon Manumaleuna with an even longer over-the-middle ball. The tight end hung on, even after being slammed by Packers' linebacker Nick Barnett. It was a gain of 26 to the Green Bay 42. Manumaleuna got up slowly and limped off the field.

On third and three from the Packers' 35, the Packers blitzed — they seemed to be blitzing at least one defender on every play now — and Bulger missed Bruce on a short middle route. However, Ahmad Carroll was called for holding, and the Rams had a first down.

On first and 10 from the Green Bay 30, Bulger dropped back as again the Packers blitzed. The Ram line picked up the extra rushers pretty well, but maybe

Bulger felt hurried because he threw one of his worst balls of the day, a long floater down the right sideline for Bruce, who had run an out-and-up route. The ball hung short and Ahmad Carroll, beaten by a step on the play, picked it off on the goal line. It was Carroll's first career interception.

Favre, taking over on the 20 after the touchback, would drive the Packers near Ram territory with one of the most disputed plays of the day. On third and 10 from the 20, Favre called signals over center, waited while Davenport went in motion out of the backfield, and then took the snap and dropped to pass. He had time against the Rams' four-man rush. Favre spotted Robert Ferguson along the right sideline and drilled a ball that Ferguson caught at the Packers' 47 just as he was pushed out of bounds by Rams' safety Antuan Edwards. Was it a completed pass or was Ferguson out of bounds when he obtained possession? Two officials converged on the spot, but neither made an immediate call. They began a hurried conversation while Aeneas Williams, the other St. Louis safety, stood nearby loudly insisting Ferguson had been out. The play was right in front of the Packers' bench. Finally a ruling came: Ferguson had caught the ball in bounds and been forced out by the defender — it was a completed pass.

The Packers, however, could not take advantage. For one of the few times on the day, Najeh Davenport was stopped on consecutive carries and then Favre missed Ferguson with a ball at the receiver's feet. Favre pled his case to an official for a defensive holding call, to no avail. Barker's punt was nearly downed inside the 5 by a diving Jason Horton, but it rolled into the end zone for a touchback.

Bulger then led the Rams on a long, time-consuming drive (13 plays, eight minutes off the clock) that ended strangely. Facing a fourth and seven from the Green Bay 24, trailing 21-10, the Rams had the chance with a field goal to make it a one-possession game.

The kicker, Wilkins, came on, setting up for a try from the left hash mark at the 32 yard line — a 42-yard attempt. Holder Dane Looker took the snap and then Wilkins took one step as if to kick and cut sharply to his left. It was a planned fake. Looker, the holder, jumped to his haunches and threw a short pass, laterally, to Wilkins, the kicker, running toward the left sideline at the 32 yard line. Wilkins made the catch, but he had nowhere to go. Al Harris wrapped him up at the Green Bay 29, and it was Packers' ball.

Harris, asked later about all the yardage gained in the game by the Rams, said: "Hey, we stopped them from scoring more points than we scored. That's what it boils down to. I don't care if they had 1,000 yards passing tonight."

The botched fake field goal was the kind of strategic error that Brett Favre might well exploit, and he did, with help from Davenport. The backup to Ahman Green continued his stellar night when Favre handed him the ball off the right side on first down. Davenport broke a tackle early by safety Adam Archuleta and then turned it up the sideline for a gain of 37 to the St. Louis 34.

On second and seven from the 31, Favre threw slightly behind Donald Driver on the left side, but Driver reached back with his right hand and made a great one-handed catch of the ball, ending with a 14-yard gain to the St. Louis 17.

Next play, Favre looked for Driver again, but this time he threw the ball well into the right corner of the end zone and Driver, having beaten Aeneas Williams (the career interception leader among active defenders, with 55), made the catch for the touchdown.

Instead of it being 21-13 — had the Rams kicked a field goal instead of faking — now it was 28-10, Packers, with the fourth quarter about to begin.

As Driver did a Lambeau leap to celebrate the touchdown with the Green Bay fans, fullback Nick Luchey lifted Favre off the ground in a big bear hug.

Still, you had to credit Mark Bulger — the quarterback wasn't quitting. After the kickoff, as the Rams faced a third-and-10 from the St. Louis 36, the Packers' continual blitzing finally caught up with them. Bulger dropped back quickly in the face of an eight-man Packer charge and he had just enough time to spot Bruce coming one-on-one over the middle against Harris. Bulger delivered the ball perfectly and Bruce raced toward the left sideline. Harris finally brought him down at the Packers' 8. On the next play, Bulger hit Faulk with a short pass that the running back converted into a score with a nifty move to shake off Packers' safety Mark Roman. It was the 135th touchdown of Faulk's career, the fourth-highest total in NFL history.

Now it was 28-17, with 14 minutes still left in the game.

What the Packers needed was a long, sustained drive, and Brett Favre gave it to them. He didn't quite get a touchdown, but the drive took 11 plays and resulted in a 27-yard Longwell field goal. Most important, it ate up nearly six minutes on the clock. Favre's passion was evident when, on the final third down before the field goal, his scramble out of the pocket came up a yard and a half short of the first down. He got to his feet berating himself.

But it was 31-17, and when the Packers' defense forced a punt, it was pretty well over. If there was any doubt, Najeh Davenport soon put it to rest, when on a fourth-and-one from the Ram 40 following the two-minute warning, Davenport took Favre's handoff off right tackle, broke through a stack of linemen at the line of scrimmage, shrugged off an arm tackle by safety Rick Coady, and took it all the way to the house, a 40-yard touchdown run that gave Davenport 178 yards on the day and the Packers a 38-17 lead.

The Packers had started the scoring with a return of an Isaac Bruce fumble for a touchdown. Curiously, they would end the scoring that way too. This time it was Darren Sharper who hit Bruce after he'd caught a pass from Bulger at the St. Louis 34. Sharper's hit jarred the ball loose, and cornerback Michael Hawthorne scooped it up and took it down the sideline untouched for a last Packer touchdown. The final score on Brett Favre Day in Wisconsin was 45-17, Green Bay.

It hadn't been quite as easy as the score indicated, but the Packers and their quarterback and gotten it done again in front of a national audience on Monday night. At the finish, Hawthorne, jubilant in the end zone after his touchdown, was called for an unsportsmanlike conduct penalty for unnecessary celebrating.

Who was the referee to call it unnecessary? Brett Favre, looking back on 200 consecutive starts and plenty of hits both on and off the field, wouldn't call it unnecessary.

"I am humbled by it," the quarterback said after the game, when asked yet again about the 200 straight starts.

The quarterback recalled that during the week he'd had a conversation with James Campen, who had been his center his first year in Green Bay, all those years ago. Campen had said that suiting up in a Packers' uniform the first time was a dream come true. Everything that happened after that was a bonus.

"I feel the same way," Brett Favre said. "Everything I've achieved after the first time is a bonus. So I'm living a dream every day."

Green Bay Packers vs. Minnesota Vikings

DECEMBER 24, 2004
Hubert H. Humphrey Metrodome, Minneapolis, Minnesota

Entire books have been written about the Green Bay Packers' rivalry with just two NFL teams: the Chicago Bears and the Minnesota Vikings. The Packers-Bears rivalry is the oldest in the National Football League and arguably the greatest rivalry in all of professional sports. That the Packers-Vikings rivalry, which began some four decades later, could be mentioned in the same breath speaks to the intensity of emotion it generates in players, coaches, and fans. Some have even argued that the Packers-Vikings rivalry is now supreme, that the Bears' recent mediocre play (with the exception of a few great seasons) has meant there is more on the line when the Packers and Vikings line up.

Fuzzy Thurston, the great Lombardi-era offensive guard for the Packers, told author Todd Mishler that, to him, the Vikings are now the top Packer rival.

"The series has gotten much more intense over the years," Thurston said in Mishler's *Cold Wars: 40 Years of Packer-Viking Rivalry.*

Thurston continued: "There are a lot more fisticuffs and talking these days, a lot more 'Let's whip each other's butts' stuff. The fans get very loud and disgusted with each other and there's a lot of yelling. As the years go by, I've hated the Vikings more [than the Bears], especially since they started playing on that stupid turf. I think it's the number-one rivalry today."

In 2003, Brett Favre addressed the rivalry in an interview with a Twin Cities paper: "I can only speak for the years I've been here, but Minnesota is as good as the Bears rivalry. And that's been a good one, too. It seems like everybody we play wants a piece of us."

The Vikings came into being when a second professional football league, the American Football League, was formed in 1960 with a franchise based in

Minneapolis-Saint Paul. The NFL's response to the upstart was to add two franchises, one in Dallas and one in Minneapolis. In January 1960, the NFL made an offer to the owners of the Minneapolis franchise, which had participated in the first AFL draft: drop out of the highly speculative AFL and join the established NFL as the 14th franchise. The owners agreed. It was too late for the Vikings — the name officially chosen in September 1960 to reflect the heavy Scandanavian influence in the upper Midwest — to play in the 1960 NFL season. So the NFL added the Dallas Cowboys in 1960 and the Minnesota Vikings played their first season in 1961.

The Vikings' head coach was Norm Van Brocklin, a former Eagles quarterback, who chose as his quarterback a young scrambler named Fran Tarkenton.

The first meeting of the Vikings and Packers was October 22, 1961 at Metropolitan Stadium in Minneapolis. It was a rout for the Packers, who were en route to an NFL championship. They dusted the Vikings, 33-7. They won every match up until October 1964, when Minnesota won at Green Bay, 24-23, on a last-second field goal.

In his history of the Vikings, *Knights and Knaves,* author Jim Klobuchar suggested there was little affection between the fiery coaches on opposite sides in the rivalry's early years.

"Vince Lombardi hated to play the Vikings," Klobucher wrote. "He had a football team with stars, discipline and championships, and in the early years Green Bay whipped the Vikings in all venues. But Lombardi was convinced that somehow Van Brocklin was schooling designated thugs on his team to maim [Packers] players. It was a suspicion that festered with special furies after Jerry Kramer, one of [Lombardi's] best linemen, suffered a leg fracture in a game against Minnesota."

True or not, it got the rivalry off to an appropriately heated start.

Speaking of heat, the Vikings moved inside in the 1982 season, when the Metrodome, named for the former vice president and U. S. senator from Minnesota, Hubert Humphrey, became the team's new home. A players' strike that season prevented the Packers from playing in the new dome; there were times in the years ahead when Green Bay's players and fans wished it had never been built. The crowd noise echoes made it difficult for opposing teams to hear their quarterback call signals at the line.

Favre addressed the subject in a 1998 interview with the *Minneapolis Star-Tribune:* "I think that every team that's come in here and played against their crowd is going to get false starts. That's part of it. So, you can complain all you want about the crowd noise and all that stuff, but that's part of it, and you've got to handle it…. Everybody had false starts against them. Trying to get off quick, trying to beat them on the count, you can't hear, so you anticipate sometimes and you get beat to the punch. That's one of the things you have to contend with when you come in here and play against their defense."

The first dome game in 1983 was a 29-21 win for the Packers. The first for Brett Favre came a decade later, in December 1992, and it wasn't a win. The Vikings beat the Packers decisively, 27-7, in the last regular-season game of the year, a loss that knocked the Packers out of a wild-card playoff berth. Favre had three interceptions in the loss.

There were many memorable games in the rivalry in the years that followed, but the one most remembered by Packers' fans was likely a Monday night game at Lambeau in November 2000. It would become known as the game of the "improbable bobble" or the "immaculate deflection."

The game — in a cold rain at Lambeau — went into overtime. That was a break for the Packers, because Minnesota had lined up for a 32-yard field goal with seven seconds left in regulation and the score tied at 20. The holder bobbled the snap and, with the kick impossible, tried to pass, resulting in an interception.

The Packers got the ball first in overtime. Moving from their own 18, they brought it to the Vikings' 43, where they faced a third and four. The call was a slant pass to Antonio Freeman. As the teams lined up, however, Favre noticed Freeman signaling him that the receiver wanted to fake the slant and go long. A dry ball had just been put in the play. Favre nodded.

"Your star player wants the ball," Favre said later, "you give it to him."

Favre launched the pass. Freeman, running downfield, dove for the ball at the 15 yard line. Vikings' defender Chris Dishman tipped the ball with his right hand. The ball then glanced off Dishman's left shoulder and down to Freeman, who was belly up on the soft field. The ball hit Freeman's facemask and shoulder before he latched onto it with his right arm.

It happened so fast no one was certain exactly what had transpired. Freeman jumped up and ran into the end zone, while the Vikings ran running for a replay. There was chaos as the officials set about trying to review the play.

Favre raced downfield, jumped on his receiver, and asked, "Did you catch it?"

The receiver replied, "I don't know if he caught it."

The quarterback had corralled Donald Driver, not Freeman.

The officials finally emerged from their conference to announce that Freeman had indeed made the catch and the Packers had won the game, 26-20. It remains one of the most exciting and unlikely game-ending plays of all time. ESPN later gave it an award as the most spectacular televised sports play of the year.

Two years later, in a December 2002 game at Lambeau, the Packers-Vikings rivalry reached a new height — or depth — when a brawl broke out at game's end.

The report the next day in the Madison *Capital Times* began: "Any doubt that the Minnesota Vikings are the Green Bay Packers' most-hated rival should have been put to rest after the melee that followed Sunday night's game at Lambeau Field."

The Packers had gone ahead, 26-22, on a 14-yard run by Tony Fisher with 1:06 left in the game. The trouble started when the Vikings, attempting some last-minute heroics, completed a pass to Chris Walsh as time was running out.

Ordinarily a player with the ball must be touched to be down in professional football, but Walsh went down to one knee in the (correct) belief that the rule allowed the taking of a knee to stop a play and allow the team to take a time-out. But no official whistled the play dead — the crew later admitted a mistake on that play — and the Packers' Antuan Edwards drilled Walsh with a hard shot. The Vikings were enraged by the hit, but nothing really happened until the following play, when Darren Sharper intercepted a pass to seal the Packers' four-point victory. During and after Sharper's return, some cheap shots were taken and punches thrown, by both teams. A total of $40,000 in fines would be handed out later. Trash-talking between Packers' quarterback Brett Favre and Vikings' defensive tackle Chris Hovan ended with them each making an obscene gesture at the other.

"Favre has arrived at a juncture of a grand career where he is as likely to beat his team with a bad throw as he is to beat the opposition with a well-aimed laser."

"This rivalry just got turned up about 10 or 12 notches," Hovan said during the following week.

It was into this charged atmosphere that Brett Favre brought the Green Bay Packers for a rare Christmas Eve game in the Metrodome in 2004. A Packers-Vikings game didn't need big stakes to be important, but as the 2004 season wound down, the game was huge: the winner would clinch the NFC North Division title and home- field advantage in the first round of the playoffs.

If Brett Favre needed any more incentive for the Vikings game, it was there. For one thing, the week marked the one-year anniversary since Brett's father, Irvin, had suffered a fatal attack while Brett was in Oakland preparing to play the Raiders.

On the actual one-year anniversary — December 21, 2004 — Brett sat down for an interview with Terry Bradshaw, the former Steelers quarterback, then with Fox Sports. Portions of the interview would air on game day a few days later; but the interview itself was done on the actual anniversary.

Bradshaw began by asking for Brett's thoughts.

"First of all," the quarterback said, "I can't believe it's been a year. I've thought about it every day. I can hear his voice."

Brett continued, "He always would call my cell phone. I'd check my voice mail and hear, 'Brett! Hey, Brett!' I'd tell him, 'Dad, you're talking to the voice mail. I'm not there.' He never got it.

"I could hear him after us losing to Jacksonville [the week prior to the Viking game, a bad loss in which Favre threw three interceptions]. Him calling. 'Well, you guys sucked. You all stunk it up.'"

Favre may have drawn more inspiration — less profound but inspiration nevertheless — from a *Minneapolis Star Tribune* story that appeared in the Twin Cities the day before the Packers-Vikings game. Headlined "Time to move over" and written by Patrick Reusse, the column suggested that in a comparison of the two quarterbacks who would play in the game, the better bet was Daunte Culpepper of the Vikings.

Reusse went so far as to suggest that the quarterback position was where the Vikings enjoyed their primary advantage over the Packers: "Culpepper has arrived as a superstar, and Favre has arrived at a juncture of a grand career where he is as likely to beat his team with a bad throw as he is to beat the opposition with a well-aimed laser."

Reusse poured it on: "That was the case again last Sunday, when the frigid Lambeau weather that made him famous could not stop Favre from again losing the eternal war with his carelessness. Now that his skills and the team around him have deteriorated, Favre's careless streak has gone from part of his charm to an increasing part of the problem in the Packers' current status as a dead-end playoff team."

It is not known for certain if Favre saw the column, but many wouldn't bet against it.

The weather for this Christmas Eve game in Minneapolis would have been dreadful — had it been played outdoors. The temperature was just six above zero at kickoff and the wind chill was eight below. Inside the Metrodome, of course, which was packed with a sellout crowd of more than 64,000, the weather was fine — 62 degrees. Favre's record in the Minneapolis dome was just three wins against nine losses, but the win column included 2003, a year earlier, when the Packers had nipped the Vikings 30-27 in the dome and the Packers' ground attack had averaged 7.7 yards per rush.

Now, almost 14 months later, the 2004 season was up for grabs, if not quite on the line. Both teams were 8-6 heading into the game and stood a reasonable chance of making the playoffs even with a loss. But a win would mean the division championship and home-field advantage in the playoffs.

Did either team have an edge? Well, the Vikings had started the year 5-1 to the Packers' 1-4, so it would appear Green Bay had more momentum. Yet after a six-game winning streak, the Packers had lost two of their last three, including the bad loss the previous week against Jacksonville. The game looked even.

The Packers received the opening kickoff and picked up a couple of first downs, overcoming an illegal block penalty in the process, and finally faced a third-and-five from the Minnesota 44 with 10:28 left in the opening quarter.

Favre took the third-down snap and dropped to pass. He had good protection early, but could find no one open; eventually defensive end Lance Johnstone got loose and hit Favre just as he prepared to pass. The ball came loose, skidding toward the right sideline, where Donald Driver tried to pick it up for the Packers. Instead, Driver inadvertently booted the ball back into Packer territory, and it finally crossed the out-of-bounds line at the Green Bay 30 for a loss of 26.

Even as his team lined up to punt, however, head coach Mike Sherman threw a challenge flag. Sherman thought Favre's arm might have been in motion, making it an incomplete pass.

The officials conferred and the ruling stood. The Packers, charged a time-out for the unsuccessful challenge, punted it away.

It was a good start for the Vikings' defense, which had given up 178 yards in the fourth quarter alone in a game a week before against the Lions.

The troubled Packers' defense would get off to a good start as well. Culpepper and the Vikings picked up a couple of first downs in their initial drive, which started from the Minnesota 29, but then a holding call in the offensive line led to punt into the end zone, and the Packers started from their 20.

The drive began nicely, with Favre faking a handoff to Ahman Green, rolling quickly to his left, and throwing hard for Driver, who gathered it in at the Packers' 35 and beat safety Corey Chavous around the corner to the left sideline, turning it up for a nice gain. The gain came back a bit when it was ruled that Driver had stepped out at the 30. Still, it was 18 yards and a first down. The Packers wouldn't get another in that drive. Two runs by Green and a missed pass to Driver later, the Packers punted.

The offensive explosion predicted by the experts had yet to materialize.

The Vikings struck first. After the second Packers' punt, Culpepper led his team on a 91-yard march for the first score of the game. The key play in the drive came on a third-and-five from the Vikings' 32. Culpepper, operating out of the shotgun, had a lot of time against a four-man Packers rush but he was eventually chased right out of the pocket by Green Bay tackle Cullen Jenkins. Throwing on the run, Culpepper hit Nate Burleson at the Viking 40. Burleson had been knocked to the ground by Packers safety Darren Sharper as the play developed, but had gotten up and after catching the pass from Culpepper. He raced to the right sideline and all the way to the Packers' 26 for a gain of 42 yards. Four plays later, on the second play of the second quarter, Culpepper, with blitzing Packers' linebacker Nick Barnett closing in, hit Randy Moss open in the front right of the end zone — Al Harris, with the coverage, had slipped and fallen. The touchdown pass was the 35th of the year for Culpepper, establishing a new Vikings' record. The extra point made it 7-0, Minnesota.

The Packers battled back with a sustained drive. Sustained? It lasted 16 plays and took over eight minutes off the game clock. Brett Favre connected on four third-down passes during the drive — one to Driver, one to Antonio Chatman, and one to William Henderson; each resulted in a first down that kept the drive alive. The fourth third-down completion came on a third-and-goal from the Minnesota 9 yard line. Favre took the snap, dropped straight back at first, and then ran several steps back toward the scrimmage line before firing, from the 13 yard line, for Driver, who was momentarily open at the goal line. Just as the ball arrived, so did Vikings' linebacker E.J. Henderson and safety Keith Newman. Driver hung onto the ball and made the catch right at the edge of goal line. The officials did not signal a touchdown. Instead, it would be fourth and goal from inside the one.

Packers' coach Mike Sherman threw a challenge flag, his second of the game. Like the first, this one was unsuccessful. While it appeared from some angles that Driver had scored, it wasn't conclusive enough to overturn the field ruling. It was fourth down.

Sherman faced a big decision. His offense had gone their last 24 first-half possessions without scoring a touchdown. They needed a spark — and if it took a gamble, so be it. Favre took the fourth-down snap and handed the ball to Ahman Green, coming to the line off the tail of an I formation. Green was hammered at the line of scrimmage by Vikings' tackle Kevin Williams, but the running back stayed on his feet, spinning left from the force of the hit and then falling across the goal line to tie the game at 7.

It had been a great drive for the Packers — and it was undone in an instant by the Vikings. After the kickoff, Minnesota had the ball on its own 32. Culpepper took the snap and dropped to throw. The Packers were blitzing and the Vikings' line did a good job of picking it up. Culpepper was able to set at the 25 and throw across the field to the left side, where Burleson had a step on Ahmad Carroll at the Minnesota 40. After the catch, Carroll swiped at the receiver to bring him down, but Burleson spun away and sprinted forward and across the field to the right, causing both Packers' safeties — Darren Sharper and Mark Roman — to miss at the Green Bay 45. Burleson then outran Al Harris down the right sideline all the way to the end zone. It had taken Green Bay 16 plays to score. It took the Vikings one. They led, 14-7, with a little over six minutes to go in the first half.

Green Bay's offense may not have yet caught its breath from its lengthy previous drive, but they mounted another. On a second-and-nine from the Packers' 38, Favre sent his lone running back, Green, in motion, then took the snap, dropped, and hit Driver with a quick release as the receiver crossed the field at the Minnesota 46. Driver added nine after-catch yards before he was tackled at the Vikings' 37 after a gain of 25.

Favre had quietly had a very good first half, to this point hitting on 11 of 15 passes for 103 yards.

On second and eight from the Minnesota 35, with Tony Fisher his lone setback, Favre took the snap and dropped quickly. He was set upon immediately by Vikings' lineman Chris Hovan, with whom the quarterback had argued following a game two years earlier. Favre got the pass off before Hovan got to him. It was a middle screen to Fisher, and the running back took it on the Minnesota 37 and advanced to the 26. The screen pass was a traditionally potent Green Bay weapon that had been missing from the Packers' arsenal in recent games. It was good to have it back.

After the two-minute warning, Najeh Davenport ran for four off right tackle to the Vikings' 22.

On second and six, with 1:23 on the clock, Favre took the snap over center and dropped straight back behind a well-formed pocket. The Vikings were rushing only four. Favre stepped up and threw over the middle, where Bubba Franks was coming from the left side. Franks caught the ball at the 3, was popped by Viking defensive back Corey Chavous at the 1, but made it into the end zone for the score. Longwell's point tied it at 14.

With little over a minute to go in the second quarter, no one would have guessed that not one but two major kickoff returns would come before halftime.

Longwell's kickoff was taken by Kelly Campbell on the right hash mark at the Vikings' 8. Campbell cut toward the middle of the field and at the 20 broke left through a good hole on a line that got him to the left sideline at the 30. From there Campbell just turned it on up the sideline all the way to the Packers' 38, where Longwell, the kicker, pushed him out of bounds.

Now there was 1:08 left in the half.

Culpepper brought the Vikings to the line. The Minnesota quarterback's last two passes had gone for touchdowns — a 12-yarder to Moss as the second quarter began and the 68-yarder to Burleson that followed the Packers' lengthy mid-quarter drive. Now Culpepper barked signals out of the shotgun. He took the snap and dropped to the Packers' 45, where he planted and pumped as if to throw long. Instead, Culpepper held onto the ball and then dumped a little screen pass to Michael Bennett on the right side. Packers' linebacker Nick Barnett had a good shot at Bennett behind the line but missed, and the former University of Wisconsin running back wound up taking it all the way up the right sideline to the end zone, giving Daunte Culpepper three touchdowns with his last three passes.

The end of the half got wilder still. The Vikings, leading 21-14, kicked off with 58 seconds left. Antonio Chatman took it for the Packers on the left hash mark at the 7. Chatman cut up between the hash marks at the 20 and was hit and nearly brought down on the right hash mark at the 27 by Vikings' corner

Brian Williams. But Chatman stayed on his feet and, as the pursuit had by then overrun him a bit to the right, Chatman cut to the left side and made it all the way to the Vikings' 34 before being brought down, a return of 59 yards.

The Packers had used all three of their first half time-outs as Favre brought the offense onto the field with 47 seconds left. On first down he hit Fisher out of the backfield for a short gain, and then, with the clock running, the quarterback unloaded incomplete on second down.

It was third and six from the Vikings' 30 with 25 seconds left in the half. Favre dropped and hit Driver on the right side at the 24, where he was pulled down.

Was it a Packers' first down? Or was it fourth and one? It was very close and there had been no indication. Confusion reigned. The clock was now under 10 seconds left in the half. Finally the officials stopped it, with four seconds remaining, to measure for a first down.

Two things happened as they measured. The Packers hurried their field goal team onto the field and Viking head coach Mike Tice went berserk. His point was it didn't matter what down it was, fourth or first — the Packers could only run one more play in any case.

"I didn't quite understand the logic of giving them a time-out for a measurement when the clock was running and they were out of time-outs," Tice said later. "What were they measuring for? To go for a first down?"

But the rules do allow for a measurement when it's too close to call and a measurement stops the clock.

On the field, Tice threw his clipboard to the ground. And Ryan Longwell kicked a 42-yard field goal to make it 21-17 Vikings at the break.

The Christmas Eve crowd had enjoyed the wild first half. Some young fans held up a banner: "OUR PARENTS THINK WE'RE IN CHURCH."

There were some Packers' fans in the Metrodome. One man in a Green Bay jersey held up a sign: "ALL WE WANT FOR XMAS ARE PLAYOFF TICKETS AT LAMBEAU."

A Packers' win would mean, if not tickets, a Green Bay home game in the first round of the post-season.

Now in the second half at the Metrodome, the Packers struck first. Having forced a Vikings' punt on the first drive, the Packers started from their own 11. On second and six from the 15, with Green the lone setback, Javon Walker went in motion left to right. Favre took the snap, faked a handoff to Green, and then threw over the middle to Walker, whose route had taken him up the right side and then posted over the middle. Walker made the catch at the 34 and took it to the Packers' 40, a gain of 25.

Those yards achieved a significant milestone for Brett Favre: he moved into third place on the list of all-time passing yards by an NFL quarterback. With

49,341 yards, Favre had passed Warren Moon. He still trailed John Elway (51,475) and the all time leader, Dan Marino (61,361).

Favre's next completion would come on a third-and-nine from the 41. He took a quick, straight drop, set at the 36, and threw over the middle for Donald Driver, who had run a down-and-in route from the right side and gathered in Favre's bullet of a pass at the Vikings' 47. Driver tacked on another 22 yards after the catch before he was brought down by Corey Chavous at the Minnesota 25 after a gain of 34.

A short pass to Ahman Green and a nice run by Najeh Davenport set the Packers up with a first down at the 11. Then, on second and eight from the 9, Favre dropped, set at the 15, looked right and couldn't find anybody, backpedaled, and then, while still backing up, threw for Walker at the goal line. The receiver grabbed it and Green Bay had its first lead of the day, 24-21.

Culpepper and the Vikings followed with a long, sustained drive of 14 plays that took up the rest of the third quarter. A false start penalty in the red zone finally stalled it, and Morten Andersen kicked a 29-yard field goal on the first play of the fourth quarter to tie it again at 24-24.

The fourth quarter would prove to be, from an emotional standpoint, one of the most volatile of Brett Favre's career.

A plunge to the bitterest depths came first. After the Vikings tied it at 24, the teams exchanged punts. The Packers went three and out, and then the Vikings, after picking up a couple of first downs, faced a fourth-and-five from the Green Bay 45 and called on Darren Bennett to punt. Bennett hit a good one, a lazy floater. The ball hit at the Green Bay 3 and bounced very high straight up into the air. Vikings reserve running back Larry Ned, who had raced down on kick coverage, swatted at it to keep it out of the end zone. After Ned momentarily saved it, the Vikings' Willie Offord got a hand on the ball, too, pushing it away from the goal line. The ball was downed at the Packers' 1 by Minnesota long snapper Cullen Loeffler.

"We could have given up. Things were tough. After the interception, I was as disappointed as anyone, but guys were resilient."

It had happened very fast and it was a terrible break for the Packers because Offord's right foot was on the goal line when he touched the ball — it should have been a touchback, giving the Packers the ball at the 20. But Green Bay was out of challenges; they had no way to question or reverse the call.

The Packers were forced to start from their own 1, with 9:37 to go and the game tied. Favre handed to Green for short yardage on consecutive plays, setting up a third-down-and-four from the Packers' 7. Favre took the snap and rolled back and right into the end zone. He was looking for Javon Walker on the right sideline, but Walker was well covered by safety Brian Russell. Favre took a couple of steps up, to the 3 yard line, and decided to take a chance. He thought that a hard, tight pass might have a chance to hit Walker while preventing any chance of a Russell interception. Favre threw the bullet, but he hadn't noticed linebacker Chris Claiborne drifting over, and Claiborne stretched his arms over his head and picked the ball off at the 15 yard line. It was Claiborne's first interception of the year and he took it into the end zone for a touchdown. The point made it 31-24, Vikings, with 8:18 left in the game.

The Metrodome went crazy.

"I gave them a big spark," Favre said later. "The crowd got into it."

The quarterback was deeply disappointed in himself. "One thing I didn't want to do today was turn the ball over. To give one away was very disappointing."

Still, there was time to regroup. What the Packers needed was a drive to take the crowd out of it, but their next series was over almost before it began. After a touchback on the kickoff, Green Bay faced a third-and-10 from their own 20. It was a huge play. Favre called signals out of the shotgun. He took the long snap, dropped back a bit more, set on the 12, and threw toward the right sideline for Driver, who had run a down-and-out route and made an excellent catch on a perfect Favre throw at the Packers' 40, a gain of 20, first down.

From there it was a steady march, a mix of runs and passes in which the first third-down situation the Packers faced was a third-and-one at the Vikings' 8. Green picked up the yard, but then it got interesting. Two incomplete passes and an Ahman Green four-yard run left the Packers' facing a fourth-down-and-goal from the Vikings' 3 with 3:42 to go. Trailing by 7, the Packers elected to go for the touchdown.

"I felt like it was a good call," Favre said later. "Of course when you don't make it, all the experts say you should have just gotten the points. But it was a gutsy call, a good call, even if we hadn't made it."

They made it. Favre called the signals as Bubba Franks went in motion right. Favre took the snap and a short drop and threw quickly over the middle for Driver, who caught it in traffic just over the goal line. Tie game!

"We could have given up," Favre said afterward. "Things were tough. After the interception, I was as disappointed as anyone, but guys were resilient." Compared with some Metrodome performances in past years, Favre said, the resiliency was the difference.

And still it wasn't over. They were now knotted at 31, with 3:34 to go.

The Vikings, after the kickoff, picked up a couple of first downs and appeared to be driving, but a holding penalty cost them dearly. They wound up punting on fourth and five from the Green Bay 46 and the Packers took over on their own 13, with just 1:35 to go in regulation time.

Favre brought the offense out. Excepting the one interception, the quarterback had played brilliantly: he was 25-36 to this point, for 280 yards and three touchdowns.

As they had throughout the game, Driver and Walker would be Favre's key targets on this last-chance drive.

"Those two guys," Favre said later. "Not just today. It's been a phenomenal year. I can't say enough about them."

Going with no huddle, Favre hit Driver first, then Walker, and then, after an illegal formation penalty, Favre dropped a screen pass to Tony Fisher, who followed great blocking all the way to the Packers' 44, a gain of 21.

Fisher got out of bounds to stop the clock. There were 38 seconds left. Favre missed Driver on first down, but on second he went right back to the receiver on a beautiful play that sent all the other receivers crossing left to right and only Driver running a cross route right to left. Favre found him at the Packers' 47 and he carried it to the Viking 38 and out of bounds, a gain of 18.

Twenty-five seconds left. Still not quite in field goal range.

The Vikings showed blitz on the next play, with eight men up tight, and when Favre took the snap they did blitz, with free safety Brian Russell getting on top of the quarterback almost immediately. But Favre had just enough time to throw to the right flat for Walker, who caught it at the 33 in front of cornerback Terrance Shaw. Walker feinted toward the inside of the field after the catch and Shaw bit on the fake; Walker then raced to the right sideline, where Shaw finally pushed him out of bounds all the way up at the Vikings' 7.

Seventeen seconds left.

Favre took three more snaps, taking a knee each time, using up a few seconds off the clock. The Vikings called time-out after the first two, and the Packers stopped the clock the last time, with 3 seconds left.

Longwell came on to try a 29-yard field goal. If he made it, it would be the ninth game-winner of his career.

Favre knelt on the sideline, watching, as Longwell lined up. When the ball was snapped, Favre stood up and, as the kick sailed through the uprights, the quarterback raised his arms triumphantly over this head. He then jumped into Coach Mike Sherman's arms. The Packers had won, 34-31.

It had been an incredible game, with 868 yards of total offense between the teams. The Packers had finally come up big in the clutch at the Metrodome.

"History has worked against us here," Favre said afterward. "I mean, I've been here a lot of times when we had the game won, I thought, and we lost. That was in the back of my mind. That drive right there.... It's what our season has been all about."

It *was* what it was all about, wasn't it? In his interview with Terry Bradshaw a few days earlier, Favre had been asked what might constitute, for him, a perfect day.

"During the season," Favre said, "it obviously would be game day. I tell guys all the time they don't pay you for the game. They pay you for practice, preparation — being a pro. If you can't play for free on Sunday, you're in it for the wrong reasons."

Wisconsin State Journal/Steve Apps

As Favre left the field after the season closer against the Bears, every Packers fan wondered: Was it for the last time?

Green Bay Packers vs. Chicago Bears

DECEMBER 31, 2006
Soldier Field, Chicago, Illinois

As the Green Bay Packers prepared to meet their arch rivals, the Chicago Bears, on the last night of the year and in the final game of the 2006 season, a question loomed as large, if not larger, than which team would win the game.

Would Brett Favre retire or would he return for another season?

On the day of the Sunday night game, the *Wisconsin State Journal* in Madison listed five things to watch for in the game. Number one was headlined: "Goodbye — and maybe hello again."

The item said, "Packers' quarterback Brett Favre might be playing the final game of his illustrious career. Then again, maybe not. You know the drill. But just in case, it might be worth altering your New Year's Eve plans to watch Favre just in case you never get another chance."

By the end of the 2006 NFL season, everyone in Wisconsin and fans throughout the NFL knew "the drill." It involved endless speculation and hand-wringing over whether Green Bay's legendary but undeniably aging quarterback would ride off into the Mississippi bayou or come back and play another year for the Packers. Everyone was desperate to know as soon as possible. Reporters pestered anyone remotely connected to Favre — his teammates, friends, acquaintances, barber, elementary school teachers, and presumably any kid who had ever valet-parked the quarterback's automobile.

Is Brett coming back?

That question didn't really arise in earnest until after the 2004 season. The 2003 season had ended with a wrenching playoff loss to the Philadelphia Eagles, when a Favre pass for Javon Walker in overtime was intercepted by Eagles safety Brian Dawkins, leading to a field goal and a 20-17 Philadelphia victory.

Though Favre was then 34 years old, there didn't seem to be any way the quarterback would let that throw and the subsequent defeat be his last in the NFL. The Monday night after the Eagles game, Brett and his wife, Deanna, were back in Mississippi watching their daughter play a high school basketball game and Brett was beginning to think about the next season.

Two weeks later, during Super Bowl week in Houston, Favre made it definite that he would be coming back. He was in town to receive an award from a candy company that had named him the NFL's "hungriest player" for his phenomenal performance against Oakland on the Monday night after his father died.

Talking to reporters about the interception, Favre said, "Do I wish I had it back? Sure." He said the Eagles "had the perfect blitz for the play we had called. To say there was miscommunication between Javon and I would be an understatement."

Favre added, "I've thrown that pass numerous times where he jumps up and catches it in traffic. I knew I had to get rid of it. You say throw it away, but in three seconds, you don't have much time to make a decision."

Favre said the devastating loss made him more determined to come back firing in 2004.

"With each game I play," he said, "each season I play, I'm running out of chances. You have to seize the opportunity when it's there in front of you. I thought we had a better opportunity this year once we got to the playoffs than last year, and our record was better last year."

The first really serious retirement talk came after the 2004 season. The Packers had won the NFC North Division title by two games with a 10-6 record and had the home-field advantage for their wild card playoff game with the Minnesota Vikings. But the Packers stumbled badly against the Vikings, losing 31-17. Favre threw four interceptions. Viking receiver Randy Moss pantomimed a "moon" of the crowd (and was later fined by the NFL). It was as bitter an end to a season as Green Bay players and fans could imagine.

By the end of February 2005, Favre had still not let the Packers know if he would be returning for the 2005 season. *Milwaukee Journal Sentinel* writer Bob McGinn was at the annual NFL "combine" — in which teams evaluate college players they may eventually draft — in Indianapolis, where he ran into Favre's agent, James "Bus" Cook, and tried without much success to get a reading on the quarterback's future.

"I don't bet, and I'm not going to bet on that," Cook told McGinn. "I don't know what he's going to do. I really can't tell you."

McGinn asked whom Favre typically consulted while making his retire-or-don't-retire decision.

"He'll talk to his wife and they'll come up with a decision," Cook said. "He may talk to me some, too, but right now he hasn't given me any indication one way or another."

One factor Favre was weighing was his wife's illness. Deanna had been diagnosed with breast cancer during the 2004 season, but seemed to be responding well to treatments.

There were plenty of reasons for Favre to come back, Cook said, but the last thing to do was try to rush his decision.

"I guess there gets to be a time in everybody's career that they get a little bit burned out or whatever. He's certainly capable of playing as good as any quarterback in the business. He had a bad game [against the Vikings], but they all do."

Cook concluded: "I think if they just let Brett decide what he's going to do and take his time, it'll be fine. I'm sure they would have liked to have heard three months ago. But nobody's put any deadlines on him or said, 'Let us know what you're going to do or not going to do.'"

In the end, he came back for 2005, but the season was a debacle. The Packers finished with a record of 4-12, far and away the worst of Favre's long career, and indeed the quarterback's first losing season since his junior year at the University of Southern Mississippi. Green Bay finished last in the NFC North.

Favre was 36 at the end of the 2005 season, and the speculation about his retirement seemed to carry more urgency. The possibility now seemed real. Maybe the only factor weighing heavily against retirement was how inappropriate it would be for such a glorious career to end on such a downer of a season — four wins, 12 losses. But was there any guarantee the 2006 season would be any better?

February passed with no word on Favre's future. March did, too. Favre was reported to be hoping that the Packers would make some trades to ensure there wouldn't be a repeat of the 4-12 season, but Packers' general manager Ted Thompson was a believer in building a team through draft choices rather than trades or the free agent market.

On the second weekend in April 2006, reporters and camera crews from Wisconsin flew down to Mississippi when word arrived that Favre would be holding a news conference the morning of his annual charity golf tournament. Several Wisconsin television stations arranged to carry the press conference live.

They believed Favre's decision was at hand — and they were wrong. He always spoke to the media prior to the golf tournament. So Packer Nation was glued to the television and holding its collective breath and the news was there was no news.

The desperate reporters asked the opinion of others. Favre's friend and former back up, Doug Pederson, said he thought Brett was going to retire. John

Madden, the former coach and colorful TV commentator, said he thought Favre might want to be traded and finish his career with a Super Bowl contender. Frank Winters thought he'd keep playing. Mark Chmura said keeping the Packers in limbo was selfish on Favre's part.

Across Wisconsin and around the country, there was no shortage of theories. But finally, the only opinion that mattered decided that 4-12 was no way to go out. Brett Favre decided to come back to play in 2006.

It proved to be a strange season. The Packers had a new head coach, former Packers' quarterback coach Mike McCarthy. Through 12 games the Packers had a 4-8 record and a repeat of the disaster of the previous season seemed a real possibility. But then, in the last month, Green Bay turned it around. The Packers won three games in a row to bring their record to 7-8 and set up a season-ending, nationally televised showdown with their fiercest rival, the Chicago Bears, on a Sunday night that was also the last night of 2006.

Heading into the weekend, the Packers had even held out faint playoff hopes. But eight separate elements in nearly as many games had to be decided in their favor for that to happen, and when the Redskins beat the Giants on Saturday it meant there would not be a post-season for the Packers.

". . . I was standing in the huddle, TV timeout, waiting for the play, and I looked around goind, 'What happened? Where did everyone go?'"

Still, the game was important. Green Bay had a chance to close on a four-game winning streak and finish with a .500 record. The Bears, with a 13-2 record, were assured of home-field advantage in the playoffs, but they needed a sound performance from their sputtering offense to enter the post-season with maximized confidence. Chicago quarterback Rex Grossman had struggled even as the defense shone and the team ran up victories. The buzz in Chicago was not really that of a 13-2 team and a Super Bowl favorite. There existed the nagging suspicion that the Super Bowl couldn't be won with a marginal quarterback. It was a big night, then, for Grossman — and also, of course, for Brett Favre.

For Favre, there was the real possibility that this would be his swan song.

John Madden, calling the game for NBC, would emerge from a meeting with Favre held the day before Sunday's game thinking that the quarterback might indeed be ready to retire.

At first, they had joked about it.

Madden: "What will you do if you don't play?"

Favre: "I may come help you. We would be great in the booth together. No offense to Al [Michaels]."

Madden: "We would have Al, too."

Favre: "Yeah, he could kind of be the third wheel."

Favre also addressed the question more seriously, noting that with the passing years his close friends on the Packers had moved on.

Favre said, "There were several times last year in the huddle, several times this year, when I was standing in the huddle, TV time-out, waiting for the play, and I looked around going, 'What happened? Where did everyone go?' Coaches, players, everybody I played with."

During their talk Madden sensed that Favre was weary, that this might indeed be it — although 24 hours later, watching Favre play against the Bears, Madden said he'd changed his mind and was now convinced Favre would return for 2007. So who knew?

What was certain was that the fans wanted him back. Even in Chicago — where the temperature at game time was a balmy 50, incredible for December 31 — there were signs held up by the Soldier Field crowd urging Favre not to retire. "4-Evre," one read, in a play on the unusual spelling and pronounciation of the quarterback's name. And another, playing off the letters N-F-L: "Never Favre's Last game." One simply said, "I Love Favre."

It was pretty sporting from an away crowd, especially considering that Favre's 21 victories over the Bears — his career mark against Chicago was 21-8 — was the second-most wins by any NFL quarterback against a single opponent. (Dan Marino had beaten the Colts 22 times.)

Favre's stats for the 2006 season were neither his best nor worst: going into the finale he had completed 56.4 percent of his passes; and thrown for 3,600 yards and 17 touchdowns. While Favre had never been blessed with the kind of receivers who had helped other Hall of Fame quarterbacks set passing records, the line up of pass catchers in Green Bay in 2006 was particularly thin. Donald Driver was still around and much appreciated, but Bubba Franks' numbers had taken a nosedive. (Franks had caught 28 TD balls from 2000-2004, and only one in the 2005-2006 seasons.) One promising young receiver would be of no help against the Bears — Greg Jennings left Chicago for Green Bay early Sunday upon learning his wife had given birth to a baby girl.

The Packers received the opening kickoff and started from their own 25 yard line. After picking up a first down on a couple of Ahman Green runs and a short Favre to William Henderson pass, the Packers came to the line with a second-and-nine from the Green Bay 38.

Favre stood over center, took the snap, and faked a handoff left to Green, his lone running back. Favre then rolled right and, with time, set at the Green Bay 32 and threw a long pass down the right side for Carlyle Holiday, a young receiver out of Notre Dame. Holiday made the catch at the Bears' 36 and took it to the 27 before he was brought down.

Holiday was playing for the absent Jennings and said later: "Brett put me in a position to make plays. I didn't know [that Jennings wouldn't play] until I got in the locker room. We all practice the same amount of reps, so you have to step up when that situation comes."

Favre found Holiday again on the game's next important play. On a third-and-eight from the Bears' 25, Favre, operating out of the shotgun, took the snap, dropped another step or two back, and then ran forward, his eyes downfield. Favre spotted Holiday open at the 12 and delivered the ball for the catch and the first down.

After Favre missed Driver on first down and a handoff to Ahman Green (who had gone over 1,000 yards for the season a few plays earlier) picked up three, Favre on third down again went to the shotgun formation. Holiday went in motion left. The ball was snapped and Favre dropped quickly even further back, setting at the 16 and firing over the middle for his veteran, Driver, who had managed to find a small opening in the end zone between two defenders. The pass was on target and just like that, Favre and the Packers had dissected the vaunted Bear defense with an 11-play, 75-yard drive that put the Packers on top, 7-0.

After the kickoff, the Packers' defense forced the Bears into a three-and-out. It was exactly the start the struggling Bears offense hoped to avoid. The Chicago fans had to be the most restless of any 13-2 team in history, but they had reason. On first down, running back Thomas Jones lost a yard and then quarterback Rex Grossman missed two passes. Suddenly it was fourth and 11. Already there were those in the stands at Soldier Field calling for Grossman's back up, the veteran Brian Griese.

The Packers took over at their own 21 after the punt. A short pass to Ruvell Martin gained eight yards on second down and then on third and two Favre went back to Martin, who, like Holiday, had not seen a lot of playing time.

On the third-down play, Favre operated out of the shotgun. He took the snap, dropped another step or two, set on the 22, and fired long down the left side. It was not Favre's best pass. Martin had two steps on Bears' corner Ricky Manning, but the ball was underthrown. Martin had to slow his stride but made the catch anyway at the Bears 38, a gain of 33 yards.

"I got some opportunities today," Martin said later, "and I'm happy I took advantage of that and just did the best I could while I was out there. I always had confidence in myself. I was just kind of waiting for an opportunity. And I got one."

Following that long gain, Favre missed on three straight passes and the Packers had to punt. Jon Ryan hit a beauty that was downed by Jarrett Bush inside the Chicago 5 yard line.

Again, Grossman and the Bears could do little on offense. Jones gained six yards on first down, but then Grossman threw incomplete and on third down was sacked for a loss back at the 4. Chicago actually caught a break when Brad

Maynard's knuckleball punt took a big Bears' roll out to the Chicago 48 yard line. It was still great field position for the Packers.

They did not, however, make it pay off. Bears' end Alex Brown sacked Favre on first down. Then on second and 18 from the Packers' 44, Favre, out of the shotgun, shuffled a slick underhand pass to Ahman Green over the middle and the Packer running back found plenty of daylight, racing to the Bears' 40 before being brought down by Ricky Manning and Chris Harris. On third and two, Green got six off right guard for a first down at the Chicago 34.

After Favre missed Donald Lee on a rollout to the right on first down, his second-down pass underscored the pitfalls of working with new receivers. With no running backs behind him, Favre took the snap, made a quick two-step drop, looked left, and threw to Ruvell Martin coming across on a short slant route. Favre threw the timing pass to a spot, but Martin inexplicably pulled his route up short. Favre's pass instead went directly to Bears' cornerback Nathan Vasher, who made the easy pick at the Chicago 28 returned it seven yards to the 35.

The Bears finally made a first down on two Thomas Jones runs to the left side. But disaster was right around the corner. On third and two from the Green Bay 45, Grossman took the snap over center, made a two-step drop while looking left all the way, and then threw a swing pass into the left flat for tight end Desmond Clark. The ball hung a bit in the air and Packers' safety Nick Collins slid in front of Clark right at the line of scrimmage and made the interception. Collins caught it in stride and made it look easy as he loped to the end zone, putting the Packers up 13-0. Then Dave Rayner's extra point hit the left upright and bounced away no good.

Collins later said that watching Grossman on videotape had helped make the interception possible.

"I was studying Rex, his mechanics, and it paid off tonight," Collins said. "I was reading his eyes. It felt great. I'm used to being in the end zone, from college and high school. My first time as a pro, it felt great. It was wonderful."

Not only were the Packers making up for the 26-0 drubbing the Bears had delivered at Lambeau in the season opener for both teams, but Green Bay looked like the playoff team.

Afterward, Grossman was at a loss to explain the poor performance of both himself and his team.

"I'm trying to figure that out myself," the quarterback said. "Everything that could go wrong, went wrong."

Those looking for an excuse might have said that finding motivation was a challenge for the Bears, since they had secured home-field advantage throughout the playoffs regardless of the outcome against the Packers. Green Bay, meanwhile, with no playoffs to look forward to, had a last chance to end the season on a high note. "It's a meaningful game for us," Mike McCarthy had said during the week. "It's our arch rival, and that's how we approach the football game."

Prior to the game, Packers' defensive lineman Corey Williams said revenging the season-opening loss in Green Bay was on the Packers' minds.

"We've got payback on those guys," Williams said. "Those guys came up early in the year and shut us out, beat us pretty good. We haven't forgotten. We've got revenge out for them, just like it would be if we'd have shut them out in their hometown."

And no doubt somewhere in the back of the minds of the Green Bay players was the possibility that this could be the final game, the swan song, of their legendary quarterback. The 2006 Packers team was very young — 21 players on the roster were under 25 years old — but history was not lost on them. If this was Brett Favre's last game, they wanted it to be memorable.

Receiving the kickoff and trailing 13-0, the Bears finally found a spark on second and 10 from their own 23. Grossman, who had been met with boos as he brought the offense onto the field, handed off to Cedric Benson off left guard, and Benson broke the play open and carried the ball all the way into Packer territory to the 47, a gain of 30 on the last play of the first quarter.

Three plays later, however, the boos were back, and even louder. Grossman, who to this point had completed one of six passes for six yards, fumbled the snap from center and the ball was recovered by the Packers' Ryan Pickett on the Green Bay 39.

One of Favre's best passes of the game would soon follow. After two handoffs to Ahman Green picked up eight yards, the Packers faced third and two from their 47. Favre took the snap out of the shotgun, dropped a couple more steps, but could find no one open. The quarterback took a step toward the line of scrimmage, then rolled hard right, throwing while in full stride on the Green Bay 42. He'd spotted Ruvell Martin open at the Chicago 37, and Martin not only made the catch, but also added 18 yards after the reception, giving the Packers a first down on the Bears' 19.

There the Packers stalled, however, and Dave Rayner, who had earlier missed an extra point, now pulled a 32-yard field goal attempt wide to the left.

Taking over on their own 22, the Bears for the second drive in a row made something good happen early. On first down, Grossman took the snap over center, dropped straight back, and threw over the middle for Muhsin Muhammad, who caught it at the 29 and then turned it up the left sideline, all the way to the Chicago 49 and a gain of 27 before Charles Woodson knocked him out of bounds.

Still the prosperity would not last for the Bears. Three plays later, on third and four from the Packers' 45, Grossman threw a lazy cross-field pass for Rashied Davis that hung in the air while Davis waited on the right sideline. It gave Woodson time to cut in front for the interception, Grossman's third turnover of the game.

The teams would then exchange punts, and with 3:43 to go in the first half, Favre and the Packers had a first down at the Green Bay 42.

The quarterback led another sustained, points-producing drive. On first down Favre dropped to pass and, under pressure, executed a nifty forward scramble, passing just before he got to the line of scrimmage and finding Ruvell Martin at the Bears' 45. The free agent out of Saginaw Valley State carried it another five yards to the Chicago 40 before he was tackled.

After two handoffs to Green got nothing, Favre faced third and 10. Out of the shotgun, standing at the Bears' 45, Favre took the snap, dropped farther still, then once again ran forward and from the Chicago 44 unleashed a bullet for Carlyle Holiday on the right hash mark at the Chicago 25, a gain of 15.

On second and seven from the Bears' 22, the Packers executed their first successful screen pass of the night. Out of the shotgun formation Favre dumped a screen to Green on the right side at the 26 yard line, and Green took it all the way to the Bears' 11 before being run out of bounds.

The Packers would not, however, reach paydirt. Favre missed Driver in the end zone on first down. Then backup running back Vernand Morency gained three yards on a run up the middle. On third down, Favre tried to find Bubba Franks over the middle near the goal line, but the ball was tipped at the line by Bears' defensive end Adewale Ogunleye. This time Rayner made the field goal and the Packers led, 16-0, with 49 seconds to go in the first half.

Incredibly, Grossman and the Bears' offense were not done messing up.

No doubt somewhere in the back of the minds of the Green Bay players was the possibility that this could be the final game, the swan song, of their legendary quarterback.

With a first-and-10 from their own 27 with 43 seconds left in the half, Grossman dropped to pass, looking over the middle for Rashied Davis. But Grossman's pass was tipped at the line by Packers' tackle Corey Williams, and the ball ended up in the arms of Green Bay corner Patrick Dendy, who caught it at the Bear 30, slipped an attempted tackle by Davis, and took the ball down the right sideline all the way to the end zone, the second return of an interception for a touchdown in the half for the Packers. Rayner's point made it 23-0 as the first half ended.

Dendy said later that Williams "got his hands on it and put me in the right position. It was clear sailing. It happened so fast. I just got it and ran."

It had been an amazing half of football — a nationally televised disaster for the Bears, sweet revenge for the Packers. Green Bay's 23-0 lead at the break was the largest halftime lead in the 90 games the two teams had played in Chicago. Favre had passed for more than 200 yards, impressive by any measure but especially when cast against Grossman's first half numbers: two of 12 passing, 33 yards, three interceptions.

The crowd chanted for Grossman's backup — "Griese! Griese!" — as the two teams ran into their locker rooms.

The fans got their wish. Brian Griese started for the Bears in the second half.

"We had to do something," Chicago coach Lovie Smith said. "We were stinking the place up."

But Griese didn't fare much better on his first drive at the helm. He threw an incompletion and then, on third-and-seven from the Bears' 35, he was sacked by Corey Williams.

The Bears punted and then the Packers, too, had to kick it away after picking up one first down.

The Bears' next series provided one of their few highlights of the night.

On a fourth-and-one from the Chicago 27, Brad Maynard came on to punt. Standing at the Bears' 15, he received the long snap, took a step as if to punt, and then straightened up. It was a planned fake. Maynard threw a pass over the middle to Chicago running back Adrian Peterson, who was wide open at the Bears' 38. He had the first down easily, but Peterson was so all alone that when he turned upfield he made it all the way to the Green Bay 35, where he was hit by Packers' receiver Carlyle Holiday, who also played special teams. Holiday's hit forced Peterson to fumble, but the Bears recovered at the 36. When a 15-yard face mask penalty against Charles Woodson was tacked on, the Bears had the ball at the Packers' 21.

Still, the Bears couldn't stand prosperity. On third and six from the 17, Griese dropped and threw for Desmond Clark on the left side. The ball wasn't thrown high enough, however, and Packers' linebacker A. J. Hawk jumped, picked it off at the 16, and returned it to the 22.

The next three series — two for the Packers, one for the Bears — ended in punts. Green Bay seemed content to watch the clock tick down, which it did. When the Bears started their fourth drive of the second half, only 1:28 remained in the third quarter. At that point, finally, something good happened for Chicago.

On third and 10 from the Bears' 25, Griese faked a handoff and dropped to pass. He planted at the 16 and threw long down the right side for Mark Bradley, a second year receiver out of Oklahoma, who had several steps on Packers' corner Patrick Dendy. Griese's pass was on target, Bradley caught it in stride and the Bears had both a touchdown and their longest play from scrimmage of the season — 75 yards. The extra point made it 23-7, Green Bay.

"I got out out of position," Dendy said later. "You get out of position and that's what happens."

As the fourth quarter started, what the Packers needed was a sustained drive that would show that the Bears were not really back in the game. Favre delivered that drive. The Packers' quarterback hit three key passes in the drive, including a pass on third and eight from the Green Bay 27 that found Driver right at the first-down marker; a third-and-10 from the 35, where he hit Holiday for 18 yards; and finally a first-and-10 from the Chicago 47, when Favre connected with Donald Lee for 15 yards and a first down at the Chicago 32.

Green Bay wound up settling for a Dave Rayner field goal, but the 11-play drive used nearly five minutes on the game clock and put the Packers ahead 26-7. It was now a three-score game.

Favre would engineer one more fine drive later in the fourth quarter. After Nick Collins picked Griese at the Green Bay 17 and returned it to the the 25, Favre and the offense took over with 8:30 to go in the game. Favre mixed runs and short passes and the Packers drove relentlessly down the field, using up more clock. At the 2:00 warning, the Packers had a second and seven from the Bears' 25.

After the next play — a run by Vernand Morency for a first down — Mike McCarthy took Brett Favre out of the game. He was replaced by backup Ingle Martin. As Favre came toward the sideline, Donald Driver grabbed him in a hug, lifting the quarterback off the ground and carrying him off the field. On the field, Martin took two snaps, kneeling each time. The Packers would run the clock down but not run up the score.

On the sideline, there were more hugs and high fives for Favre. To some observers it looked like a legendary player saying goodbye.

When the game ended, the NBC on-field reporter, Andrea Kramer, had a word with the quarterback.

Kramer said, "You took a picture with your offensive linemen, a lot of hugs, Donald Driver picking you up. What's the significance of all this?"

Favre, his helmet off, said, "Well, if it is my last game, I want to remember it."

The quarterback paused, overcome with emotion. "It's tough," he said. "It's tough. I'll miss these guys…. And miss the game. Just want to let them know that."

He paused again to gain his composure. "I wasn't planning on doing this…. Way to put me on the spot."

Kramer: "What are the emotions that are going through your mind right now?"

Favre: "I think you can see. Love to play the game, love these guys, love to compete. It just shows."

Kramer: "Is this it?"

Favre: "We'll see. I don't want to say anything right now."

It sure sounded like the end, but when Favre met the media later, he was non-committal. "If it was the last game," he said, "I couldn't be more pleased with the outcome."

Someone asked directly if he thought he'd retire.

"I'm not going to comment on it," Favre said.

In the end, he came back. But it's doubtful Brett Favre or anyone else could have dreamed of the season that lay ahead.

Green Bay Packers vs. Denver Broncos

OCTOBER 29, 2007
Invesco Field at Mile High, Denver, Colorado

Remembering his friend Ernest Hemingway and the summer they spent together watching bullfights in Spain, A.E. Hotchner wrote: "Old wine in its cask sometimes reacts to seasons, and the summer of 1959 was, by Ernest's own avowal, one of the best seasons of his life. That aura of keen enjoyment I had found so overwhelming when we had first met in Cuba eleven years before, and which since then had been steadily blunted, now had a splendid renascence."

So, too, did the fall of 2007 serve as a rebirth for Packers quarterback Brett Favre. At age 38, in his 17th season as an NFL quarterback, Favre got off to a dazzling start, leading the Packers to a 5-1 record as they prepared to face the Denver Broncos in a nationally televised game on a Monday night in late October.

If the season seemed destined to play out as an extended curtain call for Favre, a certain Hall of Famer, it was fitting that the person who had been with him since he threw his first touchdown pass in high school in Mississippi had chosen the fall of 2007 as the time to emerge from behind the curtain herself. It was, Deanna Favre had decided, her turn to speak.

The occasion was publication of a memoir, *Don't Bet Against Me!* Written by Deanna and Angela Hunt and subtitled "Beating the Odds Against Breast Cancer and in Life," the book was published in September 2007. The resulting publicity marked a sea change for Deanna Favre, who had always avoided the limelight. Suddenly Deanna was on the cover of Madison-based *Brava* magazine in October and *Milwaukee Magazine* in November. There were book signings and personal appearances and, most notably, an extended visit to the ESPN broadcast booth during the second quarter of the Packers-Broncos game October 29. She charmed the huge national television audience with her humility and humor, and amid the laughter she made her serious points about breast cancer, the insidious disease that had changed her life when she was diagnosed with it in 2004 at age 35.

Going public was anything but easy for Deanna Favre.

"I'd been receiving proposals to do a book for a couple of years," she told *Brava*. "I've been like, 'No, I don't want to be out there. I don't want to share my life. I just want things to go away.' You really don't want to relive it.

"But then I got this proposal from Tyndale [Publishers], and I said, 'Just let me think about it. Let me pray.' And I did. You see, I have stage fright, but somehow [going public with my trials] has benefited a lot of people. I have people coming up and saying, 'Thanks for sharing your story.' It felt like a calling. I'm very nervous about it, this book, but I know there's good in it, and all my proceeds are going to the Foundation to help women with breast cancer."

She started the Deanna Favre HOPE Foundation after reading one of her hospital statements and seeing that a single chemotherapy treatment cost $3,200. Deanna had good insurance and plenty of money besides, but she'd once been a single mother struggling to pay ordinary bills. Single moms get cancer too. Deanna's HOPE Foundation is a way to help them.

With it all, the story of her life has emerged, and the public has learned that it hasn't just been one big fairy tale for Deanna Favre, not at all.

Like Brett, Deanna comes from little Kiln, Mississippi. Daughter of a single mom, Deanna took the last name Tynes when her mother, Ann, married a man named Kerry Tynes, whom Deanna considers her father. Deanna would eventually have two younger siblings and serve as a role model to them and others.

She was an excellent student and gifted athlete — a beautiful girl who didn't seem to pay attention to her looks. Since Kiln had only one school, she and Brett Favre, 10 months her junior, had known each other since they were small kids. But when she was 15 and he was 14, they began looking at one another a little differently. They still played basketball and baseball together, but now there were real dates as well.

Deanna told *Milwaukee Magazine*, "I didn't care if I had a boyfriend or not. But I remember thinking, 'He's really cute. I think I could like him.'"

They both wound up at Southern Miss and Deanna wound up pregnant. Deanna had their daughter, Brittany, but Deanna and Brett didn't marry. The relationship was on-and-off for a time. Brett was getting famous and not always handling it as well as he might have. When Deanna and Brittany finally joined him in Green Bay in 1995, Deanna became convinced Brett's use of painkillers was out of control. She helped him beat the pills. They married in July 1996. Their second daughter, Breleigh, was born in July 1999, shortly after Deanna had convinced Brett that he needed to quit alcohol, too. Their marriage grew stronger, strong enough to survive some terrible tragedies — the deaths of Brett's dad and Deanna's brother, Hurricane Katrina, and the breast cancer diagnosis.

Now cancer-free, Deanna was strong enough in 2007 to take the previously unthinkable step of willingly becoming a public figure herself. Along with appearing in the ESPN broadcast booth during the second quarter of the Packers-Broncos game on Monday night, Deanna provided a voice-over for a brief film and photo montage on Brett that ESPN aired during its pre-game show. Few who saw and listened to it remained dry-eyed.

As images of her famous husband, from childhood to NFL elder statesman, flickered across the screen, Deanna said this:

"We first laid eyes on you on an autumn Sunday. You, the little boy from Dixie, drawing up plays in the Mississippi mud, never growing old. All these years later, you remain as genuine as you were that day. You are ours, because you stood by us, not only in triumph, but more importantly, in times of despair. Celebrating timeless victories, and honoring those tragically lost. As the years pass, the doubters increase in volume. 'He's too old. He's lost a step. It's time to go.' Pay them no attention. For we are survivors. Legends write their own stories. My Brett. Our Favre."

It may have been about this time — it was sometime on the Monday night of the Denver game, in any case — that a somewhat jaded Wisconsin sports writer, watching on television back in the Midwest, sent a text message around to some sportswriting buddies. It contained just one sentence: "Did Brett Favre die?"

Well, sportswriters are a cynical bunch. But there's also little question that the media could not get enough of the Brett Favre story as the 2007 season progressed. It was irresistible. The aging warrior, fighting perhaps his last campaign, somehow summoning the will to perform near the peak of his powers, week after glorious week.

Did it get to be overkill? Some in Wisconsin thought so — the majority did not. Most have never been able to hear or read enough about Brett Favre.

There were a Denver franchise record 77,160 fans in Invesco Field when the 3-3 Broncos played host to the 5-1 Packers. One interesting stat, in Favre's 17th season, was that Denver remained one of only three NFL cities in which the Packers' quarterback had never won. The others were Baltimore and Pittsburgh.

Despite the Packers' impressive record, there were some nagging questions about their offense as they got ready for the Broncos. First was Green Bay's almost total inability to run the football. The Packers ranked last in the NFL, with less than 70 rushing yards a game. The other concern, at least for some observers after the Packers-Redskins game two weeks earlier, was the strength of Brett Favre's arm. The quarterback had underthrown some long passes against Washington, though he insisted they were just poor throws rather than a reflection of diminishing powers.

To that end a broadcaster approached Favre during the pre-game warm-up on the field and jokingly asked if Brett's arm had lost some zip. Favre's answer was to plant his toes on the 50 yard line and throw a line-drive pass — the broadcaster would later call it "a laser" — at the pylon marking the goal line half the field away. The ball hammered into the pylon, Favre grinned, and that was that.

As October was National Breast Cancer Awareness Month, the Packers had made Deanna Favre an honorary captain for the game and she accompanied the captains onto the field for the coin toss to determine which team would get the ball first. Deanna later said Brett had been afraid she would actually try to call the flip, but she knew better.

Denver won the toss and elected to receive. The Broncos were forced to start from their 9 yard line after an unnecessary roughness penalty on the kickoff return. Denver's second-year quarterback, Jay Cutler, brought the offense onto the field. In recent years the team had been searching for a quarterback who could summon the magic of John Elway, the retired Denver legend. They were big shoes and some had already tried and failed to fill them. With Cutler, however, Broncos fans thought they might have a realistic candidate. Cutler's numbers were pretty good: a completion percentage of 63.2, 2,407 yards passing. and 16 touchdowns against 13 interceptions. Cutler shared an agent (James "Bus" Cook) with Brett Favre and the two quarterbacks were friendly. Could Cutler be another Favre, another Elway? Only time would tell.

It was irresistible. The aging warrior, fighting perhaps his last campaign, somehow summoning the will to perform near the peak of his powers, week after glorious week.

He looked pretty good on the first Bronco drive, connecting with tight end Daniel Graham for 12 yards and a first down at the Denver 21. Three plays later, it was the other tight end, Tony Scheffler, on the receiving end of an 11-yard first-down strike that took the Broncos out to their 43.

The drive stalled there, however, and the Broncos' fourth-down punt resulted in a touchback. Favre brought the Packers offense onto the field, but they didn't stay long.

A third-and-six pass to running back Ryan Grant out of the backfield gained only a yard and Green Bay was three and out on its first possession. Punter Jon Ryan absolutely creamed his fourth-down kick. The punt traveled 71 yards in the air, but as sometimes happens on booming punts, the ball outpaced the Packers' coverage. The Broncos return man, wide receiver Glenn Martinez, caught it at the Denver 14 and brought it back up the left sideline for 26 yards to the Broncos' 40, giving Cutler a short field for his second possession.

The young quarterback took quick advantage. He threw two passes for first downs — one to Graham, one to halfback Selvin Young out of the backfield. The latter gave the Broncos first and 10 at the Packer 38. After a short gain on a running play and a Cutler incompletion, the Broncos faced third and nine from the 37. Operating out of the shotgun, Cutler took the snap. The Packers were blitzing and Cutler backpedaled in the face of the rush. He stopped at the 45, stepped up, and threw hard to the left side of the field, where wide receiver Brandon Stokley had gotten loose on a left sideline route. Stokley caught the ball at the Packers' 20 and managed to keep his balance as he tiptoed to stay in bounds. Stokley finally stepped out at the 15. Just after doing so he was popped by Packers' safety Atari Bigby. Bigby was called for unnecessary roughness, a penalty of half the distance to the goal line.

First-and-goal Broncos, from the 8. Cutler handed to Selvin Young up the middle and the back picked up six hard yards to the Packers' 2. He gave three of them back on second down, however, when Young was dropped in the backfield after taking the handoff, bringing up a third-and-goal from the 5. Cutler took the third-down snap from the shotgun, dropped farther back, and threw from the right hash mark on the 13 yard line into the end zone for tight end Daniel Graham. Graham was covered by Bigby, and the Packer safety's feet got tangled up with Graham's causing the receiver to fall, which led to Bigby being whistled for his second penalty in only a few plays. The pass interference call gave Denver a first-and-goal from the Packer 1.

But the Green Bay defense did not roll over. A first-down handoff to Selvin Young resulted in his second loss in as many carries; this time Packer defensive end Cullen Jenkins wrapped Young up in the backfield for a loss of four. On second and five, Cutler finally took care of business. He took the snap over center, faked a handoff right, and then rolled to his left on an unprotected bootleg. He was at the 10 yard line when he released his pass for Scheffler, who was just inside the end zone and made the catch to put Denver on the board.

The point after made it 7-0, Broncos, with 3:52 left in the first quarter.

After the kickoff, Favre brought the Packers on for their second possession, which would start from the Green Bay 21. The first offensive series had done little to quell concerns about either the Packers' lack of a running game or whether Brett Favre could still air it out with long throws down the field. The first play of the second series would put one of those questions to rest definitively.

Favre brought the Packers to the line. His running backs were behind him in an I formation. His young receiver, James Jones, was split wide right, covered by Denver cornerback Champ Bailey, widely considered one of the best corners in the NFL. Favre took the snap and dropped straight back, a classic seven-yard drop that put him on the Packer 14. The Denver rush was strong but still contained when Favre took a step forward and released the ball high and long toward the right side of the field, where Jones had run a streak route and managed to get two steps behind Bailey, the great corner, who had cut his glance back toward Favre, only to find himself behind Jones in the race up the field with the ball already in the air. As the pass descended across the Denver 40 yard line, Bailey dove forward, but it was in vain, for the ball hit Jones right in stride at the 38 yard line. Bailey fell to the ground and Jones kept going. At the Broncos' 27, Jones was cut off by Denver safety Nick Ferguson, but Jones made a move back inside and eluded Ferguson, eventually taking it all the way across the field to the left sideline and ducking just inside the left end zone pylon for a 79-yard touchdown reception.

"What did I tell you leaving the press conference?" Brett Favre would ask reporters after the game. He was referring back to the Redskins game two weeks earlier, when Favre had underthrown several balls — two ending up incomplete, two that were picked by Redskin safety Sean Taylor — as the Packers narrowly defeated Washington 17-14. At a midweek press conference after the Redskin game, Favre had made a point of reminding reporters, "It's only one game" as the interview session broke up.

"It was basically two or three throws," Favre continued, after the Denver game. "I underthrew them. I took ownership of it. I knew it had nothing to do with my arm strength, it was just one of those days. What else can I say?"

Well, how about saying how you felt when you looked downfield and saw James Jones with several steps on the great Champ Bailey?

"I knew he had a step on him when I threw it," Favre said. "I think nine out of 10 times Champ Bailey outruns him. I respect the heck out of [the Denver] corners. I think on that particular play, [Bailey] was guessing. I knew [Jones] had two or three steps on him, but I knew he could make that up."

Favre continued: "When I let the ball go, I thought it was underthrown. He was open enough that I didn't want to miss. You're not going to get that opportunity too often."

Favre didn't miss. The picture-perfect pass and the great run after the reception by Jones tied the game at 7-7 with 3:29 left in the first quarter.

One highly interested fan had missed the Packers touchdown. Deanna Favre, who was in an elevator heading up to the media center to appear on ESPN's broadcast during the second quarter, didn't see her husband's brilliant scoring pass.

With the game now tied, Cutler and the Broncos came back with an impressive drive that in its way was more impressive than Favre's long touchdown strike. Starting from their own 28 after the kickoff, the Broncos moved up the field with a sustained drive that was helped by two Packer penalities, one for defensive holding and one for grabbing the face mask. Cutler also hit on two passes for first downs, the second coming on a second-and-10 from the Green Bay 31 when Cutler found Selvin Young out of the backfield with a screen pass that Young bounced out to the left sideline and wound up taking all the way to the Packers' 7, for a gain of 26 yards.

On first and goal from the seven, on the last play of the first quarter, Broncos running back Andre Hall picked up six yards and nearly a touchdown up the middle before being tackled on the 1 yard line by Packers linebackers A. J. Hawk and Nick Barnett.

After the teams switched ends of the field, Denver had a second-and-goal from the Packer 1. Cutler took the snap over center, but before he could turn to hand the ball off to a back, Denver guard Chris Kuper, who was pulling on the play to get blocking position, inadvertently swiped the ball with his right hand, knocking it out of Cutler's grasp. The ball dropped to the turf and the Packers' Nick Barnett fell on it. It was a huge turnover. The Packers had terrible field position, but they'd kept Denver from an almost certain touchdown.

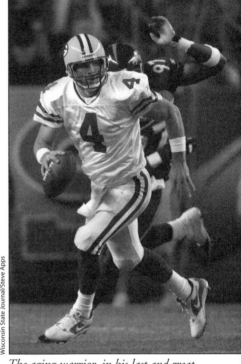

On the ensuing Packers' drive, a star was born. Green Bay's number-one running back, DeShawn Wynn, had injured his shoulder on a play in the first quarter and now Ryan Grant lined up in the Packers' backfield. Grant was a young player out of Notre Dame who had signed with the New York Giants. He'd gained over 2,000 with the Fighting Irish, but he'd struggled in New York. He'd been on the Giants practice squad in the 2005 season and then hurt his hand and been placed on injured reserve for 2006. The Packers had acquired Grant in a trade with the Giants, but

Wisconsin State Journal/Steve Apps

The aging warrior, in his last and greatest season with the Packers

going into the Broncos game he'd carried the ball only six times all year — three times against the Vikings and three more against San Diego. The overall state of the Packer running game as they came into Denver was not good.

But on Green Bay's first drive of the second quarter, something clicked. The offensive line began to open holes and Ryan Grant ran through them. Grant carried five times in a row at one stretch, and eight times overall during the drive for a total of 58 yards.

Afterward, Packer coach Mike McCarthy was asked about the reasons for the vastly improved running game.

"The players have been working hard at it," McCarthy said. "I gave those guys a chance to run the football today. We didn't do anything scheme-wise that we haven't done since day one. I thought the execution was better. I thought the offensive line did an excellent job of capturing the line of scrimmage. I thought Ryan Grant put his foot down, it was one cut, north and south, the way you're supposed to. I was pleased with the progress we made in the run game."

Everything was great about the drive — 98 yards in 14 plays — except that it fell one yard short of a touchdown. Facing fourth and goal from the Denver 1 yard line, McCarthy decided to kick a field goal. Mason Crosby booted the 19-yarder through the uprights and the Packers had their first lead of the game at 10-7.

Following a touchback on Crosby's kickoff, the Broncos had their first three-and-out of the game. Charles Woodson took Todd Sauerbrun's punt at the Green Bay 33 and brought it back eight yards to the 41.

The Packers' offense employed its newly emerging running threat, Ryan Grant, on the first five plays of the ensuing drive. Grant picked up 23 yards and two first downs in that span, and then was given a breather and replaced by Vernand Morency. On a first-and-10 from the Denver 36, Morency went off left tackle for no gain. Favre missed Driver on second down, but on third and 10 the quarterback found Greg Jennings open on the left side, and Jennings took the ball all the way to the Broncos' 16 for a gain of 20.

There had been many penalty flags thrown already in the game, and after the two-minute warning, penalties would cost the Packers. The first flag, however, was on Denver. Favre hit Morency on a screen pass to the left that gained nine to the Broncos' 7. Denver was called for a face mask penalty that gave the Packers a first-and-goal from the 3. On first down Grant got two yards to the edge of the goal line, but then on second down Packer guard Tony Moll was called for a false start before the snap. The penalty brought the ball back to the five, still second down. A handoff to Grant picked up three to the 2. Prior to the snap on third down, the Packers were flagged for another false start. This time the guilty party was tackle Chad Clifton. That made it third and goal from the Denver 7. Operating out of the shotgun, Favre had Driver open momentarily at the goal line, but the quarterback zinged the pass a bit high and left, and it was fourth down. Crosby's 26-yard field goal made it 13-7, Packers, and that was the score at halftime. Green Bay actually got the ball back at its own 37 with 19 seconds left before the break, but after another penalty — offensive holding — Mike McCarthy decided to run out the last few seconds and head for the locker room.

"I knew we had the ball in the second half," McCarthy said later, of his strategy. "I was a little frustrated in the first half. I thought some things were sloppy."

The Packers had dominated the second quarter — they had possession of the ball for 12:49 to the Broncos' 2:11 — but the only statistic that truly mattered was on the scoreboard, and it showed a game that the Broncos could still lead with just one touchdown.

With the ball to start the second half, the Packers picked up one first down on a penalty. Then on a first-and-10 from their own 33, Favre took the snap from center, dropped quickly, looked right, pumped, and then threw toward the right sideline and James Jones, who made the catch and went out of bounds at the Packers' 49, a gain of 16.

Favre was sacked on the next play, however, and three plays later, the Packers punted the ball away.

The punt was a touchback, and Cutler and the Broncos took over on their 20. From there they mounted a long, 13-play drive that, like so many others on this night, was eventually derailed by penalties. In this case, it was back-to-back offensive holding penalties after the Broncos had reached the Packers' 16 yard line with a first down.

The penalties left Denver with a first-and-25 from the Packers' 31. After an incompletion, Cutler hit Selvin Young over the middle out of the backfield and Young got 11 to the Green Bay 20. But then on third down, Packers' end Aaron Kampman got his seventh sack of the year, nailing Cutler for a seven-yard loss and forcing a field goal attempt by Jason Elam. The 45-yard kick was good and the Broncos had cut the Green Bay lead to 13-10 with three minutes left in the third quarter.

The Denver kickoff brought the 17th penalty of the game when the Packers were called for holding on the return. It meant starting from the Green Bay 10. Favre once again engineered a drive that began well as the Packers moved into Denver territory on the third play of the fourth quarter.

On third and three from the Broncos' 48, Favre, working out of the shotgun, took the snap, held his ground, pumped once, and then appeared to be getting ready to either pump or pass again when the ball slipped out of his hand. The quarterback fell on it at the Green Bay 46 and it was ruled a fumble rather than an incomplete pass. (Favre would connect on his first 12 passes of the second half without an incompletion.) That set up a fourth and nine, and Jon Ryan came in again to punt.

The only statistic that truly mattered was on the scoreboard, and it showed a game that the Broncos could still win with just one touchdown.

The punt was a touchback, and Cutler started from his 20. The second-year quarterback would throw for three first downs in a drive that got the Broncos into Green Bay territory. Later, asked about the young Denver passer, Brett Favre said he liked what he saw.

"I thought he played well," Favre said of Cutler. "He's a heckuva competitor. He has all the tools. Each week, he has progressively gotten better."

Cutler connected on first-down throws of 12 yards to Scheffler and 16 yards to Stokley, but the drive was yet again done in by penalties — a holding and a false start. Facing third and 13 from the Green Bay 44, Cutler swung a short pass to Selvin Young on the right and Young gained seven to the Packers' 37. The Broncos were on the far fringe of field goal range but decided to punt, and Sauerbrun hit a great one that was downed on the Green Bay 3. There was now 8:15 to go in the game, with the Packers clinging to a slim three-point lead.

The Packers' drive would see Ryan Grant go over 100 yards rushing, in a performance that gave Green Bay fans great hope for the rest of the season, since a decent running game had appeared to be the one thing missing from the Packers' offensive arsenal. But it was Brett Favre who really got Green Bay out of the hole they were in due to Sauerbrun's fine punt. On first down from the 3, Favre completed his 10th straight pass of the second half, finding Jennings along the left sideline at the 13 yard line. The receiver picked up eight after-catch yards and the Packers had some breathing room at their 21 yard line.

Two runs by Grant, however, left them facing a third-and-nine from the 22. Favre came through again. He took the snap out of the shotgun, dropped a few more steps back, looked downfield, and then began to roll out of the pocket right and up toward the line of scrimmage. Favre spotted Driver just outside the right hash mark at the Green Bay 39 and the quarterback let loose while on the run at the 17 yard line. Driver made the catch and the Packers had another first down.

Favre to this point was 11 for 11 in the second half, and 19-24 overall for 237 yards and a touchdown.

On second and six from the Packers' 43, Favre hit James Jones on the right side for 12 to the Denver 45. From there, however, Grant could get only a yard in two carries, and on third down Favre's perfect string of passes came to end when Broncos' end Elvis Dumervil clipped the quarterback's arm as he tried to find Jones in the right flat. The ball fluttered short of Jones and Champ Bailey nearly picked it off, but it fell incomplete.

Jon Ryan's punt was fair-caught at the Bronco 7. There was 2:27 to go in the game: a touchdown would win it for Denver; a field goal would tie. Could young Cutler take his team nearly the length of the field in just over two minutes? If so, it wouldn't be the first time: In his 12 starts at quarterback, he had three times driven his team to a winning fourth-quarter touchdown.

The Broncos were helped by yet another penalty right at the start of the drive, when the Packers' Atari Bigby was flagged for interference. It gave the Broncos a first down on their own 24.

After a handoff for no gain and an incomplete pass, Cutler faced a third-and-10 with 1:52 remaining. It was the game's biggest play to that point. The quarterback took the snap out of the shotgun and coolly found Stokely near the left sideline for a gain of 15 to the 39, where Charles Woodson rode him out of bounds.

On second and 10 from there, with 1:27 left, Cutler took the shotgun snap, dropped still farther, but then threw short over the middle for running back Brandon Marshall, who made the catch at the Denver 45. Marshall was hit but shook loose of Al Harris at the 47, cut to the right sideline, and then, at the Packers' 35, cut back inside and was finally dropped at the Packers' 26. It was a gain of 35 yards.

Marshall would figure in the very next play as well. It developed in much the same way as the one previous, as Cutler dropped, got good protection, and then threw short over the middle to Marshall at the 22. This time the back added nine yards after the catch, taking it to the Green Bay 13. But unlike the previous play Marshall was unable to get out of bounds. The clock kept running. Denver had one time out left, but appeared to want to save it lest they have to stop the clock for a field goal attempt to tie. Still, from the Packers' 13, they were thinking touchdown and the win.

There were 38 seconds left when Cutler took the next snap and he handed to Young off right tackle. It was a surprising call and worked as such; Young got nine to the Packers' 4. It was a fine run by Young, causing many missed tackles, and this time the Broncos called time-out, their last.

It was now second and one from the Packer 4 with 25 seconds left in regulation play. Cutler took the snap out of the shotgun and tried to hit Marshall in the left corner of the end. Well covered by Harris, the pass fell incomplete.

Twenty-two seconds left.

Cutler again took the snap from the shotgun, only this time he chose to run it on what appeared to be a called quarterback draw play, a risky call if true, given Denver's lack of time-outs. Cutler tried the right side, found nothing, then ran it back inside and was dropped at the line of scrimmage. The clock continued to run as Denver hustled its field goal team on the field. The holder, punter Todd Sauerbrun, knelt on the right hash mark at the Packer 11. The ball was snapped with three seconds left. Sauerbrun placed it as the clock ticked to two. Jason Elam's kick was perfect. The game was 13-13, and headed for overtime.

There would be another coin toss at mid field to see which team would get the ball first to begin the extra period. Mason Crosby and Greg Jennings came out for the Packers to call the toss. They called heads, and it came up heads. Maybe it was a good omen. The Packers could have used one. Green Bay had lost its last four road games that had been extended to overtime. For the last Packers' sudden-death win on the road, you had to go back to 1983 and a game at Tampa, which was also notable in that it was the last game announced by the bellicose and controversial Howard Cosell.

The kick came a yard deep into the end zone to Packers' wide receiver Shaun Bodiford, who brought it back 19 yards to the Green Bay 18.

It was first and 10 Packers, 82 yards from the Denver goal.

Although some had doubted his arm strength after his last game, Favre had already thrown one successful long bomb. Did he have another him?

Mark Tauscher, the veteran offensive lineman, would say later, "Whatever you doubt about him, you might as well write that he's going to do it. That's the kind of competitor he is."

They had doubted his arm strength.

Now, on the first play from scrimmage of the overtime, Favre took the snap over center. He faked a handoff to Grant and dropped back, looking briefly down the middle. Then he looked left and, planting at the Green Bay 11, uncorked a long high pass between the hash marks for Jennings, who had two steps on Denver corner Dre Bly. Jennings caught it in stride on the Broncos' 38 — the ball had traveled 51 yards in the air — and ran untouched into the end zone. The Packers had won, 19-13. It was the second-longest pass to end an overtime game in NFL history and it was yet another chapter in the legendary legacy of Packers' quarterback Brett Favre.

He had done it in front of a nationally televised audience, on a night when his wife had also been prominently featured, and he had done it in the game immediately after some critics had wondered if he would ever again be a threat throwing deep.

"The ball stayed up there a long time," Favre said later. "I thought they had good coverage right up until the end. I don't know how far it was. It seemed like 80 yards in the air."

At his press conference afterward, Favre was asked what the win meant to him.

"That one ranks up near the top," he said. "Ruvell Martin asked me, 'Where does that rank?' And I said, 'Top two.' That's just off the top of my head. But right now it's top two."

Two bombs, two perfect passes, long and on the money, one in the first quarter and one on the game's very last play.

Favre said, "Those were two of the best throws I ever made in my life."

Green Bay Packers vs. Detroit Lions

NOVEMBER 22, 2007
Ford Field, Detroit, Michigan

There was a time when the Detroit Lions and Green Bay Packers always met on Thanksgiving Day. For 13 straight years, from 1951 to 1963, the Packers traveled to Detroit to face the Lions in a holiday game that was nationally televised for the first time in 1956. Today, not watching NFL football on Thanksgiving seems as un-American as not eating turkey. One great American who was not a fan of the Thanksgiving Day game, however, was Vince Lombardi, and some observers think the great Packer coach's dislike of the game was the reason Green Bay was dropped as Detroit's regular opponent after 1963.

The Lions, in any case, will always be the team most closely associated with the Thanksgiving Day game. The association dates back to 1934, the Detroit franchise's first NFL season. Owner G. A. Richards, who had purchased the team and moved it from Ohio to Detroit, scheduled a Thanksgiving game with the Chicago Bears. George Halas's Bears were undefeated when they came to Detroit for the game. The Lions had just one loss. Fans packed University of Detroit Stadium and the NBC Radio Network carried the game. It may have been a good thing for the future of the Thanksgiving game that the opener lived up to the hype — the Bears won a thriller, 19-16.

Leading up to the Packers-Lions game in 2007, there had been 67 Thanksgiving Day games featuring the Detroit Lions. In many, as noted, the Packers figured as the Lions' opponent.

When the string of Packers-Lions Thanksgiving games began in 1951, it was the Lions who were among the NFL's elite. The Packers were still almost a decade

Twenty in a row: An amazing performance against the resilient Lions on Thanksgiving.

away from that status, but records and favorites tended (and still do) to go out the window when the Thanksgiving game came around.

The great Detroit running back Doak Walker told *The Sporting News* in 1995: "The favorite didn't always win, and some years there wasn't even a favorite. Both clubs were always up for the game and both clubs really enjoyed it. And we really had some skirmishes."

That first year, 1951, produced a barnburner. The Lions' colorful quarterback, Bobby Layne, threw four touchdown passes and the Lions defeated the Packers, 52-35, in what stood as the highest-scoring Thanksgiving game for more than three decades.

The Packers would rather remember 1956, the year Green Bay finally broke through for a Thanksgiving win and the year the game was first televised nationally. Packers quarterback Tobin Rote threw a late touchdown pass to give Green Bay the 24-20 win.

The celebrated Packers' middle linebacker Ray Nitschke recalled the game, and the national audience, in a 1995 interview with *The Sporting News*: "All of a sudden, the entire country was watching and it was more than just another game. That might have really started the tradition."

Packer center Jim Ringo concurred, saying in the same article: "We didn't get on TV much in those days, and it was really exciting. We knew that our families and friends — whether they were in Pennsylvania, Milwaukee, Texas or California — were watching. Even though we couldn't be home for Thanksgiving, we felt like they were with us."

In that 13-year span when the Lions always played the Packers on Thanksgiving, the Lions emerged with a 9-3-1 record. With the coming of Vince Lombardi to Green Bay as head coach in 1959, however, two things changed: the Lions' dominance of the Thanksgiving contest and the likelihood that the holiday game would continue to feature both Detroit and the Packers.

Ringo told *The Sporting News* that Lombardi did not think the Thanksgiving game was fair to the Packers. He had begun to complain about it to Pete Rozelle, the NFL commissioner. While a Thursday game was never easy — because of the lack of preparation and healing time from the previous Sunday — it was worse for the Packers because they lost most of a day to travel. They also, every year, were away from their families on Thanksgiving. Lombardi could not see the benefit. The 1963 Thanksgiving game — a 13-13 tie — would be the last of the annual Packers-Lions holiday meetings.

The Turkey Day game the year before, 1962, remains one of the most memorable of all time. The Packers came into the game undefeated and riding high. They had beaten the Lions in their earlier meeting that year, in a brutally tough 9-7 game that was later immortalized in *Run to Daylight*, Lombardi's collaboration with author W.C. Heinz. The book centered on one week in the 1962 season — the first Detroit game. Heinz was back home in Connecticut working on the book when the Packers and Lions had their second meeting that season. The Thanksgiving game was a debacle for the Packers, as Bart Starr was sacked 11 times for losses totaling 110 yards and Detroit triumphed, 26-14. At one point the Lions led 26-0.

Jim Ringo told *The Sporting News* that Lombardi was furious in the locker room after the game, and one would have thought so. But in his classic 1999 Lombardi biography, *When Pride Still Mattered*, author David Maraniss describes a quiet locker room in which Lombardi thought the pressure of no longer being undefeated wasn't necessarily a bad thing and that, if nothing else, the game was evidence that phoning in a game never works in the NFL. Whatever your record and reputation, you need to show up each and every week.

"Let it be an example to all of us," Lombardi said. "The Green Bay Packers are no better than anyone else when they aren't ready, when they play as individuals and not as one.... Our greatest glory is not in never failing, but in rising every time we fall."

The coach who brought the Green Bay Packers to Detroit for the Thanksgiving Day game in 2007 was in only his second season as a head coach in the

NFL. Mike McCarthy had a long way to go before there would be any comparisons made between him and a legend like Lombardi, but McCarthy had come a great distance nevertheless in the 22 months since Ted Thompson had hired him to coach the Packers.

Some had thought it a risky hire, though clearly a change needed to be made after Mike Sherman coached the Packers to a 4-12 record in 2005.

Was Mike McCarthy the man for the job? A story in the Madison *Capital Times* the week of McCarthy's hiring was headlined: "A Calculated Risk: Thompson ties his fate to unproven McCarthy."

Thompson liked McCarthy's toughness. The coach came from a blue-collar background in Pittsburgh. It's a city of hard-working people, steel mills, and saloons, and McCarthy's father Joe was a fireman who also ran an establishment called Joe McCarthy's Bar and Grill.

Mike played tight end for Bishop Boyle High School in Homestead, Pennsylvania, and played it well enough to be recruited for college ball, though by small schools. He wound up at Baker University in Baldwin City, Kansas. One year his team finished runner-up in the NAIA Division II playoffs and McCarthy was captain and all-conference as a tight end in 1986.

Out of school, he worked as a graduate assistant coach for a year at Fort Hays State University, then headed back to Pittsburgh. University of Pittsburgh coach Mike Gottfried also gave McCarthy a graduate assistant position, but it paid so little that McCarthy worked nights in a toll booth on the Pennsylvania turnpike. Gottfried was impressed by McCarthy's willingness to work long hours.

He impressed enough people around the program that when Gottfried was fired at the end of the 1989 season, the new coach, offensive coordinator Paul Hackett, asked McCarthy to stay on. He coached quarterbacks and receivers and again he must have shone, for when Hackett got the call from the NFL a few years later — the Kansas City Chiefs asked him to be offensive coordinator — McCarthy was invited along. His first NFL job was quality control assistant, but within two years he was quarterbacks coach. He progressed to Green Bay — coaching quarterbacks under the ill-fated Ray Rhodes and getting to know Brett Favre — and then spent four years with the New Orleans Saints after Rhodes was fired. He had left New Orleans and spent a year with the 49ers when Ted Thompson came calling.

"I've played for 15 years a certain way: aggressively. I don't regret the way I play or the way I approach it, and I don't think I should change."

Thompson conducted interviews with seven prospective coaches to replace Sherman. Those besides McCarthy included Dallas Cowboys' assistant head coach Sean Payton and Packers' defensive coordinator Jim Bates.

The press conference announcing McCarthy's hiring was held Thursday, January 12 in the media auditorium at Lambeau Field. McCarthy's parents and brother were in attendance and so was his 14-year-old daughter, who lived with her mother in Texas but came up for the big event.

"I kind of liked the Pittsburgh macho stuff," Thompson said of McCarthy that day. "I like the fact that he's a tough guy." Thompson also spoke about McCarthy's "command presence.... I get back to I think he's a football guy. I think he knows what he wants. He has the ability to see the big picture."

McCarthy's deal was reported to be just under $2 million a year for three years.

The new coach didn't take long to act. On Friday, the day after the news conference, McCarthy announced the firing of six assistants, including offensive coordinator Tom Rossley.

McCarthy wanted to retain defensive coordinator Jim Bates, but Bates took missing the top job hard and decided against staying with the Packers. He went on to become an assistant with the Denver Broncos.

How McCarthy would handle Brett Favre was a looming question. The two had played phone tag without speaking on the Friday after McCarthy's hiring. At that point — January 2006 — it wasn't certain Favre would be coming back for another season. But he did come back, of course, and he also came to the Packers' spring drills that began in Green Bay on May 31.

Observers wondered whether McCarthy could — or should — try to rein in his celebrated quarterback, who had suffered through the worst season of his career in 2005. The team's record of 4-12 was bad and so were Favre's personal stats: he threw 29 interceptions and just 20 touchdown passes. The interceptions were a league high.

At a press conference in mid-May, before spring practice, Favre, talking for the first time since the end of the 2005 season, said he had no intention of changing his style of play.

"I've played for 15 years a certain way: aggressively," Favre said. "I don't regret the way I play or the way I approach it, and I don't think I should change."

Asked later about those comments, McCarthy said: "I wasn't [at the news conference], so without having been there, my response is that he's always played the game the same way. He's always pushed the envelope on the side of being aggressive. And that's how I took the quotes when I saw them."

McCarthy did add this: "I'll tell you this. He's going to be coached a certain way. I believe in being aggressive, but he will be coached to play within the structure of the offense. I can assure you of that."

The quarterback and the coach eventually bonded. Winning helps. After starting the 2006 season 4-8, the Packers finished with four straight wins, including the rousing closer against the Bears. It set the table for the amazing run with which the Packers began the 2007 season, McCarthy's second as head coach.

The Packers came into the Thanksgiving Day game at 9-1, tied with Dallas for the best record in the NFC. Green Bay historians might also have noted, somewhat ominously, that it was the Packers' best 10-game start since 1962. That was the season, of course, when Lombardi's undefeated team went into Detroit for the Thursday holiday game and got clobbered.

The 2007 Lions were playing decent football heading into the game, with a 6-4 record. Their defense led the NFL in takeaways with 30. Their placekicker, Jason Hanson, was poised to become the 10th-leading scorer in NFL history if he booted two field goals.

The Lions, who won the toss and received the opening kickoff, got off to a good start. Quarterback Jon Kitna — rated eighth among league passers coming into the game — was coming off a tough game, a home loss to the New York Giants in which Kitna had thrown three interceptions. But Kitna led the Lions on a sustained drive to start the Thanksgiving game, one that used 12 plays and nearly eight minutes on the clock and went all the way to the Packers' 8 yard line before the wheels came off.

On a third down and one from there, Kitna completed a pass near the goal line, but Lion center Dominic Raiola was called for an illegal chop block that took Detroit back to the 23 yard line. On the next play, Packers end Aaron Kampman, who was having an outstanding season as a pass rusher, got to Kitna and dropped him at the Packers' 29. It was Kampman's 10th sack of the season. On fourth down Hanson nailed a 47-yard field goal through the center of the uprights and Detroit had the early lead, 3-0.

Tramon Williams made a fine kickoff return, zigzagging back and forth across the field, giving the Packers good field position at their 33 to start their first drive. But it would be a nightmare start. As Favre took the snap he moved right to hand the ball off tackle to the trailing running back, Ryan Grant. But as Favre turned, his pulling left guard, Daryn Colledge, stepped on Favre's foot, causing the quarterback to stumble. Favre nevertheless got the ball to Grant but something, perhaps the timing, was off, because the ball went right through Grant's arms and fell to the turf, where it was recovered by Detroit's Jared DeVries on the Packers' 25.

"Not the way you want to start," Favre said later. "Our defense kept us in it at that point."

The defense did rise up. After running back Kevin Jones picked up a couple of yards on first down, Kitna missed two passes and Hanson came on to kick his second field goal of the game, a 41-yarder that gave Hanson 1,618 points for his career, 10th on the all-time list.

The Packers started their next drive from their 27. Favre was riding a hot streak coming into the game — in his previous four games he'd hit 73 percent of his passes for an average yards per game of 315. In that time he'd thrown for 10 touchdowns against only two interceptions. But he struggled, and the offense struggled, during the first quarter in Detroit.

The Packers' second series was better only in that they didn't turn the ball over. It was a three and out; Favre did hit Ryan Grant with a short pass for nine yards on third and 10, but the Packers had to punt.

Taking over at his 26, Kitna once again moved the Lions into Packers' territory. Green Bay got lucky on the first play of the drive when Kitna found his wide receiver, Calvin Johnson, wide open over the middle at the Detroit 43, but Johnson dropped the ball.

The best play of the drive came on a first-and-10 from the Lions' 38. Kitna took the snap and handed the ball up the middle to halfback Kevin Jones. Finding no hole, Jones cut it to the left, sidestepped a tackle by Packers' safety Aaron Rouse, and managed to turn the corner up the left sideline. From there he made a great side-step-and-twirl move to cause Green Bay linebacker Brady Poppinga to miss as well. In the end, Jones brought the ball all the way to the Packers' 39, a gain of 23.

It was Aaron Kampman who again stepped up for the Packers' defense. On a third-and-three from the Green Bay 32, he sacked Kitna again. The six-yard loss took the Lions out of field goal range, and the subsequent punt gave the Packers their best field position of the game. Charles Woodson fielded the punt on the Green Bay 12 and brought it back 34 yards to the 46, where Lions' linebacker Alex Lewis made a tackle that might have prevented a touchdown.

The Packers, however, could not take advantage. They had by this time pretty much decided to abandon the run, but the passing game wasn't yet quite clicking. Of the decision to throw almost exclusively, Packers' offensive coordinator Joe Philbin said afterward that the Lions' defense dictated that strategy.

"Believe it or not, we were planning on running the ball a good bit," Philbin said later. "We thought they'd be a little more cautious in terms of our ability to hurt them in the passing game, but they just kept playing an extra guy down."

Starting at the 46, Favre on first down hit Donald Driver for eight — the Packers' first visit to Lions' territory — but, operating from the shotgun, the quarterback missed his next two passes and the Packers were forced to punt again.

They would end the first quarter with a total of 17 offensive yards — and none on the ground.

But Kitna and the Lions, on a second-and-seven from the Detroit 23 after the punt, helped them out.

Kitna took the snap, faked a handoff, dropped, and set to throw at the 15. Kitna releasd it long down the middle for Calvin Johnson, who was briefly open between the hash marks at the Lions' 45. Packer safety Aaron Rouse reacted quickly, however, cutting in front of Johnson and making the interception in full stride. Rouse cut right, then left, headed for the sideline, and got all the way to the Detroit 11 before he was brought down, a pick return of 34 yards.

The Lions weren't going to stymie Favre forever. On first down, back under center now rather than in the shotgun, Favre took the snap, quickly backpedaled and released the ball while retreating to Greg Jennings, who was running a short slant route on the left side. Jennings caught it at the 5 and went in standing up for the touchdown. The point after gave the Packers the lead, 7-6.

"I was hoping we'd go down and score as soon as possible," Favre said afterward. "But I figured we'd score at some point. I knew it was going to be one of those days. One of those games. We'll get some, they'll get some."

The Lions, on their next series, got some but not enough. Going into the game they had thought they might be able to probe the middle of the Packers' pass defense with a running back out of the backfield. The best play for Detroit on this drive, which again found them in Packer territory but again ended in a punt, was a 20-yard completion over the middle from Kitna to halfback Aveion Cason. It took the Lions to the Packer 44, but there they stalled and the punt went into the end zone for a touchback.

The Packers took over, and it was vintage Favre. After a screen pass to Grant was stopped at the line of scrimmage, the quarterback brought the Packers to the line with a second-and-10 from their 20. Favre took the snap over center, faked a handoff, and dropped back to the right. The rush was coming so he drifted back left away from it, then picked up his pace as two Lions closed in. Finally Favre shuffled his feet forward and looked to be ready to throw long. He did, and it was a remarkable pass, for he released it on the left hash mark at the Green Bay 17 and the ball, which was not lofted but rather drilled with a rope-like flight, hugged the left hash marks all the way up the field where Donald Driver, coming from the right, grabbed it at the Lions' 48. The laser-like pass had traveled 35 yards in the air and after catching it, Driver broke a tackle and took the ball to the Detroit 42.

On first and 10 from there, the Lions blitzed and nearly got to Favre. Outside linebacker Ernie Sims did hit the quarterback's arm as he threw and the pass fluttered away incomplete. But then on second and 10, out of the shotgun, Favre dropped a couple more steps and set at the Packer 49. From there he winged it down the right sideline for James Jones, who caught it at the Detroit 24 and was immediately pushed out of bounds.

Favre had a hot hand. Now he stood in the shotgun on another first down, and when the snap came he didn't really drop any farther. The pocket began to collapse, but before anyone got close Favre threw quickly down the left side, where Donald Driver made an excellent catch, between two Lions, at the Detroit 8, falling forward to the 5 after making the grab. On the next play, Ryan Grant got the first rushing yards of the game for the Packers when he went off tackle through a big hole and into the end zone for Green Bay's second touchdown. Crosby's kick made it 14-6, Packers, with 7:41 to go in the first half.

"I got to the point where I said I'm just going to throw it to the guys as quickly as possible. And I'll take my chances that way."

Here the Packers' kick return unit let them down. Mason Crosby's kickoff was taken by running back Aveion Cason on the Detroit 2 yard line, on the far left side of the field. Cason ran it immediately toward the middle of the field, broke through a hole at the 25, and sprinted for the right sideline, where it appeared momentarily he only had the kicker, Crosby, to beat. Crosby had an angle but Cason burst past him. Somehow, though, Packer cornerback Tramon Williams, with no angle, ran down Cason from behind, unquestionably preventing a touchdown and pulling Cason down at the Green Bay 24. It was a return of 74 yards, and still the Lions couldn't take full advantage. On third and seven from the Green Bay 21, Kabeer Gbaja-Biamila got to Kitna and sacked him for a loss of six. It was left for Hanson to kick his third field goal of the game and the Lions cut the Packer lead to 14-9.

The teams would then exchange punts, after which the Packers took over on their own 20. Grant gained two yards on first down, and then came the two-minute warning.

On the first play out of the time-out, Favre operated in the shotgun with no running backs. The Lions blitzed, but he managed to find Jennings on the right side for 10 yards and a first down.

That completion gave Favre respectable numbers on the day: 9-15 passing, for 118 yards and a touchdown. But the pass to Jennings would come to mean more than that. By game's end, it would be remembered as the first in a string of consecutive completions that eventually grew to 20, an amazing streak, a Green Bay franchise record.

Later, Favre would say that while he was happy about the record, it wasn't that big of a deal. He certainly wasn't aware of it while it was happening.

"I threw it, they caught it," he said. "Nothing spectacular. Nothing like overtime against Denver. It was kind of methodical, moving the ball down the field."

Favre continued: "I got to the point where I said I'm just going to throw it to the guys as quickly as possible. And I'll take my chances that way. You say to the other team: OK, tackle them. I know one thing: Donald Driver isn't easy to tackle."

Favre was shortchanging himself a bit. For while many of the passes in the consecutive streak were short, quick throws, he threw downfield on several occasions. And he never missed.

The pass to Jennings had given the Packers a first down on their 32 with 1:31 to go in the half. The Packers had all their time-outs to use.

The Packers began a hurry-up, no-huddle offense. Favre first hit Grant out of the backfield on the right side for a gain of 13 to the Packer' 45. Favre took the next snap, out of the shotgun, with 1:05 to go. Favre set at the 36 and threw down the right side to James Jones, who made the catch near the sideline at the Lions' 35. Jones was hit by Lions safety Kenoy Kennedy and fumbled the ball out of bounds. Detroit immediately began protesting that it should be ruled an incomplete pass, that Jones never had possession. The officials decided to review the play; while they did so, Favre and Mike McCarthy conversed on the Packers' sideline.

It was ruled a catch.

Now with first and 10 from the Lions' 35 and 58 seconds to go in the half, Favre dropped a screen pass to Grant on the right side, and the back picked up nine to the Detroit 26. The Packers hustled to the line of scrimmage and got a snap off with 35 seconds remaining. Favre hit Driver short on the left side, just a yard past the line of scrimmage, and Driver advanced it to the 19, where the Packers utilized their first time-out.

Twenty-nine seconds remained in the half.

After the time-out Favre hit Driver again, over the middle this time, and Driver took it to the 12. The Packers called their second time-out.

Now on second and three from the Detroit 12, Favre, out of the shotgun, threw over the middle and found Donald Lee for the first time that day at the Detroit 3 yard line. The tight end was wrapped up immediately in a pile on the ground. Favre sprinted up to the pile, motioning that he wanted to spike the ball and save the Packers' last time out. But the rest of the team hadn't caught up to the quarterback. Favre next signaled a time-out, but there was some thought the ball was loose on the ground, that Lee had fumbled, so no time-out was called. As the seconds ticked down it became apparent Lee had not fumbled. Favre, exasperated, motioned again for a time-out.

There were four seconds left, and the Packers really had no choice other than to try a field goal. Favre was visibly upset, but Crosby made the kick and the Packers went into the locker room leading the Lions, 17-9.

All told, it had been a very good second quarter for the Packers' offense, which had righted the ship after a disastrous first quarter. Favre finished the half with 15 of 21 passing for 184 yards and a touchdown; Driver had five catches for 79 yards. Their running game had yet to be in evidence, but that would change.

Detroit, meanwhile, had endured a half of missed opportunities. On six of their seven drives, the Lions made it into Packer territory, but never got across the goal line. Hanson's three field goals were the sum of their point production.

The Packers received to start the second half, and their opening drive looked a lot like the drive with which they closed the first half. Favre worked from the shotgun, most times with five receivers and no running back.

Favre hit six short passes to start the drive, none for even 10 yards, but they moved the Packers from their own 20 to the Detroit 47.

On second and two from there, out of the shotgun and with five wide-outs, Favre took the snap and dropped a few steps farther back. He looked right all the way and was getting some pressure from the Lions rush. Favre planted at the Packers' 46 and unloaded a long pass down the right side, where Koren Robinson had a step on Lions' corner Stanley Wilson. The ball was in the air and nearly there when they reached the 25, at which point Wilson slipped and fell and Robinson caught it in stride at the 20. Robinson continued down the sideline until he was knocked out of bounds at the Detroit 4, a gain of 43 yards.

It was Favre's 13th straight completion and proof that not all his passes during the streak were short.

On first and goal from the 4, Favre, out of the shotgun, took the snap, and as he did, Jennings, split near right, ran three steps straight into the end zone, then cut sharply toward the right sideline. Favre let the ball go just as Jennings made his cut; the receiver caught it inside the goal line for another Packers' touchdown. Crosby's kick made it 24-9 Packers with 11:13 left in the third quarter.

In the middle of the consecutive completion streak, Favre said later, he had no idea it was happening. "We were moving the ball, and passing the ball as efficiently as we have all year," Favre said. That's all he knew or needed to know.

Detroit, after the kickoff, just added to its frustration level. For the seventh time in eight drives, the Lions managed to move the ball into Green Bay territory, but once again they couldn't get a touchdown. They reached the Packers' 33 on this drive, but a couple of penalties — an ineligible receiver downfield and a false start — took the air out of the drive. Jason Hanson boomed a 52-yard field goal (the ball easily clearing the goal post) to make it 24-12 Packers with 5:15 to go in the third quarter.

It was as if Favre and the Packers couldn't wait to get the ball back. After the kickoff, a touchback, they took possession at the 20. On first down, yet again from the shotgun, Favre took the snap, dropped another couple of yards, and released a long ball down the right sideline where Greg Jennings had a slight opening between two defenders. The pass had to be perfect. Jennings caught it at the 44, where he was immediately pushed out of bounds. It was another pass in the streak with a high degree of difficulty and it was Favre's 15th in a row, setting a new personal best. The Packer franchise record was 18, held jointly by Lynn Dickey and Don Majkowski.

The streak appeared to end on the next play when Favre missed Driver on the right side, but the Lions' Travis Fisher was called for interference, making it, in effect, no play. The streak survived; the Packers got a first down at the Lions' 48.

From there, Favre hit Ryan Grant on a short pass for seven yards, and the Lions were next penalized five for encroachment. Then, on first and 10 from the Lions' 36, the Packers found their running game. Favre was over center rather than in the shotgun, and on taking the snap he handed to Grant off left tackle. Grant, who had come on so strong in the last several games, bounced it outside immediately, cut it back inside when he reached the 32, and was running almost parallel to the line of scrimmage along the 26 yard line when, at the right hash mark, he cut sharply upfield. At the 15 yard line Grant swung right again, getting to the sideline and the Detroit 5 yard line before he was knocked out of bounds.

It was the first significant running play for the Packers, but not the last: Grant would finish with 101 yards in just 15 carries.

On second and goal from the Detroit 3, Favre went back to the shotgun and found Ruvelle Martin in the left corner of the end zone with a high lofted pass that the receiver went up and grabbed for the touchdown. With the point after it was 31-12 Packers, with just under two minutes left in the third quarter. The touchdown pass was Favre's 18th straight completion, tying the Packer team record.

On receiving the kickoff, the Lions went three and out, and many thought the game was about over. That turned out not to be true, as the Lions, to their credit, did not give up.

First, however, the Packers, starting from their 34, picked up two yards on a Favre to Ryan Grant short pass and then another 15 on an unnecessary roughness penalty against Detroit. Favre's streak was now at 19.

On second and eight from the Detroit 47, on the first play of the fourth quarter, Grant gained two around right end. Then, on third and six, Favre, from the shotgun, completed his 20th straight pass, a bullet over the middle to Donald Driver, who caught it between the hash marks at the Lions' 42, where he dodged a tackle and cut it to the right sideline. Grant looked to have a shot at taking it all the way until Lion corner Keith Smith, who had a good angle, chased him out at the Detroit 4. It was a gain of 41 yards.

Favre's streak ended on the next play when he lofted a short pass for Robinson in the left end zone. The receiver caught it, but could get only one foot down in bounds. After Grant gained two, Favre threw another incompletion, missing

Jennings, and the Packers settled for a Crosby field goal and a 34-12 lead with 13:08 to go in the game.

The streak, ended at 20, was the subject of much conversation after the game. "It was like surgery out there," said Packers' back up quarterback Aaron Rodgers.

"I wouldn't say I'm amazed," Packers' coach Mike McCarthy said. "He's a Hall of Fame quarterback."

Instead of folding, though, the Lions mounted two scoring drives, something they hadn't managed all game. Kitna took them 75 yards on 10 plays in the first one, capping it with a six-yard touchdown pass to Calvin Johnson. After the Packers went three and out after the kickoff, Kitna brought the Lions right back, even more quickly this time. The second scoring drive was 67 yards in five plays. All of a sudden the score was 34-26, Green Bay, and Detroit was a touchdown and two-point conversion from tying.

There was still 6:34 to go in the game, and the crowd at Ford Field was finally into it, loud and sensing a comeback. But Brett Favre put the finishing touch on a brilliant day, engineering a 10-play drive that culminated in a Crosby field goal that put the Packers up 37-26 with less than two minutes to play. Overcoming an offensive holding penalty, Favre hit Jennings for 11 yards, Driver for nine yards, and James Jones for 20 during the drive. Ryan Grant drove in the dagger with a 27-yard run that gave the Packers a first at the Detroit 16.

Detroit had one more chance, but it ended with a fourth-down incomplete pass by Kitna. The game ended with Favre taking a knee.

The Packers were now 10-1. In the locker room, the quarterback was asked to assess the season so far.

"It's amazing," he said, and pointing to his veteran status, added, "I'm a little more aware of what this season has meant up to this point. I think we've overcome a lot. Up to this point it's been pretty satisfying. But there's still a lot of football left."

How far, Favre was asked, could this team go?

"Only one team can win it all," he said. "Hopefully, we're that team. We're given ourselves an opportunity to make a run for it."

The lion in winter: Favre exults over another first down in a snow-shrouded Lambeau Field.

Seattle Seahawks vs. Green Bay Packers

JANUARY 12, 2008
Lambeau Field, Green Bay, Wisconsin

T he Green Bay Packers finished the 2007 regular season with a 13-3 record, good enough to earn them a bye in the first round of the playoffs. But that hardly captures what was one of the most surprising, even magical, regular seasons experienced by any Green Bay team, ever.

Though the Packers had closed strong to end the 2006 season — winning their last four games — the streak had only salvaged an 8-8 record. Few knew what to expect of the 2007 team. Even Brett Favre's decision to return for another year couldn't hide the roster's inexperience.

Yet somehow, behind second-year coach Mike McCarthy, the Packers found a way first to believe, then to achieve. In the bargain, Brett Favre, who expressed as much surprise as anyone as the wins began piling up, put up numbers that were as good as any in his 16 years in Green Bay. That he did it in the twilight of his career meant that in 2007 the Packers quarterback, who was really already America's quarterback, did what many observers thought impossible: he added to his legend. It is not overstating the case to say that by the time he threw the long touchdown pass to beat Denver in overtime on Monday night in week eight of the 2007 season, Brett Favre had become a true American icon.

That Denver game and another from 2007 — the Thanksgiving Day game in Detroit — have been chronicled here. But for Packer fans the season held many other memorable moments, not least because it was all so unexpected.

The offseason had not been without controversy. Favre had announced his intention in early February to return for a 17th NFL season, telling his favored hometown area newspaper, the *Biloxi Sun-Herald,* "We have a good nucleus of young players."

But there was one player, not all that young and not on the Packers' roster, who Favre believed could make a significant difference in the Green Bay season. That was Oakland's Randy Moss, the gifted but controversial wide receiver whom Packers' fans loved to hate. Moss wanted out of Oakland. How hard Brett Favre pushed the Packers to talk to Moss, and exactly how serious any discussions between the team and Moss actually became, is difficult to ascertain because the many various rumors were rarely if ever addressed by someone in a position to know the truth. That probably only fueled the rumors, one of which had Favre so upset with the Packers' inability to land Moss that the quarterback demanded to be traded himself. That didn't happen, of course. Moss was traded from Oakland to New England in late April, and Favre remained in Green Bay.

Moss would go on to have a great year with the Patriots, who became one of the leading stories of the 2007 NFL campaign when they ran through the regular season undefeated. The other big story was, unquestionably, Brett Favre and the Green Bay Packers.

The Packers had split their four preseason games and opened the regular season at home against the Philadelphia Eagles. The Packers got off to a 10-0 lead but the unlikely hero of the game was the team's fifth — or "nickel" — defensive back, Jarrett Bush, who forced one fumble and recovered another while playing on the punt team. Bush's recovery of a fourth quarter fumble by Eagle returner J. R. Reed led to rookie placekicker Mason Crosby's winning 42-yard field goal. The Packers did not score an offensive touchdown but won, 16-13.

Brett Favre began to hit his stride in week two. Playing away against the New York Giants (who would eventually engineer a miracle year of their own), Favre led the Packers to a 35-13 win, including 21 points in the fourth quarter after the third quarter had ended with Green Bay up just 14-13. Favre threw for three touchdowns and nearly 300 yards, good enough for him to be named NFC offensive player of the week. He also passed John Elway for most wins — 149 — by a starting quarterback. It would not be the last record to topple in the 2007 season.

Week three saw the Pack back in Green Bay against the San Diego Chargers, for a game played in southern California-like weather, 73 degrees and sunny. Favre had another fine game, and was helped by once again having the services of a healthy Greg Jennings. The receiver had missed the first two games with a hamstring injury. Favre would remark often during the season how fortunate he was to have receivers who could make big plays *after* catching a pass. Jennings provided one of the first in the fourth quarter against the Chargers. The Packers were trailing 21-17 when Favre hit Jennings on a slant pass that the receiver converted into a 57-yard touchdown. Green Bay won the game, 31-24.

They won again the following week in Minnesota, beating the hated Vikings 23-16 in the Metrodome, behind another outstanding performance by their veteran quarterback. The game saw Favre become the all-time leader in both pass attempts and touchdown passes, and for the second time in the young season Favre was named the conference's offensive player of the week.

The first stumble of the year occurred the following week, when the Packers dropped a nationally televised Sunday night game at Lambeau against the Chicago Bears. Green Bay held a 17-7 halftime lead, but the Packers were eventually undone by five turnovers, including two Brett Favre interceptions, which tied him with George Blanda for the most in league history. Chicago got the win, 27-20, and the Packers fell to 4-1.

Their record improved to 5-1 the following week with a win at Lambeau over the Washington Redskins. Yet nonbelievers, and there were still more than a few in Wisconsin, pointed out that the offense had sputtered. Green Bay's defensive back Charles Woodson — who would get the NFC's defensive-player-of-the-week award — scored on a 57-yard fumble return and the Packers snuck away with a 17-14 win. Tight end Donald Lee came up big on the offensive side of the ball, turning a short first-quarter reception into a 60-yard gain to the Redskins' 3 yard line, leading to the first Green Bay touchdown. Still, Brett Favre underthrew several long passes, and the whispers began that the 38-year-old — who also had overtaken Blanda's mark for most career interceptions in the game — had lost the ability to throw deep.

It was a perception that festered for two weeks because the Packers had a bye following the Washington game, but it was convincingly shattered by Favre's performance against the Denver Broncos in a game that raised the Green Bay record to 6-1.

As exciting as Favre's overtime bomb to beat Denver had been, the finish the next week — an interconference game against the Kansas City Chiefs, the only NFL team Favre had never defeated — was almost as good. It was, in fact, the 40th time in his career that Brett Favre had brought the Packers to victory from a fourth-quarter deficit or tie.

With the Packers trailing 22-16 at Kansas City's Arrowhead Stadium, with a little over three minutes to go in the game, Favre hit Greg Jennings with a 60-yard touchdown strike to put the Packers ahead 23-22. The Packers added a late field goal and a Charles Woodson interception return to make the final 33-22.

Favre went over the 60,000-yards passing mark the following week in a lopsided 34-0 victory over the Vikings at Lambeau. The Packers were now 8-1 on the season and nonbelievers were getting scarce.

Green Bay next hosted the Carolina Panthers, with Favre throwing three touchdown passes in an efficient dismantling of the Panthers that began with Green Bay reserve cornerback Tramon Williams picking up a first-quarter Panther punt at the Packers' 6 yard line and taking it 94 yards for a touchdown. It was the longest punt return by a Packer ever at Lambeau, and it came off a "pooch" punt after Carolina had lined up in field goal formation. Favre tied another career record in the game: most games with at least three touchdown passes. It gave him 62, tied with Dan Marino.

Favre would hold the mark alone after the following week, when the Packers journeyed to Detroit on Thanksgiving and dispatched the Lions, 37-26. The more notable record from that game, of course, was Favre's 20 straight completions, breaking a Packers' team mark.

It moved the Packers to 10-1 and set up a heavily hyped showdown with the Dallas Cowboys, who also had only one loss. The game was the Thursday night following Thanksgiving week, in Dallas, televised nationally by the NFL Network. Many outraged Packer fans who didn't get that fledgling cable channel sat on sofas in friends' homes or visited sports bars to see one of the biggest regular-season games in years.

It turned out to be a bit of a letdown for Green Bay fans. Favre did not play well and left in the second quarter with minor injuries to his elbow and shoulder. The Packers ran up more than 140 yards in penalties. One of the few bright spots for the Packers was the play of Favre's back up, Aaron Rodgers, who went 18 of 26 for 201 yards and a touchdown.

The disappointment of the loss to the Cowboys may have been eased for Packers fans with the appearance, a few days later, of *Sports Illustrated* magazine's annual "Sportsman of the Year" issue. It was the 54th year the magazine had bestowed the honor, widely recognized as one of the most prestigious in all sports, and it went to Brett Favre.

"When Favre decided to return for the 2007 season," wrote Alan Shipnuck, "even die-hard Cheeseheads must have been hoping only that he would not tarnish his legacy. What no one expected was that Favre would reinvent himself yet again, enjoying one of his best years at age 38 while cajoling a talented but callow team to a stunning 10-2 record. ...It is for his perseverance and passion that *SI* honors Favre."

"The better you play, the higher the expectations become, not only of yourself, but what others expect. It can flat wear you out."

Shipnuck also took note of all the charitable good deeds both Brett and Deanna Favre had performed over the years and the bond that had been established between the Favres the city of Green Bay and the state of Wisconsin.

Those trying to get a read on Favre's future in the story might have focused on a couple of passages, one in which Deanna Favre said there was only one subject that was never raised in the Favre household.

"We don't talk about retirement," Deanna said. "Ever. This whole town is obsessed with what Brett is going to do, so at home it's off-limits because he needs to get away from it."

Brett, meanwhile, told Shipnuck that it wasn't the physical punishment that was wearing him out in this, his 17th NFL season, but rather the mental stress of playing pro football at the highest level.

"Mentally, it's much more demanding," Favre said. "Now I dwell on the negative a lot more. I'm thrilled to death we're winning, but with each game I feel more pressure to play better, to keep it going. Next play's got to be better, next game's got to be better. The better you play, the higher the expectations become, not only of yourself, but what others expect. It can flat wear you out."

The Packers came back from the Dallas loss with a vengeance the following week against the Oakland Raiders at Lambeau. When the dust settled, Green Bay had a 38-7 win and the NFC's North Division title — clinched with three games still to go in the regular season.

In week 15 of the 2007 season, the Packers clinched a bye in the first round of the playoffs by traveling to St. Louis and defeating the Rams, 33-14. History will remember the game for a different reason. It was in St. Louis that Brett Favre, with a seven-yard pass to Donald Driver, broke Dan Marino's record for the most career passing yards by an NFL quarterback. Favre threw for 227 yards in the game, including touchdowns to Donald Lee and Greg Jennings.

The Packers came down to earth the following week in Chicago, with a stunning 35-7 defeat at the hands of the Bears. Green Bay fans could rationalize that the division crown and a first-round playoff bye had already been clinched; they could also point to the terrible conditions that day at Soldier Field. Favre had always been a good cold-weather quarterback, but against the Bears it wasn't the cold that got him, it was the wind. The wind chill index dipped below zero, but it was the havoc the wind — gusting up to 40 miles per hour — played with any attempt to pass that ground down the Packers' offense. Favre had two interceptions, the Bears blocked two punts, and Green Bay fans tried to put the game out of their minds.

That task was made easier when the Pack bounced back in the last game of the regular season. At home at Lambeau, the Packers regained the form they'd exhibited for much of the season, defeating the Lions 34-13. Favre threw two touchdowns passes before exiting the game early in the second quarter.

On January 12, 2008, the Packers hosted the Seattle Seahawks in a divisional playoff match up that would send the winner to the NFC championship game.

Seattle was coming in off of an impressive 35-14 home victory over the Washington Redskins in the wild-card round of the playoffs.

The Seahawks, of course, meant Mike Holmgren. But while the return to Lambeau of the man who led the Packers to a Super Bowl victory in the 1990s would always be a story, it was less so this time. Time had marched on. For the 15,000 Packers fans who showed up at Lambeau the day before the game for a pep rally, it was much less about beating Mike Holmgren than it was about getting to the NFC championship game and just one win away from the Super Bowl.

Favre and Holmgren exchanged a friendly greeting on the field during warm-ups. The coach had on a baseball cap; the quarterback had his helmet off as they shook hands and chatted.

The day before the game, Holmgren had jokingly said the Seahawks might not send quarterback Matt Hasselbeck out to call the coin toss. It was a reference to the events of four years earlier, when a Packers-Seahawks playoff game had gone into overtime and Hasselbeck, upon winning the coin toss, announced — into an open microphone — that the Seahawks would not only receive the kickoff, but would score. Instead, Hasselbeck threw an interception that was returned for a touchdown and the Seahawks went home.

The crowd at Lambeau was in shock. The Packers had trailed by 10 points or more only twice all year (and lost both games).

Four years later, Hasselbeck was at midfield, with a grin on his face, for the coin toss. Brett Favre was there, too. The Packers won the flip, so Hasselbeck's post-toss comments were limited to a few brief words with Favre as the two shook hands before rejoining their teams.

The crowd was the largest in Lambeau Field history — 72,168. Weather was a possible factor. Not, as one might have expected, because of cold or wind — the temperature was 31 and winds only five miles an hour — but there was a possibility of light snow.

The Packers had trouble handling the opening kickoff, which bounced short around the 15 yard line. Tramon Williams tried to pick it up, stumbled, finally scooped it in his hands, and was hit almost immediately by multiple Seahawks at the Green Bay 18.

Favre brought the Packers on, but there was a considerable delay before the first play from scrimmage because a Seahawk player, Josh Scobey, had been hurt on the kickoff and had to be driven off the field.

Finally Favre brought the Packers to the line. As he called signals, tight end Donald Lee went in motion from left to right. Favre took the snap, dropped back, set himself at the Green Bay 11, and threw a short swing pass to his right, which running back Ryan Grant first bobbled, then caught. Grant's difficulty catching the ball may have contributed to his stumbling to the ground, without being hit, at the 14. As Grant struggled to his feet, he was hit hard by Seahawks linebacker LeRoy Hill, and the ball came loose. It was picked up by another

Seattle linebacker, Lofa Tatupu, on the Green Bay 10. Tatupu dodged a tackle by the Packers' Bubba Franks at the 8 and nearly scored before being brought down by several Packers at the 1 yard line.

It was as poor a start as possible for the Packers, and it got no better as Seahawk back Shaun Alexander carried over for the touchdown on first down. With just 20 seconds gone in the game, Green Bay trailed, 7-0.

It soon got worse. Tramon Williams made a nice return of the kickoff and the Packers started their second drive from good field position at their 35. Favre went immediately back to Grant, and he rolled through a good hole off left tackle, picking up 8 to the Packers' 43.

On second and three, however, Favre again went to Grant, handing off up the middle. Grant took a step left, then made a nice cut back to the middle of the field. At the 47 yard line Grant was hit by Seahawks' safety Brian Russell and again the ball came loose. This time there was a big pile up and scramble for the ball, but the result was the same: Seattle safety Jordan Babineaux had the recovery at the Green Bay 49.

The Seahawks scored six plays later, when on a first-and-10 from the Green Bay 11 Hasselbeck found wide receiver Bobby Engram over the middle near the back of the end zone. There was some debate over whether Engram got both feet down in bounds after he caught the ball and Packers' coach Mike McCarthy threw a challenge flag. In fact, Engram hadn't got both feet in, but the ruling on the field was that he'd been pushed out by Green Bay defenders. That particular call by the officials is not subject to challenge, so Seattle now led, 14-0.

The crowd at Lambeau Field was in shock. The Packers had trailed by 10 points or more only twice all year — and lost both games. Ryan Grant had fumbled only once all season — one time during a span in which he carried or caught the ball on 218 occasions.

"I wasn't really concerned," McCarthy insisted later. "There was a lot of football that was in front of us."

Afterward, Grant said: "I've been playing football for a long time and I've had my ups and downs. I've got to keep fighting no matter what."

Grant continued: "Anytime you fumble, you're going to be frustrated about it. We gave them 14 points so that's not something that you want, playing from behind."

But Grant said his teammates kept bucking him up. "I appreciate everybody staying with it, staying with me, staying on track."

They might have been helped in that task by a few words that Tom Clements, the Green Bay quarterbacks coach the past two seasons, had with Favre on the sideline after the second Seahawks' touchdown.

Favre recalled the moment later: "Right after they scored to make it 14-0 — and we really haven't been in that situation a lot, especially in the two years I've shared with [Clements] — he came over and he said, 'Hey, you don't have to get it all [back] at once.' History with me is, 'Try to get it all back right now.' Yeah, my hope was we could take the ball down and score. I think we needed to. At some point, we've got to get some points on the board. But I didn't want to make a bad situation worse. And so him giving me that simple advice made me think, 'You're right.' It was what I needed to hear at that time for us bounce back that way."

Light snow had begun to fall as the Packers took over on their own 31 after the kickoff. What may have been the most important drive of the season to that point began with Favre calling signals over center and wide receiver Greg Jennings, playing in his first playoff game, going in motion from left to right.

Favre took the snap, dropped back, set at the 25, and found Jennings open over the middle at the Green Bay 43. The receiver fell forward to the 45 as he was tackled and the Packers had their first first down.

After Grant picked up four yards on a quick pitch around right end, Favre rolled right on second down, couldn't find anyone open, and was tackled for no gain. Favre called the third-down signals out of the shotgun. After taking the snap the quarterback hit James Jones with a short pass at the Seattle 46 and the receiver did what Green Bay receivers had been doing all season: he turned a short gain into a long one. Jones cut to the left sideline and made it all the way to the Seahawks' 20, a gain of 31 yards.

On the following first down, Favre found tight end Donald Lee for a gain of five. Favre was now four for four passing, each completion to a different receiver.

Huddling with second and five from the Seattle 15, Favre called a run. But when they got to the line of scrimmage, he saw something in the Seahawks' defense that changed his mind. He signaled Jennings, who was split right, a change in plans.

"That was Brett being Brett," Jennings said later. "He gave me a look, told me to go and I went and he threw it and it worked out in our favor."

Favre lofted the ball high and Jennings was able to out-position the Seahawks' cornerback, Kelly Jennings, to make the catch at the 5 yard line, stumbling as he did so, but falling across the goal line to put the Packers back in the game, trailing 14-7.

After the kickoff, the Seahawks failed to get a first down and had to punt it right back to the Packers. The snow was falling harder and had begun to accumulate. The prediction a day earlier had been for a chance of flurries and Mike Holmgren took a light shot at the forecasters after the game.

"I'm trying to think when I lived here if the weather people were so wrong as they were last night when I looked at the television," Holmgren said. "It was the same guys. It was kind of an unusual game weather-wise and so I think if it had any effect at all — and both teams had to play in it — I think it negated a little bit of our speed on defense."

How the players felt about the snow may well have been impacted by how well they managed to perform. Matt Hasselback cited a negative impact: "It was tough to see people. That was crazy weather out there."

Green Bay tight end Bubba Franks said: "It was pretty. That was beautiful out there."

Favre said he had been waiting his whole career for a game in the snow: "I wanted to play where you couldn't see the field."

It wasn't quite so bad that they couldn't see the field, but it quickly got intense enough that during play stoppages the Lambeau ground crew began sweeping snow to help identify the yard-line markings.

After a Seattle punt, the Packers took over on their own 36 with 5:52 to go in the first quarter. With a quick toss to Donald Driver on first down that netted three yards, Brett Favre passed John Elway to move into second place (Joe Montana is first) among all NFL quarterbacks for most post-season passing yards.

The drive almost ended on the next play, when Favre, out of the shotgun, threw a slant pass to James Jones that went right through the receiver's hands and into those of Seahawk safety Jordan Babineaux, who seemed to simultaneously slip and bobble the ball, which fell incomplete.

On third and seven, Favre hit Bubba Franks short over the middle, and Franks made a nice run to near the first down. On being tackled Franks reached the ball forward with his right arm; the question was where the ball would be spotted and whether it would be a first down. A measurement showed it inches short, but Favre, conferring on the sideline with McCarthy and watching a replay on a Lambeau big screen, pointed to the screen and encouraged McCarthy to throw a challenge flag on the spotting of the ball, which the coach did. The Packers won the challenge and the drive stayed alive.

From that point — first and 10 at the Green Bay 46 — it was the Ryan Grant show. Favre completed one short pass — a five-yard toss to Jennings — but the other five plays were runs by Grant, who had begun the game so disastrously but was making up for it with a vengeance. One carry was for 26 yards; the following gained 15 and gave Green Bay a first and goal from the Seattle 1. Grant, naturally, took it in on the next snap. He was on his way to 201-yard, three-touchdown performance.

The 14-14 tie matched the highest number of first-quarter points in NFL post-season history, and the Packers were hungry for more. They didn't quite get it done in the first quarter, but it was close. After the kickoff, Seattle ran the ball twice to end the quarter.

On the first play of the second quarter, a second down and 19 (there had been a holding penalty) from the Seahawks' 15, Hasselbeck rolled right and hit tight end Marcus Pollard with a short pass as the receiver was approaching the right sideline. Pollard turned it upfield and was then hit hard by Packers' safety Atari Bigby; the ball came loose and was recovered by Green Bay's Aaron Kampman at the Seattle 18.

The Packers quickly capitalized on the turnover. Favre first dumped a short pass to Grant, who turned it into an 11-yard gain to the 7. The running back next took a handoff from Favre off left tackle and moved the ball to the 2. Favre took the following snap out of the shotgun and Jennings, split right, made a nifty inside move before cutting outside to the corner, where Favre had laid up a soft, well-timed pass. Jennings caught it for the score and said later, "He threw a perfect ball."

Favre's numbers to that point: 10 of 11 passing, 88 yards, and two touchdowns.

Now it was the Seahawks who needed to stop the bleeding, and they did. Hasselbeck led them on a sustained drive that was aided early by a roughing-the-kicker penalty on Green Bay's Brandon Jackson during a Seattle punt. It kept the drive alive and Hasselbeck took advantage, though the Seahawks could not quite punch the ball into the end zone. The 11-play drive ended with a 29-yard Josh Brown field goal that cut the Green Bay lead to 21-17.

If Hasselbeck's 11-play drive, executed in the snow, was impressive, his former teammate Brett Favre did him one better after the kickoff. Favre took the Packers on a 14-play drive, and the drive's penultimate play would be destined to live in Packers lore forever. If a single play could stand as a representation of how Brett Favre played football, it was that play.

He'd led the Packers down the field with a mix of short passes and runs by Ryan Grant. Favre hit Jones and Jennings on the drive and Driver twice. With just 1:19 left until halftime, the Packers found themselves facing a third-and-8 at the Seahawks' 14.

As the snow continued to fall, Favre called signals from the shotgun. The backfield was empty except for the quarterback. Favre took several steps forward as he called signals, emphasizing an instruction that quickly brought tight end Donald Lee off the line and into the backfield, presumably to block.

The ball was snapped and the Seattle rush came quickly. The pocket began to collapse and Favre pumped his arm even as Seattle defensive tackle Brandon Mebane got a hand on him. The quarterback eluded Mebane and ran right. As he did so he stumbled, almost falling, his gaze directed at the ground. But Favre regained his balance, looking up as he did so, and as he ran he flipped a sidearm, almost underhand toss to Lee, who had come out of the backfield and was open at the Seattle 12. Lee caught the ball, took it to the Seattle 3, and the Lambeau crowd went wild. They had just witnessed Brett Favre at his best. On the next play, Ryan Grant took it in for a touchdown that gave the Packers the halftime lead, 28-17.

Along with the career-defining play at the end, Favre's first- half stats were stellar: 15 out of 19 passing for 133 yards and two touchdowns.

Seattle at least had the consolation of receiving the second-half kickoff. They needed to come out strong but didn't; instead, Hasselbeck missed on three consecutive passes and the Seahawks were forced to punt.

In a nightmare scenario for Holmgren and Seattle, the Packers picked up right where they had been before the break. After starting from their 34, on a third-and-four from the 40, Favre took the snap out of the shotgun and immediately rolled out hard to the right. He threw on the run for Jennings, who had a step on defender Marcus Trufant along the right sideline. It wasn't a perfect ball — Favre's pass was slightly underthrown — but Trufant slipped and Jennings made a good catch at the Seahawks' 40 and took it to the 36. It was a reflection of what Favre had learned and what had buoyed the confidence of the Packers' offense all season: Brett didn't have to be perfect on every throw. His receivers could — and most often would — make plays.

On first down from the 36, Favre called signals over center, with his backs in an I formation. With the snap, the offensive line began clearing to the right, and Favre handed off to Grant, the second man in the I. Grant almost at once cut the play back to the middle, seeing that the Seattle linebackers, known for their quickness, had sensed a run right and moved fast to stop it. Grant found a huge hole in the left middle of the field and burst through it. He ran untouched until he slipped slightly in the snow and was tackled from behind by Seahawks' safety Brian Russell at the 12, a gain of 24 yards.

After Grant lost a yard on first down, Favre took the snap out of the shotgun, dropped back and threw a short swing pass right to Brandon Jackson, who immediately cut to the right sideline, outracing the one man he had to beat, linebacker LeRoy Hill, and taking it in for a Packers touchdown — the first touchdown pass to a running back Favre had thrown all year. The score made it 35-17, Green Bay.

Seattle didn't quit. Hasselbeck took the offense on an impressive drive — 14 plays that ran nearly eight minutes off the clock — but for the second time in the game a long Seahawks' possession failed to produce a touchdown. This drive fizzled at the Green Bay 9, and Josh Brown kicked a 27-yard field goal to make it 35-20.

The snow at this point was falling as hard as it had all game.

The Packers' offense took over on its own 35 with 2:46 to go in the third quarter. On third and three from the Green Bay 42, Favre took the snap under center and handed to Grant off left tackle. Grant took it quickly to the left sideline and then turned up field, churning untouched for what might have been a touchdown had Seattle's Jordan Babineaux not tripped Grant up with a diving tackle from behind at the Seahawks' 15. It was a gain of 43 for Grant, who again demonstrated that the two early fumbles had not messed up his head.

Instead it was the collective Seattle mindset that seemed spooked. The offense couldn't cross the goal line and the defense couldn't stop the Packers. On first down from the 15, with Grant getting a breather, Brandon Jackson gained 10 off right tackle, setting up a first-and-goal from the 5.

After the teams switched sides to begin the fourth quarter, Grant lost a yard off left tackle. On second and goal from the 6, Favre rolled to his right, was pressured by linebacker Julian Peterson, but managed to sidestep him. Favre then threw low and incomplete for Donald Lee just over the goal line, but linebacker LeRoy Hill had banged into Favre after he released the ball and Hill was called for roughing, giving the Packers a first down at the 3. It took Grant two carries to push it over, and when Mason Crosby kicked the extra point, Green Bay led 42-20. The Packers had scored the most points of any Green Bay team in a postseason game.

The game had much of the fourth quarter remaining, but there would be no more scoring. Brett Favre seemed to sense it was over as he came off the field following Grant's last touchdown. The Mississippi boy bent down and put his hands on some Wisconsin snow, packed it into a ball, and delivered it into the back of a startled Donald Driver. Of course, Driver retaliated, with a slightly bigger missile that hit Favre near the top of his helmet.

"It was fun," the quarterback said.

It was fun, and the Packers were in the National Conference championship game. It was a moment to relish, even in the locker room afterward, when someone brought up an article that had appeared during the week in a Biloxi newspaper saying that Favre was leaning toward not retiring and instead coming back for an 18th NFL season.

"I haven't decided on next year," Favre said. "And I think if you read the article, I don't think there's anything in there that says, 'Hey, I'm coming back.' I said I want to continue this playoff run further."

By this time, however, the quarterback had learned that his every word on the subject of his future would be brought up again and again for deep analysis.

Favre said: "I'm not surprised by anything I do taking on a life of its own."

Epilogue

Any doubt that Brett Favre had passed from the ranks of famous quarterbacks into an echelon of celebrity known to only a very few was erased when word that he had decided to retire broke early on the morning of March 4, 2008. It was a "stop the presses" moment in a new media age.

Web sites instantly bannered the news. In Wisconsin, talk radio programs were immediately given over to the topic. TV news producers scrambled to line up guests and program special shows devoted to Favre's legacy. Newspapers hurried to prepare special sections remembering the Favre era.

The national media was no less frenzied. ESPN's *SportsCenter*, an hour-long show which has become a good barometer of what the sports world is talking about at the close of any given day, devoted all but three of its noncommercial minutes to Favre's retirement. Even though Favre wouldn't address the media himself for another couple of days, it was, as more than one writer noted, "All Favre, all the time."

Many of the articles and the talking heads on the TV shows tried to place Favre in the pantheon of great NFL quarterbacks. Did he deserve consideration as the greatest? If not, was he in the top five? Whenever the talk became too clinical, about whether Favre could engineer a comeback like Joe Montana or release a pass as quickly at Dan Marino, somebody else would state what really, in hindsight, seemed to matter most: What really made Favre special was his love for the game and his unmixed joy in playing it.

He said he never played for records, but there they stood, regardless:

Most touchdown passes: 442.

Most passing yards: 61,655.

Most passing attempts: 8,758.

Most wins by a starting quarterback: 160.

Most consecutive starts by a quarterback: 253 (275, including playoffs).

Most 3,000-yard passing seasons: 16.

Most pass completions: 5,377.

Most seasons with 30-plus touchdown passes: 8.

Most consecutive post-season games with a touchdown pass: 18.

Most NFL MVP awards: 3.

On the day of what would be Favre's last game before announcing his retirement — January 20, 2008 — the *New York Daily News* ran a lengthy story headlined: "The Best Ever? NFL's greatest pass judgment on Favre's place in history."

Retired quarterback Boomer Esiason said: "In my world, Joe Montana is the number one quarterback of all time."

Former Green Bay general manager Ron Wolf listed Favre in the top five. (Otto Graham topped Wolf's list.)

Former Giants coach Jim Fassel had Favre second.

Joe Montana refused to make a list.

Dan Marino was perhaps most honest of all. He laughed and said, "If you ask me, I would tell you I'm the best."

Cris Collingsworth, the receiver turned NBC analyst, put Favre 10th. "I've seen him make mistakes in big games," Collingsworth said. But he added: "But he's won, he's always played, he brings passion in an era when passion seems to be more about money and things not related to football than it does about the game."

The retirement press conference was Thursday, March 6. Alan Shipnuck, the *Sports Illustrated* writer who had authored the "Sportsman of the Year" piece a few months earlier, described the decision, and the moment, like this:

"There is plenty left in Favre's rocket right arm, but the expectations of the sport's most passionate fan base exhausted him, and he was weary of the preparation time required to summon his best. So last Thursday, Favre made another visit to Lambeau Field. This time the old stadium was ghostly quiet except for a windowless room packed with reporters and photographers for his retirement press conference."

It wasn't long before that room was filled with the sound of sobs. It could not have been otherwise. In his fourth sentence, Favre reminded himself that he'd made a promise not to get emotional. You might as well have told him not to fist-pump after throwing a touchdown pass. Of course he cried. It had meant too much to him for too long and even though he believed he was making the right decision, he wept when he talked about giving it up.

"It's a unique situation," Brett Favre said, "in that at 17 years I had one of the better years of my career, the team had a great year, everything seems to be going great, the team wants me back, I still can play, for the most part everyone would think I would be back, would want me back. That's a unique situation going into an 18th season.... But this year, and this is not the first year, but it really to me and Deanna was more noticeable, the stress part of it. It's demanding. It always has been, but I think as I've gotten older I'm much more aware of that. I'm much more aware of how hard it is to win in this league and to play at a high level. I'm not up to the challenge anymore. I can play, but I'm not up to the challenge."

In the days that followed, there was speculation that Favre hadn't meant it, that he hadn't really thought it through, that as the enormity of the decision dawned on him he would change his mind. Some fans tried to read as much into an appearance on David Letterman when Favre said he knew he'd miss it come fall.

Apart from Letterman, however, he was seldom seen in public in the weeks after his announcement. He had once told Peter King of *Sports Illustrated*, one of the reporters he liked best, that when he retired, "You'll never find me. I'll disappear."

That's not so different from what Favre told *USA Today* prior to the 2005 season, when the retirement talk had already begun to seem tiresome.

"Some people live for being known," Favre said, "for sitting and being seen, but I always joke that I'm going to be like Don Meredith and suddenly be gone."

Meredith was the former Dallas Cowboys quarterback whose already considerable fame went through the roof when he starred opposite Howard Cosell in the first years of *Monday Night Football*. Meredith later went away quietly to live with his family in New Mexico, almost never gave interviews, but was wonderfully happy and genuinely surprised when *Sports Illustrated* tracked him down in July 2000. *SI* noted that Meredith was "stunned" to learn that he was considered a recluse.

"I don't understand that," Meredith said. "I don't feel reclusive. I actually feel kind of normal."

Might that be in Brett Favre's future? Some who know him best wouldn't bet against it. Life that's been filled with so much passion and drama seems to demand more out of a second act.

But even those who expected some kind of dramatic second act from Favre could not have anticipated what played out in the summer of 2008, just months after the quarterback's emotional retirement press conference. The media storm that had accompanied Favre's retirement was dwarfed by the frenzy that developed when word began to circulate that Favre was rethinking his decision to retire.

When it became clear that Favre was serious about playing again, and that the Packers were not certain his return was the best thing for the team, fans in Wisconsin and around the country found themselves taking sides. When, in early August, the previously unthinkable happened and Brett Favre was traded to the New York Jets, many fans of both Favre and the Packers seemed stunned.

But in the next several days, as the dust began to at least partially settle, many seemed to come to terms with the idea that whatever the future held for Brett Favre as a New York Jet, his legacy as a Green Bay Packer was secure and unassailable. Just as, for Favre, it had always been about playing the game, so most fans would choose to remember the great games of his career.

On a Milwaukee radio station, lineman Mark Tauscher was asked to try to summarize what he would take away from his years of playing with Favre. Tauscher said he would remember, above all, the quarterback's love of the game and his passion for playing it.

"It rubbed off on you," Tauscher said.

It rubbed off on everybody.

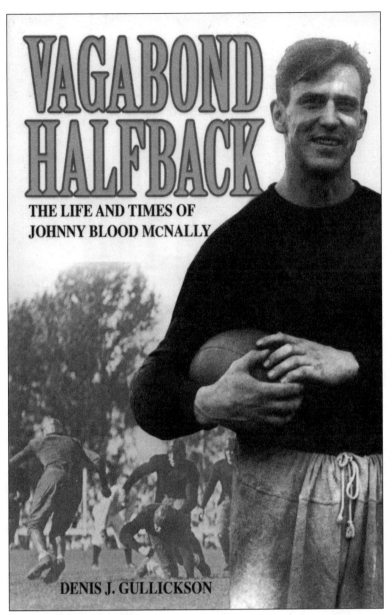

Vagabond Halfback
The Life and Times of Johnny Blood McNally
Denis J. Gullickson

The outrageous, larger-than-life tale of the man whose story inspired the movie *Leatherheads*. He was a poet, a lady's man, a drunk —and one of the greatest Packers of all time. The only published account of the conflicts and triumphs of Johnny Blood, whose exploits off the field often eclipsed his gridiron glory.

Paper | 6 x 9 | 232 pages | $18.95 | ISBN 978-1-931599-73-3

For this and other great Trails Books titles, call (800) 258-5830 or visit us online at www.trailsbooks.com

Mudbaths and Bloodbaths:
The Inside Story of the Bears-Packers Rivalry
Gary D'Amato & Cliff Christl

The definitive book on the NFL's oldest and fiercest rivalry! The story of the Packers-Bears blood fued is the history of professional football itself, and you'll enjoy the entire saga from its origins in the 1920s to today, told by the players and coaches themselves.

Paper | 6 x 9 | 288 pages | $16.95 | ISBN 978-1-879483-95-8

For this and other great Trails Books titles, call (800) 258-5830 or visit us online at www.trailsbooks.com

After They Were Packers
Jerry Poling

Where do the heroes go when the cheering ends? In his follow up to the best-selling *Downfield!* Jerry Poling reveals the lives of the 1997 Super Bowl champions after they left the Packers. Also included are former greats Lynn Dickey, Don Majkowski, and others from before the "New Glory Years"

Paper | 6 x 9 | 288 pages | $19.95 | ISBN 978-1-931599-72-6

For this and other great Trails Books titles, call (800) 258-5830 or visit us online at www.trailsbooks.com